The Preaching of Jesus

The Preaching of Jesus

Gospel Proclamation, Then and Now

William Brosend

WJK WESTMINSTER
JOHN KNOX PRESS
LOUISVILLE · KENTUCKY

First edition
Published by Westminster John Knox Press
Louisville, Kentucky

10 11 12 13 14 15 16 17 18 19—10 9 8 7 6 5 4 3 2 1

Book design by Drew Stevens
Cover design by Mark Abrams
Cover Image: Mary Evans Picture Library

Library of Congress Cataloging-in-Publication Data

Brosend, William F. (William Frank).
    The preaching of Jesus : Gospel proclamation, then and now / William Brosend.
        p. cm.
    Includes bibliographical references (p.   ).
    ISBN 978-0-664-23215-3 (alk. paper)
    1. Preaching. 2. Jesus Christ—Preaching. I. Title.
    BV4211.3.B758 2010
    251—dc22

2009028354

PRINTED IN THE UNITED STATES OF AMERICA

For Fred B. Craddock,
preacher, teacher, mentor

Contents

Foreword

MARCUS BORG

Few people are as well prepared by education and experience as Bill Brosend to write a book on *The Preaching of Jesus* and what we might learn not only from the content of his proclamation but also from its style. A New Testament scholar whose PhD from the University of Chicago focused on the parables of Jesus, Brosend is also a professor of homiletics (preaching) in a divinity school preparing students for ordination. Once a Baptist pastor and now an Episcopal priest, he must of necessity preach what he teaches.

There is much to learn from this book: The stunning fact that around 150 thousand sermons are preached each week in the United States— but with what effects? A compelling sketch of Jesus' message about the kingdom of God. Significant insights about how Jesus preached and what contemporary preachers might learn from his way of preaching. Cultural commentary about then and now. Exemplary sermons from some of today's most skillful and powerful mainline American Protestant preachers. This book combines thought with the pleasure of hearing these voices.

In the rest of this foreword, my purpose is to guard against a possible misunderstanding of its title and several of its most central terms. The words "preach," "preaching," "preacher," and "sermon" have acquired common meanings over the centuries that are quite different from anything that would apply to Jesus and his time. Their most common meanings in our time: *preaching* is what *preachers* (commonly ordained) do, and what they do is *preach sermons.*

In this sense, Jesus wasn't a preacher, and he didn't preach sermons. More than one thing is meant. To begin with the least important, he wasn't an "ordained" preacher. Though he was occasionally addressed as "Rabbi," the term had not yet become a designation for somebody who was "ordained" as a rabbi. The term simply meant "teacher." Indeed, the word "preacher" does not occur in the NRSV translation of the New Testament.

ix

There is a further reason for saying that Jesus was not a "preacher" in the common modern sense of the word. It is an ecclesiastical term, a word whose meaning has been shaped by its use within the church. A preacher is not only a religious functionary, but also preaches about religious matters to religious assemblies. But, though Jesus occasionally taught in synagogues, he spoke mostly outside of them—in the countryside and small towns of Galilee, and primarily to the peasant class.

Moreover, his message was more than religious, even as it was deeply religious: it was about "the kingdom of God"—*on earth*, as already in heaven, as Brosend ably and passionately affirms. Jesus combined what we separate into religion and politics. And that's why he was executed.

In modern speech, common church words other than "preacher" and "preaching" also have distorted meanings when applied to Jesus. For example, it is common to speak of "the ministry" of Jesus—and then we think of ministry as what ministers do, and Jesus becomes a "minister," a pastoral person. But Jesus was not a pastor. It is also common to speak of "the mission" of Jesus—and then we think of mission as what missionaries do: trying to convert people to Christianity. But Jesus was not trying to convert people from one religion to another.

To return to preaching and sermons: not only was Jesus not a preacher in the modern sense of the word, but he did not preach sermons as we understand that word. Like the word "preacher," the word "sermon" does not occur in the NRSV translation of the New Testament. Though scholars and Christians alike regularly refer to the "*Sermon* on the Mount" in Matthew 5–7, Matthew does not. Nor does any other Gospel refer to Jesus as preaching a sermon.

Instead, Jesus most commonly taught with short provocative sayings (which scholars call "aphorisms") and with short stories, the parables. Aphorisms and parables are not sermons in the modern sense of the word. They are teaching devices carefully crafted to engage an audience.

Aphorisms. For the most part, we need to imagine the aphorisms—the provocative short sayings—as spoken one at a time and not strung together one after the other. For example, try to imagine Matthew 5–7 (the "Sermon" on the Mount) as an oral sermon spoken all at once. It is impossible to do so. Instead, it is a collection of short aphorisms spoken on many different occasions. Exceptions might include sayings using a parallel structure, such as a string of beatitudes or antitheses. But in general, the aphorisms are great one-liners.

How did Jesus use them? It is impossible, or at least very difficult, to imagine him saying a great one-liner all by itself and then letting it hang in the air until he walked away in silence. It is also impossible, or at least very difficult, to imagine that an itinerant oral teacher like Jesus would use a great aphorism only once; he would have used each aphorism many times. It is much easier to imagine that individual aphorisms were either oral texts for a more extended teaching or used as invitations to interaction, with hearers asking, "What do you mean?"

Parables. What we have in the Gospels are plot-summaries of stories that Jesus would have told many times and at varying lengths. For example, the parable of the Prodigal Son is the longest parable, and it can be read aloud in about three minutes, without rushing overly much. It is easy to imagine that a good storyteller like Jesus could have expanded the story to ten or fifteen minutes or even longer without losing a crowd's interest.

The parables of Jesus, like the aphorisms, are invitational forms of speech that stir the imagination: they invite the hearers into the world of the story or the perspective of the aphorism, and encourage them to imagine the world and life as different from how they seem to be. So too they probably invite interaction with the audience. In the parable of the Prodigal Son: What do you think of a son who behaved that way? Of a father who welcomed him home so grandly? Of the elder brother, who objects?

Yet though Jesus was not a preacher who preached sermons in the modern senses of these words, there are lessons to learn from his way of speaking to and engaging his audiences. There is much to be learned from the wisdom and rhetoric of Jesus—for clergy and laity alike. That is what this insightful and helpful book is about.

Acknowledgments

This project first took shape in conversation with the late editor and publisher Harold W. (Hal) Rast. Along the way many colleagues and friends, students, and parishioners encouraged, critiqued, questioned, and guided me in ways beyond simple summary. Thank you to all, and to the following, particular thanks: Students of the School of Theology, Sewanee, and of the Preaching Excellence Program of the Episcopal Preaching Foundation, who listened to the lectures that brought sense to the project. Jack Keller and David Lott encouraged me to stop talking and start writing, and the Conant Fund of the Episcopal Church provided a grant to help me do so. My wonderful collaborators, Fred B. Craddock, Michael Curry, Thomas G. Long, and Barbara Brown Taylor, read and responded to early versions of the manuscript and contributed their own words to bring theory to life. Marcus Borg and Fred Craddock challenged me to remember who this book was for and to write for them, not at them. Student assistant Elaine Ruth read and corrected the manuscript with care. Above all, and beyond anything I could ever deserve, Christine and Emily accepted my absences and preoccupation with grace and understanding.

Feast of St. Augustine, 2009
Sewanee, Tennessee

Introduction

A beautiful Sunday, wonderful attendance, and your very best homiletical effort was not unrewarded as you stand in the narthex after the service:

Thank you, pastor. A nice sermon.

Thank you.

Nice sermon, pastor.

Good morning, pastor.

Thank you for the sermon. It meant more to me than I can say.

Thank you.

Pastor, that was the best sermon I have ever heard.

Good morning.

How, pray God, are we to make sense of these responses? Was it the best sermon in the history of Christianity, or an offering that caused the listeners to nod their heads in an noncommittal "Good morning" after nodding their heads as they dozed through the homily? And how, pray God, are we preachers supposed to discern the difference?

Students invariably ask two questions in the course "Introduction to Preaching": What makes a sermon "good"? and "Who are the 'best' preachers today?" As a professor of homiletics, I am supposed to have an answer to these questions, but I wonder how you, dear preacher, would answer?

What makes a sermon "good"? What are the criteria, and who gets to decide? How can we preachers, week after week, determine if we have prepared a good sermon? Upon what basis would we judge a sermon? Is there an example, someone, somewhere out there, who week in and week out is preaching sermons that inform, move, and transform their hearers? The basic argument of this book is that there is such a person, whose sermons you know very well. In fact, you have copies of them all over your office and your home, maybe even in the glove compartment of your car. The example, certainly, is Jesus.

Remember the 1960s? I know—if you remember the '60s, you weren't there. But whether you lived it or read about it, you remember.

It was the Beatles, Woodstock, and the summer of love. It was freedom rides, race riots, and a "Letter from a Birmingham Jail." Hippies and Jesus freaks, psychedelics and charismatics, "Up with People" and "Down with America," protests and pray-ins. The 1960s, which arguably began with Kennedy's inauguration and ended with Nixon's resignation, was a decade of tumult, change, and coming of age, inside and outside the church. And it was a decade of truly incredible preaching. Remember?

Yes, there was Martin Luther King's "I Have a Dream," and there was also Fred Craddock's *As One without Authority*.[1] Many cheered and others cursed the proclamations of liberal firebrands William Sloane Coffin and Jesse Jackson, while still others gathered in stadiums and around televisions for Billy Graham revivals. And it was not limited to the (in)famous: powerful preaching was imitated in pulpits great and small. Stands were taken, for and against, and each in the name of Jesus. As Charles Marsh, Tim Tyson, and others have shown, in town and country churches we never heard of, preachers we never knew bravely followed the logic of their faith into conflicts over race, war, and the role of women in church and society—all the way to the unemployment line.[2]

At the same time, and perhaps for some similar reasons, New Testament scholars were beginning to rediscover Jesus, first in the parables and then in "history." The impact was less immediate—you can have a revolution in less time than it takes to write a monograph—but Jesus was making a comeback. The beginnings of the comeback are rooted in the Parables Seminar of the Society of Biblical Literature, where scholars Norman Perrin, Robert Funk, John Dominic Crossan, Dan Via, and others built on the work of Amos Wilder to produce an explosion of literature on the parables of Jesus. One direction taken by many in the seminar concerned locating the authentic parables attributable to the historical Jesus and distinguishing them from those stories or portions thereof added to Jesus' own stories, which are attributable to the evangelists or the early church, work begun by Joachim Jeremias in the 1940s and best known in the 1972 English translation of the revised, third edition.[3] This historical-literary approach to the parables and other sayings of Jesus focused in the 1980s on Jesus as a figure within a particular sociohistorical context, and finally into a full-blown third, or renewed, quest for the historical Jesus.

As the literary concerns moved to the background, the study of Jesus within history was invigorated by two factors: the rediscovery of the simple but long-forgotten fact that Jesus was a Jew (surprise!), and the appropriation and application of the insights of what came to be known as social-scientific criticism. The study of Jesus within Judaism, led by the pioneering work of E. P. Sanders and guided, if often only through the work of others such as Sanders, by the incomparable scholarship of Jacob Neusner, reclaimed Jesus as a Galilean Jew from decades of wandering in the mythical and mystical mists of Greco-Roman religion. Social-scientific criticism shares the concerns of much of the older look at "everyday life in Bible times," but with a rigor grounded in historical sociology, anthropology, and economics, all informed by the discoveries of material culture brought to the surface by a new generation of archaeologists.

All this is well-known, as are the decidedly mixed and frequently vituperous results of the renewed quest. From peasant Jewish cynic to Chalcedonian Christian, the "historical" Jesus has been called just about everything, always with biblical warrant, rarely with hermeneutical modesty. While it is a study I will engage, it is not a battle that I want to join: first, because I find the very concept of a "historical Jesus" multiply problematic; and second, because the focus of this study is *how* Jesus was depicted as saying what he says in the Synoptic Gospels, and not on whether or not he said this, that, or the other. This is not because I have no interest in the historical questions, but because the *rhetorical* questions have, almost without exception since Wilder's *Early Christian Rhetoric*, been entirely ignored.[4]

This brings us round to the real issue at hand: what happened to Christian preaching since the 1960s? More particularly, what happened to what one might refer to as the public voice of the pulpit? Not the absence of the Coffins and marginalization of the Jacksons, but the widespread silence of pulpits mainline and otherwise on issues controversial and matters problematic. The case in point I cannot get off my heart and mind is the difference in pulpit responses to preparations for the First and Second Iraq Wars, in 1990–1991 and 2002–2003. Remember? Certainly, between those wars was September 11, 2001, but 9/11 is not enough to account for the change in pulpit response. Something about the preachers changed as well, and about the postmodern models preachers were using to shape their messages. Without pointing fingers and naming names, because I would have to include myself, I think it fair to say that many of us lost our way, our public voices if not our homiletical courage; as regime change in Iraq moved to quagmire and on to civil war, and back again, most of us have yet to find it.

The whys, and maybe the ifs, are not really at issue, no more than finally are conclusions about the historical Jesus. Blame it on the lectionary, the "triumph of the therapeutic," the turn to spirituality, or some other source; wherever one chooses to assign responsibility is unimportant. Once again the issue is *how*: What is the rhetoric that characterizes the preaching of Jesus in the Synoptic Gospels? How may our preaching of Jesus today learn from it? The current study will explore those two questions, and their implications. It is intended to fill a gap in our study of Jesus within history, to offer a way forward by finding a way back into public proclamation.

If what you seek is what you get when looking for Jesus within history, I want to primarily look for the rhetorical styles attributed to Jesus. Although my goal is possibly presumptuous, my historical claims are limited. On the one hand, I am interested in the rhetoric attributed to Jesus in the Synoptic Gospels because I believe it should inform the rhetorics of preaching today. On the other hand, I am not concerned to demonstrate that one saying, set of sayings, or strand of the tradition is more or less historically reliable than another. For the purposes of this project, I am not interested in determining the probabilities that Jesus may have said this, that, or the other. I am principally interested in *how* Jesus is depicted as saying what he says. I am not naive enough to think that the what and the how are unrelated, just that they can be separated in an exercise like this one. Moreover, I recognize that the tradition and the evangelists shaped both the how and the what. Yet there is something important to be learned from this as well.[5] *How* the tradition and evangelists chose to depict the Jesus *they* proclaim as proclaiming his own message is not insignificant; it could, I believe, inform *how* those who would proclaim Jesus today shape their own proclamation.

The Preaching of Jesus is grounded in the conviction that contemporary Christian preaching can be strengthened, enriched, and emboldened by careful study of the preaching of Jesus reflected in the Gospels of Matthew, Mark, and Luke. John, as is so often the case, is another matter altogether; while the rhetoric of Jesus in the Fourth Gospel is well worth a study of its own, that is a study for another time. But this distinction is rhetorical, not historical, and it is not a claim about the appropriateness of using the Fourth Gospel in reconstructions of Jesus within history.

The first chapter of this study begins with a brief survey of the literature on Jesus within history that has informed my own reconstruction, and an explanation of who I understand Jesus to be. The remainder of the chapter is devoted to a characterization of the rhetoric of Jesus as found in the Synoptic Gospels, and a preliminary statement of the implications of that rhetoric for contemporary proclamation. The chapters to follow develop this characterization in considerably more detail, first exegetically, grounding the claim in the proclamation of Jesus in the Synoptic Gospels, and then homiletically. Each chapter concludes with a sermon modeling the focus of that chapter. I cannot say how deeply indebted I am to my mentors and friends Dr. Fred Craddock, Bishop Michael Curry, Tom Long, and Barbara Taylor for sharing these sermons, knowing that they will be critiqued. The conclusion further explores the homiletical implications and challenges that the rhetoric of Jesus offers us all, and it shares a sermon of my own.

1

Jesus the Preacher / Preaching Jesus

Jesus came preaching. Mark told us as much from the beginning: after baptism, temptation, and the Baptist's arrest, "Jesus came to Galilee, preaching [*kēryssōn*] the Gospel of God" (Mark 1:14 AT). A few verses later, in typical Markan brevity and without bothering to tell us more about the content of Jesus' message, we learn the reaction: "They were astounded at his teaching, for he taught them as one having authority, and not as the scribes" (1:22). Authoritative and astounding! Not exactly Sunday morning's "Nice sermon, pastor."

Jesus came preaching. Charles Campbell, echoing John Howard Yoder, has challenged us to account more fully for this simple statement in our homiletic and in our preaching, and he is right.[1] What does it mean that Jesus chose preaching as his primary means of ministry, and of resistance to empire, temple, and adversary? What does it mean that Jesus chose preaching not only for our understanding of him, but also for our proclamation of him? That is the essential question of this chapter and the chapters to follow.

Jesus came preaching. Not the most obvious strategy, then or now. Matthew's and Luke's account of the temptation show Jesus' rejection of what many would consider more promising approaches.[2] They were not, however, more faithful approaches, and the choices Jesus made invite us to consider our own choices in preaching Jesus. Are we to be effective, or faithful? Or might we be both?

1

Jesus came preaching, and he came to a particular time and place, one suited for the strategy he chose. Military resistance to empire was foolish, as the Jewish War would prove a generation after the crucifixion. The adversary had stepped aside, if only for a season: "When the devil had finished every test, he departed from him until an opportune time" (Luke 4:13). And the temple? Its fate was soon enough sealed: "Do you see these great buildings? Not one stone will be left here upon another; all will be thrown down" (Mark 13:2). Words made sense. They were, after all, only words, at least as far as empire and adversary were concerned. Temple knew better, but in debate after debate it proved phenomenally powerless to resist the resister. "Then some of the scribes answered, 'Teacher, you have spoken well.' For they no longer dared to ask him another question" (Luke 20:39–40).

Jesus came preaching, in particular, and we will also want to be as particular as we can. Jesus came preaching "the Gospel of God." He preached the present moment; he preached that God's reign is here. Jesus preached repentance; he preached faith. Good stuff all, but to tell the truth, this study is not as interested in *what* Jesus said as it is interested in *how* Jesus is depicted in the Gospels as having said it. Not that what and how are ever unrelated.[3] This chapter begins with a reconstruction of Jesus within history, so that Jesus' rhetoric is placed within some sense of its historical context. That rhetoric, as evidenced by Mark, Matthew, and Luke, is analyzed in the hope of determining its dominant characteristics. Finally, attention turns to contemporary preaching about Jesus, and suggestions are made for how the rhetoric of Jesus might be more fully employed in preaching about Jesus.

As soon as someone says "the historical Jesus," someone else says "the Christ of faith"; then the debate, at least since Bultmann, is on. As far as I have been able to tell, it rarely gets anywhere. Because the distinction, and many others like it (Borg's "pre" and "post"-Easter Jesus, for example), are overwhelmed by the formulations, and by the implications read into them by frequently unsympathetic audiences. What was intended as a designation for the sake of precision becomes a label for use in political/religious/theological debates. The "historical Jesus" was, in the foundational uses by those engaged in the renewed quest, meant to distinguish at least the following: Jesus as he could be known from multiply attested sources, biblical and otherwise (Crossan); Jesus as he could be known "scientifically" by reliable historical evidence, biblical and otherwise (Wright and Meier); Jesus as he can be known to believers before and after Easter (Borg); Jesus as he "really" was (Johnson).[4] These in themselves are caricatures, but they are not tendentious nor highly polemical. It is when one moves from, say, the "real" Jesus to the "only" Jesus, when reconstructions of Jesus within history are presented as historical and/or biblical absolutes, that a line has been crossed. And it has been crossed.

It is better, I have come to believe, to speak of our reconstructions as presenting Jesus "within history" rather than "the historical Jesus." The former formulation admits to distinction between the biblical and historical, without claims to whole or simple truths. All believers have, to varying degrees, some idea or a set of ideas about who Jesus was and is for them. This is especially true for preachers. To speak and write of Jesus "within history" is to make explicit that understanding, without making claims for Jesus "as he actually was," which is an unrecoverable reality from a historical perspective, and a not necessarily helpful one from a homiletical perspective. All this suggests the second reason I prefer to write of Jesus "within history" rather than "the historical Jesus." This is finally a work of homiletics, not history, and the Jesus we here seek to recover is Jesus the preacher, in order to better understand how the preaching of Jesus may inform our preaching about Jesus. In this sense history is secondary to rhetoric, which is not to say that history is unimportant.

Reading, teaching, and writing about Jesus the preacher has convinced me that my own reconstruction of Jesus within history is a dialogue between rhetoric and Scripture, homiletics and history, and that it is important to be explicit about that reconstruction, its sources, and its implications. So before outlining the central rhetorical claims about the preaching of Jesus, and the implications that rhetoric has for contemporary preaching about Jesus, I share my own understanding of Jesus within history. It is not an understanding that has emerged in a vacuum, but through years of study, teaching, writing, preaching, and ministry. Thus it is a little messy and also unabashedly informed by the wisdom of many others.

Over the last two generations of New Testament scholarship, scores of authors—in articles, monographs, books, and multivolume studies—have presented reconstructions of Jesus within history of varying degrees of rigor, complexity, and persuasiveness. What these reconstructions have in common, without exception to my knowledge, is an almost complete disregard for the rhetoric Jesus used (or is said to have used) in his preaching and teaching. With the singular exception of Amos Wilder, to a scholar they make the following two claims as if the claims were self-explanatory and there was little more to be said on the subject: (1) Jesus was a teacher/preacher. (2) Jesus' favorite mode of preaching was the parable. Marcus Borg, in developing his understanding of Jesus as a teacher of "alternative wisdom," is representative:

> The forms of speech most frequently used by Jesus as an oral teacher were aphorisms and parables. Aphorisms are short, memorable sayings, great "one-liners." Parables, of course, are short stories. Together aphorisms and parables are the bedrock of the Jesus tradition, and they put us most directly in touch with the voice of the pre-Easter Jesus. Strikingly, the most certain thing we know about Jesus is that he was a storyteller and speaker of great one-liners.[5]

Jesus as after-dinner raconteur is not what Borg means; yet after only a few additional comments about form, he moves on to content. But if the wisdom of Craddock noted in the introduction (above) is correct, and it most certainly is, that *what* and *how*, content and form, can never be separated, must it be left to the homiletician to consider both? Apparently so. My own effort will first outline my understanding of who Jesus was, followed by a summary of my analysis of the rhetoric of Jesus in the Synoptic Gospels.

JESUS WITHIN HISTORY

Sanders began his 1985 study with a list of eight "almost indisputable facts" about Jesus.[6] My list in this study makes four claims:[7]

1. Jesus was a Galilean Jew.
2. Jesus was a preacher who proclaimed a kingdom and resisted a crown.
3. Jesus was a teacher actively reshaping a tradition for a new day.
4. Jesus knew the probable outcome of his ministry of resistance and transformation, and he did not capitulate to empire, temple, or adversary.

Jesus Was a Galilean Jew

That Jesus was fully and faithfully Jewish is as certain as it is often forgotten, and our collective debt to scholars Jacob Neusner, Geza

Vermes, E. P. Sanders, A.-J. Levine, and others is great. I hold Sanders's 1985 study *Jesus and Judaism* as especially pivotal, and my own reconstruction is as indebted to Sanders as to anyone. Here we want to recognize two facts: Jesus was Jewish, and he was a Galilean, not a Judean Jew. Having quoted Borg with tongue in cheek, it is only fair to let him have a second say:

> Jesus would have participated in the practices of "common Judaism." He would have learned the stories, hymns, and prayers of the Jewish tradition. He would have observed and celebrated the great Jewish holidays, three of which were pilgrimage festivals, ideally to be spent in Jerusalem [Passover, Pentecost, and Tabernacles]. . . . It is reasonable to think that Jesus at least occasionally went on pilgrimage to Jerusalem to observe these festivals. Though we do not know much about daily and weekly religious practices at the time of Jesus, it is probable that he, like most Jews, prayed the Shema twice daily, upon rising and going to bed. He no doubt observed the sabbath, which included attending the synagogue for Torah study and prayer.[8]

This sketch, though not universally shared, is generally accepted by most biblical scholars. Meier is even more detailed, and focuses on the practice of Judaism in Galilee in particular:

> The Jewish faith that was shared by pious Galileans in the countryside would have been, for all its fervor, fairly simple and straightforward. Like most traditional religion handed down by largely uneducated groups in rural areas, it would have focused more on basic practices rather than theoretical details debated by the religious elite. In the case of Judaism, the basic practices included circumcision of infant males, kosher food laws, the main purity rules, sabbath rest, and, when possible, pilgrimage to the Jerusalem temple on the great feasts to take part in its sacrifices. . . . The oft-repeated assertion that Galilean Jews were lax in their practice, alienated from the Jerusalem temple, and constantly rebellious does not seem to have held—if it ever held—during the adult life of Jesus.[9]

Three points from Borg and Meier merit further attention. First is the question of Jesus' understanding and practice of Torah, something that his teaching and frequent controversies with the "scribes and Pharisees" call into question. Second is the oft-repeated assertion about lax Galilean religious practice, and third is the matter of Galilee as a seat of rebellion and resistance, and the impact such activity may have had on Jesus and his followers.

How do we best understand the relationship of Jesus to the tradition in which he was raised and formed? Though my answer to this question is already implicit in my third claim (Jesus was a teacher actively and intentionally reshaping a tradition for a new day), it must be addressed in the first claim as well. Matthew, as an example, is well and rightly understood to have in part shaped his telling of Jesus' story with a keen eye for that tradition, with frequent references to Jesus' acting, or others acting upon him, as it was "spoken" or "written."[10] Jesus himself says in the Sermon on the Mount, "Do not think that I have come to abolish the law or the prophets; I have come not to abolish but to fulfill" (Matt. 5:17). Yet it is also in this same chapter of Matthew that we encounter the six antitheses, "You have heard it said. . . . But I say to you . . . " (5:21–48). Is not this Jesus echoing prophetic and wisdom critique, if not of the Torah itself, then of its interpretation and application? Thus even the disputes and controversies are consonant with the tradition. For example, is the "Powers'" (Wink[11]) attempt to silence Jesus' followers (Luke 19:39) not unlike the Powers' attempt to silence the prophet Amos (Amos 7:12–13)? Sanders has concluded that though there were at least two points of clear conflict (Sabbath and temple),

> the setting of Jesus' work within Judaism, therefore, is not to be understood as one of polar opposition between a man of good will and men of bad intent. It is not reasonable historical explanation to say that Jesus believed in a whole list of non-controversial and pleasant abstractions (love, mercy, grace) and that his opponents denied them. . . . Jesus does not "fit" into Judaism as its moral and spiritual antithesis (as some polemical passages have led some to think). There was, rather, a firm context of agreement, and within that context a conflict.[12]

One cannot overstate the importance of understanding this "firm context of agreement," not only for Sanders's work, but also for any reconstruction of Jesus within history. Jesus was Jewish, and there is no basis inside or outside the Gospels for claiming that he ever understood himself or his mission apart from his Jewishness. We have learned not to collapse first-century Palestinian Judaism into a singular reality, but that does not change the point. Jesus was Jewish. This is where we start.

Yet Jesus was also Galilean, and the differences between Judean, Galilean, and Samaritan, who all shared an Israelite history, are of at least biblical proportions (John 4:9b). The place and relationship of Samaritans within Palestine generally and vis–à–vis Judean and Galilean Judaism in particular are problematic, but not of real concern to this study. The conclusion of Meier may be affirmed: "We can already exclude one popular presentation of the Samaritan religion in the 1st century A.D.: namely, that it was a type of syncretistic polytheism combined with Jewish elements. Far from being polytheistic in practice or belief, the Samaritans tended to represent a rather conservative expression of Israelite religion, more rigorous than many Jews in their observance of the Sabbath and more wary of religious innovations."[13]

The relationship of Galilee to Jerusalem and Judea is more critical for this study, and fortunately not as widely disputed as Samaritan religion and culture, though agreements are not unanimous. As observed, two issues pertaining to Galilee are important for my argument: Was Galilee "Jewish"? To what extent was it a seat of rebellion and resistance? Meier has already declared the inappropriateness of assertions about lax religious practice in Galilee, but there are historical issues as well. While we will not join the debate between Horsley, Freyne, and others,[14] the question of whether or not Galileans were of non-Jewish descent is significant, even if Jesus' own family had recently migrated to Galilee, something presumed by Luke 2:4. If the ancient Israelite population of Galilee had been exiled by the Assyrians (2 Kgs. 17) so that the residents approximately one hundred years before Jesus' day needed to be circumcised when the Hasmonean king Aristobulus I gained control of the territory (Josephus, *Antiquities* 13.318), did Jesus grow up in a truly Jewish milieu?

Recent archaeological findings challenge Josephus, as well as Freyne and Horsley. Dunn, drawing on Reed, summarizes:

> All these data refute Horsley's idea of a Hasmonean aristocracy imposing themselves over a continuing Israelite population and point clearly to a wave of Judean settlements spreading over a depopulated territory.
>
> To this has to be added what Jonathan Reed calls four indicators of Jewish religious identity: stone vessels (chalk or soft limestone), attesting a concern for ritual purity, plastered stepped pools, that is Jewish ritual baths (*miqwaoth*); burial practices, reflecting Jewish views of the afterlife; and bone profiles without pork, indicating conformity to Jewish dietary laws. . . . In the light of such finds we

can hardly do other than speak of the characteristically *Jewish* population of Galilee in the late Second Temple period.[15]

If Galilee in the time of Jesus must be understood as thoroughly
Jewish, it was nevertheless a distinctive Judaism. To begin with, the
temple in Jerusalem was not a constant sight, but a site of pilgrimage,
the frequency of which is also a matter of debate. This makes Torah,
not temple, the focal point.[16] And during Jesus' lifetime, Galilee was
governed by Herod Antipas after the death of Herod the Great, while
Judea was governed directly by Rome's procurator. This difference has
encouraged some to overread the Hellenistic and Roman influence on
Galilee, and perhaps to underestimate the Roman influence on Judea.
The proximity of Nazareth to Sepphoris is frequently mentioned, but
scholars dispute the significance of this proximity, and even the importance of Sepphoris itself. Dunn points out that Reed's research shows
findings in Sepphoris consistent with the findings throughout Galilee;
he writes, "The conclusion that Sepphoris contained a predominately
Jewish and devout Jewish population is hard to avoid."[17] But Antipas
established Sepphoris as a provincial center, and excavations indicate a
theater, fortress, courts, bank, and arsenal.[18] Speculation has run the
gamut, with Jesus the carpenter helping to construct Antipas's new
city, to the idea that Nazarenes rarely if ever had reason to visit the city.
Claims are made for its importance, while others claim it was only a
minor city, not on a major trade route, and it is recognized that Antipas
himself abandoned Sepphoris for Tiberias. What is clear is that Sepphoris is never mentioned in the New Testament.

Though Sepphoris is not mentioned in the Gospels, scholars cite
revolt, resistance, and varying degrees of tension and conflict between
the Roman authorities and the temple aristocracies appointed by them
against the people of Judah and Galilee (e.g., Luke 13:1–2; 23:6, 19;
Acts 5:36–37), if not conflict to the extent found in Josephus. How
much should we make of these waves of resistance? To what extent
did they influence the development and ministry of Jesus of Nazareth?
This again is a matter of debate, and to some degree will be a point of
discussion throughout this book.

"In order to have a revolt, you have to have revolting conditions,"
said William Sloane Coffin.[19] How revolting were the conditions in
Galilee, and in Judea, and what impact might these conditions have
had on Jesus? Here as elsewhere, we must settle for summaries of an
ever-expanding but already voluminous literature (for which we should

give thanks!). In a word, conditions were awful. That is why there were revolts and insurrections. Two important realities, one unlike and one much like our own, are crucial. First was the reality of an essentially zero-sum economy. As the expression goes, there was only so much to go around, and if one person or social class got more, that meant that someone or some other class got less. The notion of increases in productivity was nonexistent. Wealth had a fixed source, land, and apart from the occasional pearl of great price or treasure hidden in the field, that land had to be worked, and whoever owned it received its produce.

Second, and growing out of the first, was an extraordinary socioeconomic stratification, such as that to which we are, God forgive us, beginning to return.[20] We do best to think of this socioeconomic stratification as a pyramid with an enormously wide base and a small peak. The emperor and his retainers are at the peak, 1 to 2 percent at most, with an equestrian class of a few percent, landowners, then merchants, at which point the pyramid explodes to account for the bottom 70 to 85 percent, the largest class by far being the expendables: slaves, day laborers, beggars. It is impossible to exaggerate the degree of desperation. Horsley says:

> Peasants are by definition always under the political-economic rule and exploitation of landlords or rulers. As comparative studies have shown, however, protests, renewal movements, and revolts tend to arise when actions by rulers impact villagers so severely as to cause their nascent disintegration. The Roman conquests and installation of Herodian client kings apparently had just such an impact on Galilean villagers.[21]

The scope, frequency, and intensity of revolt just before and during Jesus' lifetime is a matter of interpretation; the relevant texts are almost all from Josephus, a writer who must always be read and applied with caution and care. Horsley continues to argue that, "for generations both before and after the ministry of Jesus, the Galilean and Judean people mounted repeated protests and revolts against the Romans and their client rulers, the Herodian kings and Jerusalem high priests."[22] In marked contrast, and clearly in response to Horsley and others, Meier writes,

> I emphasize this point of relative peace and stability in Galilee because all too often Jesus is portrayed as an angry social rebel emerging from a seething cauldron of intolerable social and economic injustice. Such a portrait, however attractive to modern academics, gives

the historical Jesus a type of social conscience and political concern for which there is precious little proof in the Gospels. It also paints a dubious picture of the conditions in Galilee and the sensibilities of the Galileans during the public ministry. Significantly, around the turn of the era, Jews revolted a number of times against the powerful Syrian and Roman empires, despite the fact that revolt sometimes seemed madness. In contrast, the Jews of Galilee never attempted an insurrection against the much less powerful Antipas.[23]

Wright concurs that revolt was more likely in Judea, though it was "by no means impossible in Galilee."[24] Dunn points out that the presence of Roman troops in Galilee, and so the level of potential provocation, was modest; "the main political impact on the villages of Galilee, and Jesus for most of his life, would have been in terms of taxes."[25] Not that taxes were an insignificant issue, for the multi-tiered (Roman, Herodian, temple) taxation, exacerbated by the system through which they were collected, added significant burdens on the already subsistence-level lives of the peasantry.

Firm conclusions are difficult, in part because ideology is not only an issue for our reading of modern academics. Josephus certainly, but Matthew, Mark, and Luke as well, wrote from a point of view and for particular purposes, including socioeconomic and sociopolitical concerns. For this study, thankfully, it is not necessary to adjudicate all the interpretive differences. That the conditions in Galilee were "revolting," and that revolts did occur, is more important than documenting the frequency and intensity of such revolts.

Jesus was a Galilean Jew. He grew up in difficult and often desperate times; the memory and rumor of revolts near (Sepphoris) and far (Judea) were undeniably important. But the conditions rather than the revolts were most often reflected in Jesus' proclamation and teaching. Jesus was raised in a Torah-centered rather than temple-centered form of "common Judaism,"[26] in a village that would have emphasized first-century family-values.

Jesus Was a Preacher Who Proclaimed a Kingdom and Resisted a Crown

The chapter began with the less-than-startling claim that Jesus was a preacher, and that his preaching was first summarized by Mark (1:15) as "The time is fulfilled, and the kingdom of God has come near;

repent, and believe in the good news." Almost every word in this sentence has been the subject of a monograph or book, so the content of Mark's summary is anything but clear. Yet an outline of Jesus' message as summarized is possible:

1. There is an emphasis on the present moment.
2. There is a symbolic/metaphorical evocation of the divine claim and presence.
3. There is a call for a decisive response and an invitation to embrace the message.

Much of the discussion of the first part of the statement, "the time is fulfilled [*peplērōtai ho kairos*]," is coupled with the meaning of "near" (*ēngiken*) in the second part. It often focuses on determining chronicity, despite our wonderful sermons as seminarians about the difference between *kairos* and *chronos*. Something quite different, something timeless, is instead in view. To put it simply, Jesus is saying, "Now!" This is it: whatever "it" you have been waiting for, the season of waiting is past. This is the time of fulfillment, so be fully and completely present to the moment and to the momentous things that are happening all around you. "A number of sayings and actions of Jesus argue strongly for the view that Jesus at times spoke of the kingdom as already present in some way or to some degree in his ministry."[27]

The second part of Jesus' statement is about the kingdom of God. We have learned that "reign" is a better translation than "kingdom," but probably for the wrong reasons. Jesus was certainly speaking metaphorically, but the semantic field in view was the first century, not the twenty-first. *Basileia* would likely be taken to mean a sovereign territory ruled by a king,[28] and Jesus was claiming that God was king, surely a biblical thing to do.[29] A tempting question, therefore, is to ask the extent to which Jesus understood God's kingship to reach. To only "the lost sheep of the house of Israel" (Matt. 15:24) or "to the ends of the earth" (Acts 1:8)? Tempting, but mistaken. Because whether we take "kingdom" to be a symbol, a metaphor, or some other trope, it was certainly figurative. How one understands the figure can be as basic or as complicated as the interpreter chooses; for the purposes of this study, a basic approach, in four parts, is called for.

First, as Sanders points out, *"We know perfectly well what he meant in general terms: the ruling power of God."*[30] The central point of comparison in the metaphor claims, with the psalmist, that "God is king," and its central claim is not terribly difficult to understand. "We should all agree that 'kingdom' is a concept with a known core of meaning: the reign of God, the 'sphere' (whether geographical, temporal or spiritual) where God exercises his power."[31] Second, N. T. Wright points us in a helpful direction when he suggests that, in speaking of kingdom, Jesus was thinking narratively, and the narrative in mind was the story of Israel. "When Jesus spoke of the 'reign' or 'kingdom' of Israel's God, he was deliberately evoking an entire story-line that he and his hearers knew quite well; second, . . . he was retelling this familiar story in such a way as to subvert and redirect its normal plot."[32] Jesus was consciously connecting his proclamation to his listeners' own story, but with a decisive shift. Third, and this is where the fun comes in, Jesus' rhetorical shift wonderfully complexified the matter by continually setting the root metaphor, kingdom of God, in figurative tension with other metaphors in parables and allegories, symbolic discourses and similitudes. It is one thing to say, "The kingdom of God is near" (Mark 1:15) and something quite else to say, "The kingdom of God is as if . . . " and then launch into a parable (Mark 4:26–32), or to say that the kingdom of God belongs to little children (Mark 10:14). This metaphorical juxtaposition of "the kingdom of God is like" works not by addition, but by multiplication. Fourth, the open-ended quality of the metaphorical juxtapositions created by Jesus is exegetically profound and homiletically suggestive, leaving the interpreter/proclaimer with not only work to do, but also a model for how to do it: connecting our proclamation to our listeners' story, and making a claim for the presence and rule of God, but making it in story and symbol.

The third part of Jesus' statement is "Repent [*metanoiete*]," an imperative call for a decisive response to the proclamation of the kingdom. It is found on the lips of John the Baptist (Matt. 3:2), the Twelve (Mark 6:12), Jesus (Luke 13:3, 5), and even the "rich man" in Jesus' story about poor Lazarus (Luke 16:30). It is prominent in the proclamation of Peter, Philip, and the apostles in Acts (2:38; 3:19; 8:22); in Paul in Acts (17:30) and his Epistles (2 Cor. 7:10); and in the Letters to the Seven Churches in Revelation 2 and 3. The root meaning is a change of mind (*meta-noia*), but the root is likely in the Hebrew Bible's understanding of repentance as "turning [*šûb*]." It is a call to change, with an implicit sense of leaving behind or letting go, but also a turning to.

"Believe [*pisteuete*]" is also an imperative and paired with "repent" because Jesus calls for a turning from and a turning to. Unlike other studies, we are not concerned with the linguistic and semantic backgrounds of these terms,[33] but with how Jesus employed the terms as a part of his rhetorical strategy, a topic that will be visited specifically in chapter 3. The focus here is that Jesus' proclamation expected a response, which Mark characterized as "repent and believe."

None of this is out of keeping with scholarly consensus, though what has been left out, especially the relation of kingdom to eschatology, was admittedly left out for just that reason. The second half of my second claim, that while Jesus proclaimed a kingdom, *he resisted a crown*, is more problematic. So it is important to understand what I am not trying to do in this claim. Most important, I am not making any claim regarding Jesus' self-understanding, or in the terms of persistent debate, Jesus' "messianic self-consciousness." I am inherently skeptical of psychologizing approaches to biblical characters and materials in exegesis and in preaching; thus I am not staking a claim for how Jesus may or may not have understood himself in relation to God's history with Israel. Nor am I making an absolute claim about how Jesus is depicted in the Synoptics; the distinction between "resist" and "refuse" a crown is important here. But whether we try to seek coherence in the biblical witness under a rubric like the "messianic secret" or not, Jesus is consistently and persistently depicted as focusing the attention on God and God's kingdom, not on himself. Even when he does appear to be referring to himself, it is most often in the third person, usually as "the Son of the Man [*ho huios tou anthrōpou*]" (AT). The full significance of this form of (self)-reference will be explored in chapter 4. For this claim it is enough to note how rarely Jesus refers directly to himself in Matthew, Mark, and Luke (see the appendix). John is another matter altogether.

> We have to conclude as likely that Jesus made no attempt to lay claim to any title as such; also that he rejected at least one which others tried to fit him to. We can sharpen the point a little. It would appear that Jesus saw it as no part of his mission to make specific claims for his own status. The nearest we have to such a claim is his use of the non-title *bar 'naša* (son of man), too ambiguous to be a demand for explicit faith in himself, more an expression of his own hope for vindication. Allusion to his own role comes out more as a by-product of his proclamation of God's kingdom; his role was a role in relation to that, rather than an assertion of his own status as such.[34]

Jesus was a preacher who proclaimed a kingdom and resisted a crown. He chose preaching as his primary form of resistance, taking an omnipresent and oppressive reality and metaphorically subverting it into a striking claim of God's presence and power, all while making few, and even then usually indirect, claims for himself.

Jesus Was a Teacher Actively Reshaping a Tradition for a New Day

Whether Jesus is viewed as a sage in the tradition of Solomon and Ben Sira,[35] or a disciple-gathering philosopher modeled on the great Hellenistic rhetors,[36] no one disputes that Jesus was a teacher. "The Jesus discovered in the quest was above all a teacher. This is hardly surprising since the gospels report that he taught and what he taught, as well as what he did. . . . So important have the teachings of Jesus been, and still remain, that to a considerable degree the history of the quest is the quest of Jesus the teacher."[37] It is often observed that "teacher" is the preferred designation of Jesus in the Gospels,[38] but little distinction is made between the usages. The majority could be described as neutral and benign, a mild honorific as at Luke 8:49 (par. Mark 5:35), "Your daughter is dead, do not trouble the teacher any longer." Other uses seem more caustic, as when the scribes and Pharisees say, "Teacher, we wish to see a sign from you" (Matt. 12:38), and in addressing Jesus during what might be called the Temple Inquisition, in Matthew 22 and parallels. And whatever else we may conclude about references to Jesus as teacher in the Synoptics, on one recorded occasion Jesus refers to himself as *didaskalos* (Matt. 26:18/ Mark 14:14/Luke 22:11): "He said, 'Go into the city to a certain man, and say to him, "The Teacher says, My time is near; I will keep the Passover at your house with my disciples."'"

My claim is not just that Jesus was a teacher, however, but also that Jesus was a particular type of teacher, a teacher actively reshaping a tradition for a new day. This may help to account for the variety of tones with which the designation "teacher" is used about Jesus. Everyone, other than teenagers, loves a "good teacher" (Mark 10:17). Not so subversive teachers.

Though the parallels noted by Robbins, Crossan, Betz, and others between Jesus as presented in the Gospels and Hellenistic philosophers and rhetors are instructive, Jesus was Jewish, and his teaching is best understood in relation to Jewish sapiential tradition. Jesus was a wisdom teacher, and as Witherington and Borg have argued (an interesting convergence), he was a teacher of *alternative* wisdom. "As a teacher of wisdom, Jesus undermined the world of conventional wisdom and spoke of an alternative. The two are intrinsically linked: the first must be deconstructed in order for the second to appear."[39] Only one who teaches from within a tradition may subvert it; an outsider attacks; the difference between subversion and attack is significant for understanding Jesus historically and rhetorically. As a teacher of alternative wisdom, Jesus' mode of subversion was a matter of form and content, style and substance. The form and style were indirect and figurative, the parable being the most obvious and frequent example. The content and substance was uncompromising, demanding, and daunting. "Be perfect, therefore, as your heavenly Father is perfect" (Matt. 5:48).

Significantly, this Matthean summary comes at the end of six antitheses that have come to epitomize Jesus as a teacher reshaping his tradition. "You have heard that it was said to those of ancient times. . . . But I say to you that" comes in one variation or another six times as Jesus discusses murder/anger, adultery, divorce, oaths, vengeance, and love of neighbor and enemy (Matt. 5:21–48).[40] A first reading of the antitheses may suggest a repudiation of the tradition; yet closer reading sees Jesus as deepening and extending the tradition, not rejecting it.[41] Wright is correct to point out that the distinction Jesus makes is not between "outward" and "inward" ways of keeping the law. "They emphasize, rather, the way in which the renewal which Jesus sought to engender would produce a radically different way of being Israel in real-life Palestinian situations."[42]

As we will see in later sections and chapters, Jesus' conversation with his tradition shaped his message in decisive ways, and the oft-heard, off-hand claim that "there was nothing new in Jesus' teaching" has basis in his teaching itself. "Do not think that I have come to abolish the law or the prophets" (Matt. 5:17) and "Today this scripture has been fulfilled in your hearing" (Luke 4:21) are cases in point. But Jesus did decisively critique the tradition; he sharply critiqued the appropriation and practice of the tradition by many of his contemporaries, thus standing in a long line of interpretive tradition from the prophets to the rabbis.

Jesus Knew the Probable Outcome of His Ministry of Resistance and Transformation, and He Did Not Capitulate to Empire, Temple, or Adversary

The claim of this section is not, let me emphasize, a claim about Jesus' "messianic self-consciousness" or self-understanding. It is a claim about

Jesus' words and actions within their sociohistorical milieu. As we have already seen, the extent to which Galilee was a particular hotbed of resistance and revolt is disputed.[43] Significantly, those who argue that it was not a seat of rebellion do so in part because of the thoroughness of Roman/Herodian suppression in the period immediately before and during Jesus' lifetime. More significantly, no one questions that whatever resistance and revolt there was in first-century Palestine was quickly, brutally, and absolutely crushed.

Jesus' anticipation of his death is often, and unhelpfully, limited to those passages referred to as "passion predictions" (Mark 8:31–33; 9:31–32; 10:32–34; and par.). But these passages are better explored under the rubric that Dunn terms, "Did Jesus give meaning to his anticipated death?"[44] an issue not central to this study. Consideration of the claim of this section also tends to be overshadowed by the evangelists' own purposes, and the centrality of the cross in Paul and other early Christian writings in and out of the New Testament. In Mark the Pharisees and Herodians are seeking to "destroy" Jesus by 3:6. Paul "decided to know nothing among you except Jesus Christ, and him crucified" (1 Cor. 2:2). And by the writing of the Letter to the Hebrews, it begins to seem that the only reason Jesus was born was to die. "But as it is, he has appeared once for all at the end of the age to remove sin by the sacrifice of himself" (9:26b). Moreover, from what we know of the earliest liturgies until now, the focus on Jesus' self-offering and self-sacrifice in the Great Thanksgiving tends to overwhelm any other reading of what Jesus may or may not have anticipated the outcome of his ministry to be.[45] If we set all this aside, with what are we left? Quite a bit, in fact.

Turning from psychology to historical reconstruction is helpful, looking at what Jesus is reported to have said and done, and not at what or whom he might have understood himself to be.[46] Three points from the earlier discussion of Jesus as a Galilean Jew seem most important in reconstructing the socioeconomic and political realities in Palestine during Jesus' ministry. First, the extreme socioeconomic stratification reduced close to 85 percent of the population to what we might call a hand-to-mouth existence, the sort of people for whom the petition "Give us this day our daily bread" (Matt. 6:11) was a matter of survival. For them a parable built around Leviticus 19:13b, "You shall not keep for yourself the wages of a laborer until morning," as in the Laborers in the Vineyard (Matt. 20:1–15), would have deep resonance.[47] Contributing to this desperate situation was a triple system of taxation (imperial Rome, regional Galilean or Judean, temple) that claimed upward to or beyond 50 percent of produce or income.[48] Second, the governing authorities were doubly oppressive, not just the Romans but also their collaborators or appointees. Be it Hasmonean or Herodian, and in the case of Judea after Herod's death and the uprising(s) that followed, direct Roman rule by a procurator, Palestine was to greater and lesser extents intrusively occupied territory. And the temple authorities, whose motives we also do well not to explore in the absence of any source even slightly unbiased, cooperated and collaborated with the Romans in ways that our contemporary notions of church-state separation must work to understand. It follows, third, that for many in Judea and Galilee, and not just in Samaria, the temple itself was a mixed symbol, not only of tradition, heritage, and pride, but also of collaboration and oppression.

Into this world at this time with these realities, these Powers, Jesus came preaching. He proclaimed what has been variously characterized as a "domination free order" (Wink) or a "brokerless kingdom" (Crossan), but which Jesus himself is most often depicted as calling the kingdom of God/heaven. This very phrasing was an implied challenge to empire, and Jesus' response to queries about taxation (Matt. 17:24–27; Mark 12:14–17; and par.) and his discourses on authority (Mark 10:42–45 and par.) would have done little to change that impression. And given the cooperation/ collaboration between empire and temple, Jesus' continuing disagreements and disputations with temple and religious authorities was a challenge to the established order, which was finally a Roman order. This culminated in the pronouncement of judgment upon the temple (Mark 11:11–22, which will be discussed in chap. 3), the temple inquisition of Mark 12 and parallels, and the eschatological discourse of Mark 13 and parallels—all unequivocally challenging the place and future of the temple. Finally, there is Jesus' ministry of resistance to the adversary, first engaged in the "temptation scene" (Mark 1:12–13/Matt. 4:1–11/Luke 4:1–13) and dramatically repeated in exorcisms and healings. Empire, temple, and adversary sought to silence or co-opt Jesus, without success. And so they collaborated to kill him.

Despite these gaps just where one desires clear evidence from Jesus, from the logic of the situation important inferences are valid: (a) Jesus was not executed because he happened to be at the wrong place at the wrong time; (b) since there is no evidence that his disciples or anyone else talked him into going to Jerusalem, he went freely and deliberately, indeed with a sense that his vocation made the trip unavoidable; (c) the events in Jerusalem, though having a distinct character, are of a piece with the Galilean mission, indeed, its climax; (d) in going to Jerusalem he who in Galilee understood himself to be the finger of God put himself and his mission into the hands of God.[49]

Jesus was a Galilean Jew who proclaimed a kingdom and resisted a crown. He was a teacher actively reshaping a tradition for a new day, and who knew the probable outcome of his ministry of resistance and transformation, yet did not capitulate to empire, temple, or adversary. With this rudimentary understanding of who Jesus was in history, we may now turn to how Jesus shaped and shared his proclamation.

THE RHETORIC OF JESUS

"The rhetoric of Jesus" is a loaded phrase, needing some explanation in order to be placed within the world of New Testament studies, rhetoric, and homiletics. First is the meaning of the prepositional phrase. While this study is interested in Jesus within history, it will not make or defend claims about the degree to which any saying may or may not be attributed to the "historical" Jesus, nor distinguish between Jesus' words, traditional or redactional additions, and an evangelist's shaping for narrative, theological, or other reason. In other words, for (over?)simplicity's sake, the rhetoric attributed to Jesus in the Synoptic Gospels will be treated, and referred to, as the rhetoric *of* Jesus. This should not be misconstrued as an attempt to make indirect claims for the historical reliability of one form of a saying of Jesus over another. It is rather an acceptance that the canonical text is as far back as we need go in this project. Second is the understanding of rhetoric implicit in my analysis. I confess to a homiletical hybrid, informed by studies of classical rhetoric, *new* rhetoric, rhetorical criticism, and homiletics. The goal is not as confused as the method, however. I want to understand how Jesus is depicted as employing language, not how the evangelists employ language in their depiction of Jesus. It is the rhetoric of proclamation, not the rhetoric of composition, that concerns me.

Mark 10:17–30, the account of Jesus' encounter with one who has "many possessions," is an excellent place to begin consideration of the rhetoric of Jesus in the Synoptic Gospels, in part because Matthew (19:16–30) and Luke (18:18–30) reproduce Mark with considerable fidelity.

> [17]As he was setting out on a journey, a man ran up and knelt before him, and asked him, "Good Teacher, what must I do to inherit eternal life?" [18]Jesus said to him, "Why do you call me good? No one is good but God alone. [19]You know the commandments: 'You shall not murder; You shall not commit adultery; You shall not steal; You shall not bear false witness; You shall not defraud; Honor your father and mother.'" [20]He said to him, "Teacher, I have kept all these since my youth." [21]Jesus, looking at him, loved him and said, "You lack one thing; go, sell what you own, and give the money to the poor, and you will have treasure in heaven; then come, follow me." [22]When he heard this, he was shocked and went away grieving, for he had many possessions. [23]Then Jesus looked around and said to his disciples, "How hard it will be for those who have wealth to enter the kingdom of God!" [24]And the disciples were perplexed at these words. But Jesus said to them again, "Children, how hard it is to enter the kingdom of God! [25]It is easier for a camel to go through the eye of a needle than for someone who is rich to enter the kingdom of God." [26]They were greatly astounded and said to one another, "Then who can be saved?" [27]Jesus looked at them and said, "For mortals it is impossible, but not for God; for God all things are possible." [28]Peter began to say to him, "Look, we have left everything and followed you." [29]Jesus said, "Truly I tell you, there is no one who has left house or brothers or sisters or mother or father or children or fields, for my sake and for the sake of the good news, [30]who will not receive a hundredfold now in this age—houses, brothers and sisters, mothers and children, and fields with persecutions—and in the age to come eternal life."

Traditional analysis divides the passage into three sections: 17–22, the dialogue with the inquirer; 23–27, the first dialogue with the disciples on entering the kingdom; 28–30 (31), the second dialogue with the disciples on leaving, following, and receiving. This should not be taken to suggest the passage is weakly linked rhetorically. Applying Robbins'sociorhetorical method, which asks the reader to consider five aspects, or "textures," of biblical material , reveals an especially rich passage.[50] The scene begins with a man running to Jesus, kneeling, calling Jesus "Good Teacher," and asking what he should do to inherit eternal life. The dialogue with the disciples concludes with Jesus promising that they will have eternal life in the age to come.[51] Further connecting the unit is the threefold reference to Jesus "looking upon" his interlocutors: first the man, whom he looks upon and "loves" (v. 21); then the disciples as a group (v. 23); and finally Peter (vv. 27–28). Moreover, while the man had many possessions (v. 22), and the disciples have given up everything (v. 28), the latter shall gain it all one hundredfold *in this age*, albeit "with persecutions" (v. 30).

Vivid language of movement characterizes both the narration and the discourse: while Jesus is "going out," the man "runs toward" him (v. 17 AT). Jesus soon tells him to "go," "sell," "give," and "come" and "follow" (v. 21). But the man "departs" (v. 22 AT). Jesus says it is hard to "enter into" the kingdom not once but three times in the space of three verses (vv. 23–25 AT), twice with specific references to those with riches. Peter speaks of the disciples' "leaving" and "following" (v. 28 AT), and Jesus affirms their leaving with a promise of things to come (v. 30). There is also a tough edge to the language: "kneeling" (v. 17), "guarding" (v. 20), "saddened" and "sorrowful" (v. 22), "hardness" of entry (vv. 23–24; AT in sentence).

The breadth and depth of the intertexture in this passage is notable. Most obvious is the oral-scribal intertexture of the quotation by Jesus of five of the Ten Commandments, and the fascinating addition of a sixth ("You shall not defraud") not found in the Decalogues of Exodus and Deuteronomy. The proverbial "eye of the needle" must surely have at least some Galilean significance to belie desperate preachers' attempts to squeeze a scrawny camel through a mythical Jerusalem gate. The title used by the man for Jesus, "Teacher," resounds through the Gospels, and the adjective he uses the first time, "Good," is rejected by Jesus here in the absolute, but used elsewhere to describe the manner of living that Jesus proclaims ("good" soil, Mark 4:7; "the good person out of the good treasure of the heart produces good," Luke 6:45a). The place of the Ten Commandments in the teaching of Jesus, with the notable resonance at Luke 10:25–37, is significant, as is the phenomenon of "leaving everything" as a condition of discipleship. So also the attitude toward wealth and possessions that left the disciples "shocked" when Jesus said it would be hard for those with riches to enter the kingdom (Mark 10:24, 26 AT), something echoed in the Letter of James (4:13–5:5).

This passage stands at the crossroads of Robbins' third aspect of a text, the social and cultural textures. For instance, very little solo running goes on in the Synoptic Gospels—this man, the Prodigal's Father, and Zacchaeus—and even less kneeling. The man with many possessions is the only one who does both. In a culture that makes profound distinctions between what honors and shames a person or family, the entire description of the man's approach to Jesus, his initial address, and Jesus' response, "Why do you call me good?" is fraught with significance. The questions raised by Jesus' challenge, "You lack one thing," continue to reverberate in our own social and cultural setting, as do the questions raised by Jesus' triple insistence on how hard it will be for a person with possessions to enter the kingdom. The reader is forced to wonder about the understanding of discipleship behind the text. Further, all of the intertextual questions about wealth and possessions should also be asked of the social and cultural textures.

How one addresses the issues raised above will tell as much about the interpreter's ideological orientation as it will about the text itself. Wealth and salvation, the hindrance of riches, sacrifice as necessary for discipleship—these are powerful and vital ideological issues. There is also the ideological issue of how one characterizes the "kingdom" that Jesus states is hard to enter.

The passage begins with the question that arguably is *the* question of the gospel: "What must I do to inherit eternal life?" Jesus adds a second issue of sacred texture by stating, "No one is good except God" (AT). The entire passage is focused on questions of eternity, divinity, faithfulness to tradition, sacrifice and reward, and not least what we should do with the statement that "nothing is impossible with God" (10:27 AT).

The previous few paragraphs are standard-issue sociorhetorical criticism of a biblical passage, deeply indebted to the work of Vernon Robbins. The primary concern is with how the author, Mark, has used and shaped an event and sayings of Jesus from the tradition as a key moment in his Gospel, how the verses relate to other verses in Scripture, and what Mark's shaping tells us about conditions and concerns of his community and intended audience. For this study, that is all background. What must come to the foreground is what we can see about the rhetoric of Jesus in the passage, and not just the rhetoric of Mark.

The first striking feature is that almost everything Jesus says comes either in response to and/or in conversation with someone else. The initial responses are to his inquirer (vv. 17–21), then to his perplexed disciples (vv. 24–27), and finally to Peter (vv. 28–30). But the conversation, or dialogue, is not just with the inquirer and the disciples; it is also explicitly with the tradition, and implicitly with the culture. By citing commandments from the Decalogue, Jesus invites Torah into the conversation. In referring to the difficulty of entering the kingdom, and the particular difficulty that those with possessions will encounter, Jesus brings to the surface class distinctions and invites further reflection on the place of wealth and possessions in the life of faith. This multilevel conversation, hardly atypical in the teaching and preaching of Jesus, will be referred to in this study as *dialogical.*

In the midst of the conversations, we also encounter pronouncement; indeed later form critics, building on Bultmann's understanding of the passage, will refer to it as a "pronouncement story." Jesus makes six specific declarations:

1. "No one is good but God alone" (v. 18).
2. "You lack one thing; . . . then come, follow me" (v. 21).
3. "How hard it will be for those who have wealth to enter the kingdom of God!" (v. 23).
4. "Children, how hard it is to enter the kingdom of God! It is easier for a camel to go through the eye of a needle than for someone who is rich to enter the kingdom of God" (vv. 24b–25).
5. "For God all things are possible" (v. 27).
6. "Truly I tell you, there is no one who has left . . . who will not receive a hundredfold, . . . and in the age to come eternal life" (vv. 29–30).

The pronouncements differ considerably—two are about God; one is particular to Jesus' first interlocutor; two are about the difficulty of entering the kingdom, with specific focus on those with many possessions; and one is to the Twelve—but all are definitive. Jesus is not asking, even in the middle of dialogue; Jesus makes claims, theological and soteriological. Here, and throughout the Synoptic Gospels, Jesus' rhetoric can be well described as *proclamatory.*

A third feature of the passage, while not as prominent, is often observed, sometimes as perplexing: Jesus' refusal to accept the inquirer's flattering sobriquet, "Good Teacher." As we have seen, the noun is not the problem since it is a common designation and even self-designation (Mark 14:14) of Jesus. But despite the also-noted positive use of the adjective, here it is repudiated and becomes the basis for a proclamation: "No one is good but God alone." This fits into a pattern described in the previous section: while Jesus "proclaimed a kingdom," he "resisted a crown." Neither here nor elsewhere in the Synoptics when Jesus is asked, "What should I do to inherit eternal life?" does he say, "Believe in me." Instead, Jesus points to two things, Torah and

God, and says, "Follow me," an invitation to discipleship well attested in Jewish and Greek literatures, which need not carry anything like the messianic weight often given to it.[52] Jesus' rhetorical strategy in the passages suggests a rhetoric that is only *occasionally self-referential.*

Finally, and most obviously, is Jesus' use of figurative language. Although Mark 10:17–30 is not the best example of this characteristic, it is representative. Four figures are clearly present: (1) *metaphor:* "treasure in heaven"; (2) *repetition for the sake of emphasis:* "How hard it will be, . . . how hard it is"; (3) *proverb:* the camel and the rich person; (4) *hyperbole:* "will not receive a hundredfold." Other examples arguably include use of the diminutive "children [*tekna*]" at verse 24, the proverbial feel of "for God all things are possible," and "you lack one thing," an example of litotes, a form of ironic understatement. In any case, it is more than fair to say that Jesus' rhetoric in this passage is *persistently figurative.*

Dialogical. Proclamatory. Occasionally self-referential. Persistently figurative. The thesis of this study is that the rhetoric of Jesus in the Synoptic Gospels has four distinct and consistent aspects. Jesus' rhetoric is dialogical, proclamatory, occasionally self-referential, and persistently figurative. While the exegetical, rhetorical, and homiletical foundations and implications for this claim will be developed and explored in the chapters to follow, it is important to further ground the claim at the outset.

1. *Dialogical.* Jesus is depicted as teaching and preaching in response to challenges, questions, and traditions. These dialogues are both implicit, as in Luke 4:16–30 when the people of Nazareth express their amazement to each other at the grace of his words and Jesus responds to the undercurrent,[53] and explicit, as in Mark 2:18–20 when the disciples of John and the Pharisees ask Jesus why his disciples do not fast. Jesus is often portrayed as responsive to specific questions, a well-known example echoing Mark 10:17–20 and Luke 10:25–28 found at Matthew 22:34–36 and parallels: "When the Pharisees heard that he had silenced the Sadducees, they gathered together, and one of them, a lawyer, asked him a question to test him. 'Teacher, which commandment in the law is the greatest?'" Not all the questions initiating dialogue are overt, however. In Mark 9:33ff. Jesus responds to what he seems to have overheard. "Then they came to Capernaum; and when he was in the house he asked them, 'What were you arguing about on the way?' But they were silent, for on the way they had argued with one another over who was the greatest. He sat down, called the twelve, and said to them,

'Whoever wants to be first must be last of all and servant of all.'" In this same scene Luke says that Jesus was "aware of their inner thoughts" (9:47), also a basis for response in Luke 6:8 (Mark 3:5) and elsewhere.

The dialogical nature of Jesus' rhetoric is not limited to conversation with inquirers, puzzled disciples, and provocative challengers. Indeed, a case can be made that the most obvious dialogues are second in importance to the dialogue with tradition, culture, and empire. Torah is inevitably present, as in the encounter with the rich person in Mark 10, and most famously in the six antitheses of Matthew 5:21–48. But Torah is also in the background, reflected through the culture: "Why do John's disciples and the disciples of the Pharisees fast, but your disciples do not fast?" (Mark 2:18). And Torah also provides background to the conflict with empire: "Render to Caesar" and the like. How one worships God alone, without provoking retaliation from the empire, was not an abstract question under Roman rule. The dialogues of the Synoptic Gospels differ from those in the Fourth Gospel, and even more from dialogues of Socrates or other putative models from antiquity. Rightly understood, however, they are an important feature of the depiction of Jesus' preaching and teaching, with important implications for our preaching today.

2. *Proclamatory.* Jesus is consistently depicted as making bold and authoritative pronouncements. Mark begins his account of Jesus' teaching ministry by telling us, "Jesus went into Galilee, proclaiming the gospel of God, and saying, 'The time is fulfilled, and the kingdom of God is near. Repent and believe in the gospel'" (Mark 1:14b–15 AT). Mark continues the emphasis by describing the crowds as reacting to Jesus' teaching as having authority (1:22, 27), though at this juncture the reader has not yet heard the teaching. The rest of Mark's Gospel depicts the authoritative quality of Jesus' proclamation; from opening encounters (2:1–12) to final conversations (14:17–42), Jesus is consistently depicted as making clear and bold pronouncements.

This proclamation comes in a variety of forms. In the "synagogue sermon" of Luke 4:14–30, we encounter a number of them. "Today this scripture has been fulfilled in your hearing" (4:21) is both in absolute terms and in dialogue with the tradition (Isa. 61:1–2; 58:6). Soon the proclamation becomes figurative and proverbial: "Doctor, cure yourself," and "Truly I tell you, no prophet is accepted in the prophet's hometown" (Luke 4:23–24). Returning to the tradition, but this time in the form of midrash, Jesus reminds his listeners—to their outrage—of Elijah and Elisha's ministry to non-Israelites (4:25–27; 1 Kgs. 17;

2 Kgs. 5). All the while the proclamation is dialogical and, as is often the case for Jesus, controversial and provocative.

Jesus' proclamation is frequently ironic, the Beatitudes (Matt. 5:1–11) coming most easily to mind. But it is not always so: at times his preaching is so direct that the reader wants to duck and cover. Almost the entirety of the Sermon on the Mount falls under the category of "proclamatory," from the opening macarisms through the antitheses and the extraordinary "Be perfect, therefore, as your heavenly Father is perfect" (5:48). The rest of the sermon is filled with verbs in various forms of the imperative, from the admonition to "Beware" how one practices one's piety in 6:1 to the warning to "Beware" of false prophets at 7:15. The audience in Capernaum was right: Jesus preaches with authority (Mark 1:27).

3. *Occasionally self-referential.* The frequent use of self-reference in the Fourth Gospel is one of the main differences between the rhetoric of Jesus in John and in the Synoptic Gospels. But regardless of that comparison, it is striking how infrequently Jesus is depicted as speaking about himself directly in Matthew, Mark, and Luke. Further, his rhetorical goal in the more frequent indirect references, as in the "Son of Man" sayings, is a topic of considerable dispute. What we find more often are references to Jesus' commanding that his identity and actions not be made known (e.g., Mark 1:44; 3:12; 5:43), Jesus' resisting flattery (10:18), refusing to perform signs (8:11–12), and by virtue of his itinerancy, regularly retreating from the recognition that his deeds and words create (e.g., Mark 1:45).

In our calculations about the place of self-reference in his rhetoric, Jesus' use of story is also worth noting. Traditional interpretation has tended to identify Jesus with characters in his own parables and allegories, but that is often a history of misreading. The strategy of teaching in parables directs the listener away from the speaker and to the story. So, for instance, in the Allegory of the Seed and Soils (Mark 4:1–7), in both the story and the later interpretation (4:13–20), the sower disappears after the first verse, hardly a formula for christological claims.[54]

This rhetorical strategy has a second impact: when Jesus does refer to himself, both directly and as "the Son of the Man" (AT), the sayings carry an added impact. After thirteen chapters and sixty-one verses of Jesus demurring, declining, silencing, and withdrawing, the "I am [*egō eimi*]" of Mark 14:62 explodes in the reader's ears as it did before the council. The following Son of Man saying quotes the prophet Daniel (7:13) and continues the cacophony, forcing the reader to ask again

what Jesus means in "the Son of the Man" references earlier in the
Gospel, a topic to be explored in chapter 4.

4. *Persistently figurative.* Jesus never misses an opportunity to elab-
orate, illustrate, or sharpen his message through metaphor (Matt.
15:24–26), hyperbole (Mark 9:42–50), parable (Mark 4:26–29), allegory (Luke 20:9–19), and other rhetorical figures. Whether the mode
of discourse is hortatory (e.g., the "narrow door," Luke 13:23–30) or
didactic (e.g., the instructions on table etiquette, Luke 14:7–14), in
dialogue (the lawyer in Luke 10) or proclamation (e.g., "counting the
cost," Luke 14:25–33), while confronting opponents (allegory of the
vineyard owner and tenants, Mark 12:1–11) or encouraging followers ("My yoke is easy," Matt. 11:28–30)—the language attributed to
Jesus is invariably figurative. Amos Wilder has emphasized this use of
language as a key "to the mystery of his being."

> In his modes of speech we may recognize yet another clue to the
> mystery of his being. In certain ages of culture we know how ear-
> lier artistic forms, whether in painting or music or poetry, come to
> a moment of perfection in some great master. He is able both to
> exploit all the initiatives of his predecessors and at the same time to
> relate himself and the forms he employs to a new occasion. So in
> Jesus, it is as though many ancient tributaries of speech, many styles,
> merged in him. The discourse of prophet, lawgiver, and wise man
> meet in him. He unites in himself many roles. . . . Jesus' speech had
> the character not of instruction and ideas but of compelling imagi-
> nation, or spell, or mythical shock and transformation.[55]

Nowhere is this more obvious than in the figure most characteristic
of Jesus' proclamation, the parable, but it is hardly limited to parable. A
trio of examples from the Gospel of Luke will suffice until chapter 5.

> As they were going along the road, someone said to him, "I will fol-
> low you wherever you go." And Jesus said to him, "Foxes have holes,
> and birds of the air have nests; but the Son of Man has nowhere to
> lay his head."
>   To another he said, "Follow me." But he said, "Lord, first let me go
> and bury my father." But Jesus said to him, "Let the dead bury their
> own dead; but as for you, go and proclaim the kingdom of God."
>   Another said, "I will follow you, Lord; but let me first say farewell
> to those at my home." Jesus said to him, "No one who puts a hand
> to the plow and looks back is fit for the kingdom of God."
>   (Luke 9:57–62)

Foxes have holes. Let the dead bury the dead. Never look back. Good news, right? Yes, but good news for those with "eyes to see and ears to hear." My guess is that most of those who preach the twenty-first-century equivalent of Jesus' message will have some explaining to do, actually a lot of explaining to do. Pointed metaphors require explanation. We are not called "reporters"; we are called "preachers." And we explain ourselves because the preaching of the one we proclaim was *persistently figurative*.

THE RHETORIC OF PROCLAMATION

> What is the matter with preaching today? Trying to answer that question is a little like flushing out a covey of quail. One hardly knows where to shoot. What's gone wrong with preaching? Is it content, style, language, purpose, relevance, delivery? All of the above? Everybody has an opinion, a pet peeve, about sermons—at least everybody who still cares enough to raise a critique. Sermons are boring or sensationalist, trivial or pompous, irrelevant or trendy, too caught up in "Bible speak" or not biblical enough, too long or too short, too worldly or too remote, and on and on.[56]

Long goes on to point out that such critiques of preaching are hardly limited to our era. The volume for which he wrote was compiled to reflect anew on Harry Emerson Fosdick's 1928 article, "What Is the Matter with Preaching?"[57] And the feeling that something, some *thing* is wrong with contemporary preaching, is widely shared.

David Buttrick offers typically trenchant questions. "By all objective standards, *the pulpit has lost public influence*. Certainly preaching is no longer as socially significant as it once was. . . . How can we account for the collapse of the pulpit? At least 150 thousand sermons are preached each week in North America, but to what avail? How can we account for the loss of pulpit impact? What's the problem?"[58] Whatever the causes, the consensus of a shift in the pulpit's prominence and influence is widely shared. How to address the problem, if it even can be addressed, is something else again. In 2005 the Louisville Institute, a program of the Religion Division of the Lilly Endowment (Inc.), based at Louisville Presbyterian Seminary, gathered a distinguished group of preachers and practitioners to discuss planning a consultation and then conference on "The Public Voice of the Pulpit." Participants agreed on the importance of the issue, acknowledging that in large measure the

pulpit seems to have lost its public voice, but they could not frame critical questions in a way thought productive enough to proceed. Participants knew that there was a significant problem, but they did not know
how to address it. Neither consultation nor conference was held.

The challenge here is to resist being overwhelmed by the issue, to
resist seeking easy resolution by limiting consideration to any one sermon or any one preacher. All of us preach effectively from time to time,
and some of us preach effectively week in and week out. What might
help most of us preach effectively most of the time?

> The truly great preachers in this world are people whose names no
> one will ever know, because their sermons both arise from and are
> entirely absorbed by local communities of listeners who labor with
> them to embody God's word. In cases such as these, the success of
> a sermon is not measured by how many people said they liked it,
> nor by a preacher's own sense of accomplishment, but by how the
> spoken word cleared a space for people to be met and set in motion
> by the Spirit of the living God.[59]

Truly great preaching, Taylor maintains, will happen only in community. It is not a one-off dazzler for a convention or conference, but
a "weekly wrestling match." It always takes two to tango, engaging
speaker and hearer. The question then seems to become something
of a dilemma. If preaching that "avails" must come from the community being shaped by the preaching, and the community shapes the
preaching, which comes first, preaching or community? Put more cyni-
cally, if 150 thousand sermons are preached every Sunday, and nothing
changes, did anyone hear them?

Central to the thesis of this project is that dilemma or not, there
is a way forward, and the clearest example of this way forward is the
preaching of Jesus. Those of us who wrestle weekly will be well served
by considering the characteristics of Jesus' rhetoric and contrasting
what characterizes his preaching with what too often characterizes
our own. The preaching of Jesus has been characterized as dialogical, proclamatory, occasionally self-referential, and persistently figurative. Rarely can the same be said of contemporary North American
preaching. We struggle to be relevant and responsive; we fear to speak
without qualifications; we talk about ourselves much more than we
should; and loathe as we are to admit it, we are sometimes simply boring. If the preaching of Jesus is dialogical, proclamatory, occasionally
self-referential, and persistently figurative, our preaching about Jesus

may all too often be characterized as unresponsive, indecisive, self-indulgent, and unimaginative. A little extreme? Yes, but there must be some reason why our collective 150 thousand weekly sermons are making so little difference.

Dialogical or Unresponsive?

Here is a true story: A Baptist preacher was going on at what appears to have been too considerable length when the preacher's young son stood up on the pew in frustration and asked one and all, "Does anybody here have any idea what he is talking about?" While the son in question was relocated to the balcony for the remainder of the pastor's tenure, his question can be taken in a number of ways. What I have understood to have been heard by the congregation was, "Does anyone care about what he is saying?" The presumed answer, perhaps even for the preacher in this instance, was "No." The issue was, and generally is, not whether the listeners understand what the preacher is talking about, but whether what the preacher is talking about aligns in any meaningful way with what the listeners care about.

As we have seen, this was not a problem for Jesus. The radically dialogical nature of his preaching virtually guaranteed an alignment of concerns, and not only when he was responding to specific questions. There are no questions, except Jesus' own rhetorical questions, in the Sermon on the Mount, but there is no better example of the dialogical nature of Jesus' preaching than Matthew 5–7. From the blessings of the distressed, dispossessed, and distraught, to the challenge to do, not just say, in response to the Sermon—Jesus is in dialogue with tradition, culture, and the lives of his listeners.

Dialogical preaching does not mean a return to our ill-fated experiments with "dialogue sermons" in the 1970s. No one has to stand up in the middle of your sermon and ask, "What do you want us to do about it, preacher?" Dialogical preaching means asking yourself, often and repeatedly, in the beginning, middle, and end of preparing your sermon: What questions do I imagine my listeners will bring with them? What questions will arise in the hearing of Scripture and sermon? It means taking listener and context as seriously as we take the biblical text. There are a variety of ways to do this, all guided by one question: "What does the Holy Spirit want the people of God to hear from these texts on this occasion?"

I will not ask you to "close your eyes" because I hate that, and it makes it hard to keep reading, so simply imagine for a moment those with whom you preach. Who is sitting where? What was *their* week like? How attentive or distracted are they this morning? From all of your interaction and ministry with them, how might they hear the lesson(s) for the day? Have you noticed in Sunday school or youth group, in a meeting, at a wedding, wherever, that certain themes or theological claims provoke a greater or lesser response? These are the sort of questions we must ask ourselves throughout the sermon-preparation process. The issue, preacher, is not just what you think the Scripture is about; that is to ask, "What does the Holy Spirit want me to *say* about these texts on this occasion?" This is the easier question but the wrong question. Dialogical preaching is not about our speaking but about their hearing. One of the most faithful ways our preaching can become more like Jesus' preaching is to take seriously how responsive his preaching was to the concerns, questions, needs, and hopes of his listeners.

Proclamatory or Indecisive?

I have said earlier that one of many forces driving this project was the experience of the difference in the run-up to the First and Second Gulf Wars. In 1990–1991, believers of every faith, creed, and confession gathered to pray, to petition, and to protest, in this country and abroad. I will always remember the shock of going to a Wednesday evening service in January 1991 and hearing that the first bombs were falling on Baghdad. Parishioners were crying, almost keening. "But we prayed so hard on Sunday!" one of them said. "How can this happen?" Not so in 2003. There were a few protests, but as near as one could tell, even fewer sermons. Had 9/11 robbed the pulpit of its voice? Looking back, we must surely agree that it did, but were the now-admitted manipulation of intelligence data and the post-9/11 cultural trend in support of the Bush administration's policies the only explanation?[60] I do not think so. What one might call the domestication of preaching was much longer in coming.

"Repent! Believe!" Jesus says. And this:

Do to others as you would have them do to you. If you love those who love you, what credit is that to you? For even sinners love those who love them. If you do good to those who do good to you, what credit is that to you? For even sinners do the same. If you lend to those from whom you hope to receive, what credit is that to you? Even sinners lend to sinners, to receive as much again. But love your enemies, do good, and lend, expecting nothing in return. Your reward will be great, and you will be children of the Most High; for he is kind to the ungrateful and the wicked. Be merciful, just as your Father is merciful.

(Luke 6:31–36)

Clearly this sermon snippet is dialogical, but it is also decisively pro-clamatory. Jesus does not say, "Love some a little and others a lot" or "Be sure to give the poor a fair interest rate." Jesus knows exactly what we are thinking and doing and is telling us to change. It is fairly abstract at the beginning and end, "Do to others" and "Be merciful," but the application is as specific as it can be. Jesus chides, scolds, and promises, and there is no mistaking what behavior he is after.

Frankly, I do not know what we are afraid of. Do we think our listeners do not have some idea how we think on crucial and controversial issues? Do they not already know something of our political leanings, our social concerns and commitments, and our personal top ten "Thou Shalt Nots"? Must everything that matters be saved for "adult forum" or some other setting where we cannot be accused of abusing the power of the pulpit? And come to think of it, if we are not occasionally accused of pulpit abuse, are we likely then not saying much of anything that matters?

One of the most wonderful and infrequently used words in the Gospels is "to have compassion." Sometimes the NRSV translates it as "mercy," but in contemporary English by far the preferred translation is "compassion." It is what the Samaritan has for the injured man, what the prodigal father has for his lost son. The Greek loans itself to our word "spleen" but refers more specifically to the bowels, so that an overly literal translation might be "a feeling from the very depths of our being." A desperate preacher might talk about "with passion." I am that preacher, because a homiletical concern to be "fair and balanced" in the pulpit has led to preaching that lacks passion. Students refer to this, referencing the Greek term *splanchnizomai*, as "gutless" preaching.

None of this should be taken as license for name-calling, score-settling, saber-rattling, or personal assaults. Nor does it suggest that every sermon should be devoted to "taking a stand" on an "issue." It does mean that when a stand is called for, when a controversy needs to be addressed, when a text is challenging the community, the preacher deals with it, faithfully, fully, and well. It calls us to remember that proclaiming the good news involves a call to discipleship, that after "Repent!" comes "Believe!" and that our listeners often need help in imagining what a faithful life looks like. Proclamatory preaching is not pulpit-pounding, Bible-waving bravado. It is decisive and clear, with our being willing to risk not always hearing "Nice sermon, pastor" from listeners on the way out the door.

Occasionally Self-Referential or Self-Indulgent?

You have heard it. You have done it. Preachers often begin with reference to how difficult they find the Scripture lesson and tell all the ways they thought of trying to get around it. Then they share a book they read or tell of a professor they had who changed their way of understanding the passage so that it no longer seemed so overwhelming. Next they tell of a relative or friend who practiced just what is being preached, and they conclude with a few lines from a favorite poet or songwriter who perfectly captures the heart of the message just shared. What do we know? We know that the preacher struggles as we do. We know that the preacher is well educated and well read. We know that the preacher has exemplary friends and family members. And we know that the preacher is not just a left-brained problem-solver, but has an artistic and literary side as well. In other words, we know too much about the preacher.

Teaching on this topic has proved it to be the one characteristic of Jesus' preaching in the Synoptic Gospels most misunderstood and most resisted. Students bring me every example of self-reference in the Synoptics and say, "See!" as if I claimed that Jesus was *never* self-referential. Or they complain that if they never refer to themselves, their congregations will never get to know them, or think that they lack a faith of their own. But I never say never: I say rarely and occasionally. One might also say, thoughtfully and judiciously, that when Jesus does speak self-referentially in the Synoptics, the impact is significant.

> The seventy returned with joy, saying, "Lord, in your name even the demons submit to us!" He said to them, "I watched Satan fall from heaven like a flash of lightning. See, I have given you authority to tread on snakes and scorpions, and over all the power of the enemy; and nothing will hurt you. Nevertheless, do not rejoice at this, that

the spirits submit to you, but rejoice that your names are written in heaven."

At that same hour Jesus rejoiced in the Holy Spirit and said, "I thank you, Father, Lord of heaven and earth, because you have hidden these things from the wise and the intelligent and have revealed them to infants; yes, Father, for such was your gracious will. All things have been handed over to me by my Father; and no one knows who the Son is except the Father, or who the Father is except the Son and anyone to whom the Son chooses to reveal him."

(Luke 10:17–22)

If this passage were in the Fourth Gospel, it would blend right in. In the Gospel of Luke it jumps off the page—*I* watched Satan; *I* have given you authority; *I* thank you, Father; all things have been handed over to *me*—this is atypical in the Synoptics, strikingly so.

Self-referential preaching is inherently powerful, unless the preacher dilutes the power by overuse. Beginning each sermon with some variation on "A funny thing happened to me the other day," consistently using one's family life in sermons so the congregation gets to know you, and constantly mentioning incidents from one's ministry so they know you are doing your job—this can dull the ear. Moreover, such referencing sends the unintentional message that to be a person of faith is to be like the preacher, an accidentally Pauline "What you have heard and seen in me, do." *Don't,* so that when it is time to be self-disclosing, and not casually self-referencing, the rhetorical power has not been drained away.

Persistently Figurative or Unimaginative?

Late-night scrolling of the Internet gives us away. We *need* a good story to help our sermon. Sometimes, more sadly, it is a weeklong search for a way to massage the Scripture lessons to fit the good story we already have. Either way our practice often concedes the point: we know that story and figure are essential to effective preaching, and we struggle to make it happen.

Where do you think Jesus got his material? Were there scriptwriters behind the scenes feeding him his lines? Did he have a first-century copy of McCartney's *Illustrations* to thumb through? Or did he fabricate the stories, analogies, images, and metaphors himself? Fabricate? Doesn't that mean made-up, as in false? No, in rhetoric it means made-up as in "created." In Aristotle the creation of stories, whether from history

(Scripture and tradition for us) or nature, comes under the heading of "proof [*pistis*]."[61] In Dodd's classic definition of the parable, the story is "drawn from nature or common life."[62] Jesus looked around, paid attention, and shaped his stories from the material all around him, every day. This does not mean that he stood on the side of the Jericho road and watched the priest and Levite pass by, or heard the Pharisee's prayer in the temple. He made them up, fabricated the parables from the stuff of everyone's everyday lives.

You may think that you are not naturally creative or poetic. Then you will have to work at it like the rest of us. While at its highest level the fashioning of stories, parables, metaphors, and other types of illustrative material contains an element of artistry, at its foundation is skill, teachable and learnable skill. It requires practice, coaching, and correcting, but allows for growth and development. The ancients used rhetorical handbooks, copied by students in the *gymnasium*, or grammar school, to lay this foundation. Looking for shortcuts on the Internet is not the same thing. Working at the craft of your preaching is.

So preacher, which do you choose? Dialogical, proclamatory, occasionally self-referential, and persistently figurative—or unresponsive, indecisive, self-indulgent, and unimaginative? Not much of a choice, but by now you know what I am after. In the chapters to follow, we will explore in more exegetical depth how Jesus' preaching is dialogical, proclamatory, occasionally self-referential, and persistently figurative. With the help of sermons from four of the finest preachers any of us have ever heard, we will explore, rhetorically and homiletically, how our preaching can be more like Jesus' preaching.

2

Dialogical Preaching

"Pastor, I was wondering. Where do you get your sermons from?" Not such an innocent question, given the abundance of cyber-ready resources available, but assume that the questioner had a less cynical purpose: she wanted to know where you found the ideas that come to life in your preaching. You might say, "The lectionary," which would defer the real question for a moment or two, but that is not what she is after. She wants to know where *you* are coming from, what is motivating and capturing your interests, how you are interacting with the lectionary, yes, but above all, how you are interacting with *her*.

The thesis of this chapter is that we preachers will preach best if we learn to look at the same source material that Jesus turned to: Scripture, tradition, culture, and the lives of our listeners. In each of the Gospels the teaching and preaching of Jesus is regularly depicted as offered in response to questions, situations, challenges, charges, and traditional teachings. The task of the present chapter is first to explore examples of the various ways in which the preaching of Jesus is shown in response to tradition, question, challenge, and implicit situation; and next to develop how contemporary preaching may be enriched by the models of responsiveness seen in the Gospels. In the last section we will read and analyze a sermon by Dr. Fred Craddock, to better see what "dialogical preaching" looks like today. More than one homiletician has pointed out that to be effective, preaching must be responsive to the situation, needs, and questions of the audience and not just those of the preacher.[1] We will find no better model than the one the Synoptic Gospels show of Jesus. "Dialogue sermons" are safely buried in the attic underneath my plaid, three-piece polyester suits and other remnants of the 1970s. "Dialogical sermons" are due for a revival.

THE DIALOGICAL CHARACTER OF JESUS' PREACHING

If the first hallmark of good preaching is authentic responsiveness to the needs and interests of the audience, what in rhetoric is called "pathos," Jesus was an undeniably good preacher. In the Gospel of John, Jesus is more likely to tell the listeners what they need to know, and not what they asked about: the dialogue with Nicodemus in John 3:1–12 is the best-known example. But in the Synoptic Gospels, Jesus responds readily to specific spoken questions, as well as to implied ones, and responds also to Scripture, tradition, and culture.

Scripture

In the Sermon on the Mount, Jesus inaugurates a conversation with the Hebrew Bible that never really ends. He says first, "Do not think that I have come to abolish the law or the prophets; I have come not to abolish but to fulfill. For truly I tell you, until heaven and earth pass away, not one letter, not one stroke of a letter, will pass from the law until all is accomplished" (Matt. 5:17–18). But this clearly does not mean that he expects a rote and unreflective obedience to Torah, for what follows are the six antitheses: "You have heard that it was said. . . . But I say to you. . . . " Following Sanders, we saw in chapter 1 that calling for a higher standard of behavior than is found in the letter of the Law does not mean a repudiation of the Law. But what then does it mean? How should our own conversations with Scripture be influenced by what we see of Jesus' conversation? An example or two will be helpful.

Matthew 12:1–8 and parallels recount a challenge and riposte in which Jesus brings Scripture into a conversation with the Pharisees about keeping Sabbath. In the first place, what Pharisees were doing in a grain field in Galilee on the Sabbath is an interesting question (following Jesus? lying in wait for grain-plucking Galileans?), but we will leave it as a narrative requirement: if they were not, we have no story. The challenge to Jesus, "Look, your disciples are doing what it is not lawful to do on the sabbath," leads to an interpretation and application of Scripture and concludes with a "Son of Man" saying that will be considered in chapter 4. Here our interest is in the appropriation of the story of David and Ahimelech from 1 Samuel 21. David, fleeing from Saul, came to the city of Nob, whose location is not clear to us, but given what is found there—a priest, bread offered to God, the ephod, and Goliath's sword—was obviously a holy city with an important shrine. David asks for food and weapons, and Ahimelech, who "came trembling to meet David" (1 Sam. 21:1), allows David to take the bread of the Presence and the sword, for which Ahimelech and all in the city will later be killed (1 Sam. 22:16–19).

The challenge of the Pharisees presumes that the disciples were reaping (*therizein*) the grain, clearly a Sabbath violation, though the word used, "pluck" (*tillein*), does not carry that meaning. Jesus accepts the premise, and rather than arguing that what the disciples are doing is not a Sabbath violation, argues by analogy that sometimes more than rote obedience is called for. Over time the tradition came to understand that it was a Sabbath day when David came to Nob, and perhaps that tradition had become fixed by Jesus' day.[2] Otherwise the analogy seems less compelling but its use more interesting. While the pericope ends with a dramatic Son of Man saying about the Sabbath, Jesus uses Scripture to make a subtler point, bringing into tension the behavior of none other than David with Torah. "Have you not read what David did when he and his companions were hungry? He entered the house of God and ate the bread of the Presence, which it was not lawful for him or his companions to eat, but only for the priests" (Matt. 12:3–4). Jesus continues with a second analogy about the actions of priests on the Sabbath, from Numbers 28:9–10, showing a tension within Torah itself: offering a sacrifice is presumably work yet is specifically commanded for the Sabbath. Scripture, Jesus implies, tells stories of what can be understood to be technical violations of Scripture.

Not so long ago the human sexuality behavior issue roiling the church was divorce. When (never? after the children are grown?), who (laypeople? priests? bishops?), and why (abuse, adultery, or abandonment? incompatibility?) were critical issues. Unlike current debates about human sexuality, Jesus is actually recorded as having something to say about divorce, in Mark 10:1–12/Matthew 19:1–12. Once again our interest is more exegetical than ethical.

The passage is multiply dialogical, as is often the case, with the Pharisees serving as interlocutors: "Is it lawful for a man to divorce his wife?" (Mark 10:2). Jesus does not take the bait but asks them to answer their own question. Referencing Deuteronomy 24:1–4, they say, "Moses allowed a man to write a certificate of dismissal and to divorce her" (10:4). Jesus replies, "Because of your hardness of heart he wrote this commandment for you" (10:5). That is not a compliment. What follows is striking and suggestive for our understanding of Jesus' hermeneutic. Reaching back before Moses and Torah to "the beginning of creation," Jesus quotes from Genesis: first, "God made them male and female" (Mark 10:6/Gen. 1:27); then, "For this reason a man shall leave his father and mother and be joined to his wife, and the two shall become one flesh" (Mark 10:7–8a/Gen. 2:24). The pronouncement, "Therefore what God has joined together, let no one separate" follows (Mark 10:9), and the passage concludes with an addendum of explanation to the disciples (10:10–12). Once again Jesus uses Scripture to argue against a proffered understanding of a passage of Scripture.

But now we are forcing a question: did Jesus, in his dialogue with Scripture, ever call for its abrogation? In a passage to be examined below (Mark 7:1–23) in consideration of Jesus' conversation with tradition, the answer seems to be yes. But the issue is complex, for it is Mark, in an aside, who writes, "Thus he declared all foods clean" (7:19), and not Jesus himself, who uses metaphor, not declaration, to make his point. Sanders, in a chapter on "Jesus and the Law," holds that only the saying, "Let the dead bury their own dead" (Matt. 8:22/Luke 9:60) is a technical violation of the Law. "We have found one instance in which Jesus, in effect, demanded transgression of the law: the demand to the man whose father had died. Otherwise the material in the Gospels reveals no transgression by Jesus. And, with the one exception, following him did not entail transgression on the part of his followers."[3]

The Synoptic Gospels depict Jesus in an ongoing conversation with Scripture. And it is a complex conversation because Jesus appears, in what we will later come to refer to as "rabbinic" fashion, to include the whole of Scripture in that conversation. When asked about appropriate behavior on the Sabbath, Jesus does not limit himself to the Decalogue, or even to Torah, but recalls a pivotal story in the David cycle. When asked about divorce, Jesus does not limit himself to Deuteronomy 24, but reminds us of God's purposes in creation. So the preacher, I will argue later, should not confine the conversation to the focal passage(s) of the sermon and the obvious incidents of what Robbins calls "oral-scribal intertexture,"[4] but should bring to bear the whole of Scripture in the interpretation of the passage.

Tradition

An interesting biblical counterpoint to Jesus' dialogue and pronouncement on divorce is the story of Hosea and his wife, Gomer. In Hosea 1
the prophet is told, "Go, take for yourself a wife of whoredom" (1:2),
which he does, and they have three children. In Hosea 2 prophetic ora-
cle replaces the narrative style of chapter 1, and the couple appears to
have divorced: "Plead with your mother—plead, for she is not my wife,
and I am not her husband" (2:2). Gomer has (re)turned to prostitu-
tion: "For their mother has played the whore; she who conceived them
has acted shamefully" (2:5). Then, in a return to narrative in chapter 3,
"The LORD said to me again, 'Go, love a woman who has a lover and is
an adulteress" (3:1), which Hosea does.

God uses the life and family of Hosea to act out the drama of God's
relationship with wayward Israel. Clear enough. But what are we to
make of the fact that God commands the prophet to break the Law?
Specifically Deuteronomy 24:3–4, the same passage from which Jesus'
interlocutors about divorce quote, and prohibitions against prostitu-
tion (Lev. 19:29; Deut. 23:17) and regulations prescribing death in
cases of adultery (Deut. 22:22)—all these are contravened by God's
commands to Hosea. The prophetic critique of Torah and tradition
seems foundational for Jesus' own practice. One reason to mention
Hosea is that Jesus is depicted by Matthew as familiar with the prophet.
In the passage explored above, Matthew 12:1–8, prior to the Son of
Man saying, Jesus quotes a version of Hosea 6:6, "I desire mercy and
not sacrifice" (Matt. 12:7). Discussion of tradition almost inevitably
overlaps with discussion of Scripture because the tradition is always in
dialogue with Scripture, and often it is a quite challenging dialogue.

Mark 7:1–23 (par. Matt. 15:1–20) contains some of the sharp-
est language this side of Matthew 23:1–36 ("Woe to you, scribes and
Pharisees, hypocrites!"). In both passages Jesus is attacking his opponents, in highly agonistic rhetoric, over their reading and applying of
the Law. Mark 7:3–4 provides as narrative aside information that Matthew 23 incorporates into the denunciations. "For the Pharisees, and
all the Jews, do not eat unless they thoroughly wash their hands, thus
observing the tradition of the elders; and they do not eat anything from
the market unless they wash it; and there are also many other traditions that they observe, the washing of cups, pots, and bronze ket-
tles." These details provide the background for Jesus' discourse on true
purity (cleanliness) that culminates in a declaration: "It is what comes

out of a person that defiles" (Mark 7:20). In between comes Jesus'
analysis of the struggle between Scripture and tradition, contrasting
the commandment to honor parents with the practice of proclaiming
one's property as dedicated to God in order avoid responsibility for the
care of one's parents.[5] Jesus' denunciation is clear, not only for evading
filial duties, but also for "thus making void the word of God through
your tradition that you have handed on" (7:13). Traditions that void
God's word are invalid and hence in contrast with Jesus' own mission
to fulfill God's word (Matt. 5:17).

Recall the parable of the Pharisee and the tax collector, in Luke 18:9–
14. The Pharisee "prays" that he fasts "twice a week" and gives "a tenth
of all [his] income" (18:12), both works of supererogation not called for
in Torah. Jesus is not impressed any more than he is impressed in the
other Synoptic mention of tithing, Luke 11:42/Matt. 23:23. "For you
tithe mint and rue and herbs of all kinds, and neglect justice and the
love of God; it is these you ought to have practiced, without neglecting
the others." In the dialogue with traditional practice, as in the dialogue
with Scripture, Jesus is sharply critical of readings that "have neglected
the weightier matters of the law" (Matt. 23:23). On the other hand,
those who share Jesus' reading of Scripture and tradition are welcomed,
even praised.[6]

One final aspect of tradition will be mentioned in passing but
explored in chapter 4: how did Jesus respond to traditional expectations of the coming of "messiah"? That the depiction of his entry to
Jerusalem (Mark 11:1–11 and par.) suggests a certain level of awareness
is undeniable; but whether the following actions in the temple should
be read as prophetic or messianic is a question of interpretation that we
will consider in the next section of this chapter. The larger issues raised
by the "Son of Man" sayings we will defer to chapter 4.

Culture

How does one distinguish between tradition and culture in examining
biblical materials? To be honest, somewhat arbitrarily. The passages I
have chosen to interpret as representing Jesus' dialogue with culture
overlap in many instances the dialogue with tradition and Scripture. As
noted above, that is the nature of intertextuality.

The blessings of Matthew 5:1–11 and the blessings and curses of
Luke 6:20–26 are a complex conversation with cultural attitudes and

expectations. Grounded in classic prophetic reversal formula ("Every valley shall be lifted up, and every mountain and hill be made low," Isa. 40:4), Jesus expresses a similar attitude proverbially in sayings about last/first (Matt. 19:30), humbled/exalted (Luke 14:11), and saving/losing (Mark 8:35). The Lukan version (6:20–26) is shorter and sharper:

> Blessed are you who are poor, for yours is the kingdom of God.
> Blessed are you who are hungry now, for you will be filled.
> Blessed are you who weep now, for you will laugh.
> Blessed are you when people hate you, . . . exclude you, . . . defame you. . . .
> But woe to you who are rich, for you have received your consolation.
> Woe to you who are full now, for you will be hungry.
> Woe to you who are laughing now, for you will mourn and weep.
> Woe to you when all speak well of you, for that is what their ancestors did to the false prophets.

The poor, hungry, grieving, and hated are blessed; the rich, filled, laughing, and well regarded are cursed. It is common to speak of Jesus challenging the conventional wisdom of his day, wisdom that viewed prosperity as a mark of divine blessing. There are two things wrong with this common wisdom: it simplifies the attitudes and outlooks of Jesus' day (they had heard of Job), and it pretends that our cultural assumptions are quite different, when in fact they are not. If Bill Gates and Joe Six-Pack arrive simultaneously at a five-star restaurant or First Church, the reactions of the *maître d'hôtel* and head usher would be indistinguishable.

In Luke, Jesus considers certain traits and characteristics (Matthew's list is longer): wealth, food, grief, and honor. Much is made of the amount of attention Jesus pays to wealth and possessions, as if our current cultural convention not to talk about money in church except for one brief annual stewardship season could obscure the truth that we, like Jesus' listeners, are preoccupied with thoughts and worries about wealth and possessions. Jesus talked about it because his listeners were thinking about it—the essence of dialogical preaching. For some, the preoccupation was like our own, how to get and spend ever more. For others, the hungry and dispossessed, the preoccupation was a matter of survival. Perhaps only in the current age of obesity can we fully appreciate the irony of "Woe to you who are full now." The reversal of weeping/laughing sharpens the note of eschatological reversal, the "consolation [*paraklēsis*]" mentioned and the laughter anticipated presumably at the last day.

Honor is a more complicated issue because the freight carried by the reality that the term points to was significantly greater in Jesus' culture than in contemporary Western cultures, though it can still be found in the Middle East and elsewhere. Honor, and its companion value, shame, were and are means of cultural valuation and control. In a world in which the vast majority of people lived at subsistence levels and below, in small communities where everyone really did know everyone else's business, the more modern expression "All I have left is my good name" was true. As a result, one's good name was of inordinate value.

> "Honor" is the value of somebody in the eyes of others. It is a value rating that is always a part of the competition within the community, where the individual is subject to the evaluation of the others. Honor and shame are intimately connected with place: they are the status of somebody in his or her place. It is possible to be honorable in a humble position, and one can incur shame by going beyond one's place, not respecting one's position within the community.[7]

Integrally related to the values of honor and shame for the culture of Jesus' day was the place of family. Moxnes and other social-scientific critics distinguish levels of kinship—household, family, tribe, and clan—distinctions we will not make. Instead, our focus is on the way Jesus engaged the cultural assumptions of his day about honor and family. Three well-known passages make the point:

> He came to his hometown and began to teach the people in their synagogue, so that they were astounded and said, "Where did this man get this wisdom and these deeds of power? Is not this the carpenter's son? Is not his mother called Mary? And are not his brothers James and Joseph and Simon and Judas? And are not all his sisters with us? Where then did this man get all this?" And they took offense at him. But Jesus said to them, "Prophets are not without honor except in their own country and in their own house."
>
> (Matt. 13:54–57)

This first passage, found also in Mark 6 and in a quite different version in Luke 4, brings issues of family, community, and honor into sharp focus. Put simply, from the perspective of the community, Jesus is bringing shame on his family by, as Moxnes put it, "going beyond one's place." Jesus challenges this conventional wisdom with proverbial wisdom of his own, using a saying that specifically names the cultural value at issue, honor (*timos*). The result in Matthew and Mark is a standoff, though Mark comments that Jesus "was amazed at their unbelief" (6:6). In Luke's extended version, passions are so inflamed at this challenge to traditional cultural values that the good citizens of Nazareth "got up, drove him out of the town, and led him to the brow of the hill on which their town was built, so that they might hurl him off the cliff" (4:29). No wonder Jesus moved to Capernaum.

> When his family heard it, they went out to restrain him, for people were saying, "He has gone out of his mind." . . . Then his mother and his brothers came; and standing outside, they sent to him and called him. A crowd was sitting around him; and they said to him, "Your mother and your brothers and sisters are outside, asking for you." And he replied, "Who are my mother and my brothers?" And looking at those who sat around him, he said, "Here are my mother and my brothers! Whoever does the will of God is my brother and sister and mother."
>
> (Mark 3:21, 31–35)

I place this passage second because while in Mark's chronology it happens three chapters before the scene above, it seems to be much in response to it. Only Mark uses the language of seizure and restraint (*krateō*), and only Mark tells us that the gossip in town was that Jesus was crazy, the Greek *exestē* literally meaning "outside himself." In any culture, when a child acts in ways that cause the neighbors to gossip, the reaction of the family is to sit the child down and ask for less inflammatory behavior. Assuming that Jesus' family had to walk a rugged thirty miles or so, the rumors about Jesus must have been quite disturbing—but not nearly as disturbing as Jesus' response to his family. We are not told that he went to greet them, welcomed them, or responded in any of the ways appropriate to his or most cultures. Instead, he rejected the premise that his family had any claim on him at all; he challenged the very idea that family is defined by kinship ties. In the last passage he warns his followers not to expect anything better in their own lives.

> [The Lord said,] "From now on five in one household will be divided, three against two and two against three; they will be divided:
>
> father against son and son against father,
> mother against daughter and daughter against mother,

mother-in-law against her daughter-in-law and daughter-in-law
against mother-in-law."

(Luke 12:52–53)

What is Jesus up to? The Lukan passage begins with the challenge, "Do
you think that I have come to bring peace to the earth? No, I tell you, but
rather division!" (Luke 12:51). This level of rancor and these challenges
to traditional cultural values have led Crossan to see parallels with the
behavior of Cynic philosophers and to describe Jesus as a "peasant Jewish
Cynic."[8] Jesus was not challenging traditional values for the fun of it, or in
an anarchic way. He challenged the culture because he found many of the
values of the culture to be incompatible with his vision of the kingdom of
God. He did not just tear down; he built up. Jesus "directly attacked the
central values of his social world's conventional wisdom: family, wealth,
honor, purity, and religiosity,"[9] in order to clear the way for his own proclamation—but that is the topic of the next chapter.

Listeners

Not everyone who approaches Jesus in the Synoptic Gospels does so to
"test [*peirazō*]" him (Matt. 16:1). It only seems that way. Some have
legitimate questions and needs (Luke 12:13). But Jesus does not limit
himself to responding to specific, spoken questions or challenges; he
also replies to what he is aware of only indirectly (Mark 8:17; 10:42)
and with, perhaps, what one might call prophetic discernment. "At
once Jesus perceived in his spirit that they were discussing these questions among themselves; and he said to them, 'Why do you raise such
questions in your hearts?'" (Mark 2:8). The Synoptic Gospels consistently depict Jesus responding to direct and implied challenges, spoken
and unspoken questions, and the lived reality of his audience.

Luke 13 is a particularly apt case study. The chapter can be divided
into the following divisions:

13:1—5, "Worse Sinners"
    13:6–9, Parable of the Unfruitful Fig Tree
13:10–17, Healing on the Sabbath
    13:18–21, Parables of the Mustard Seed and Leaven
13:22–23, "Will Only a Few Be Saved?"
    13:24–30, Narrow Gate and Locked Door
13:31–35, Herod the Fox; Jesus and Jerusalem

Admittedly, the skillful compositional hand of Luke is present throughout the chapter, from the careful alternation of encounter, dialogue,
and parable to the affirmation at the very center of the chapter: "and
the entire crowd was rejoicing at all the wonderful things that he was
doing" (13:17). But Luke's rhetoric of composition serves Jesus' rhetoric of proclamation, and serves it well.

The first scene, verses 1–5, shows Jesus responding to current events,
first the actions of Pilate and second what was likely a construction
accident. But in responding to the events, Jesus also responds to the
tradition and, one suspects, to the implied question of his audience.
"Do you think that because the Galileans suffered in this way they
were worse sinners than all other Galileans? No, I tell you" (13:2–3a).
The parable of the Unfruitful Fig Tree follows, illustrating what Jesus
means by "Unless you repent."

The next scene shifts to "one of the synagogues," and (cue the
ominous music) "on the Sabbath" (13:10). A woman "appears [*idou
gynē*]." She has a spirit (*pneuma*) that has crippled her for eighteen
years. Jesus sees her, calls her over, declares her healing—"Woman,
you are set free from your ailment" (13:12)—and lays hands on her.
The woman is no doubt happy, but synagogues have proved to be
enormously tough crowds. Sure enough, the "leader of the synagogue"
was "indignant because Jesus had cured on the Sabbath" and "kept
saying to the crowd, 'There are six days on which work ought to be
done; come on those days and be cured, and not on the sabbath day"
(13:14). We'll ignore the patriarchal deflection of criticism from
healer to healed, the obvious fact that the woman "appeared" when
the healer was there, and the coincidental fact that it was the Sabbath.
Our interest is in the way Jesus responds not to what is said *to* him but
to what is said *about* him.

We assume that the synagogue leader is not whispering. We are told
that Jesus does not respond by turning the other cheek. "You hypocrites!" he begins, and then looks to a combination of tradition and
common sense—"You feed your animals on the Sabbath"—to make
a "how much more" argument about healing on the Sabbath. "Ought
not this . . . daughter of Abraham . . . be set free . . . on the sabbath
day?" (13:16). The principle at work in the juxtaposition of passages
seen above (Torah commandment and David on the lam) is also at
work in Jesus' action and accompanying proclamation. Given Jesus'
understanding of Sabbath, one common in the Judaism of his day, the
idea that it is forbidden to do good on the Sabbath is nonsensical.

The twin kingdom "similitudes" of mustard seed and leaven use the rhetorical commonplace of lesser to greater to underline Jesus' reading of Sabbath. Kingdom discourse trumps Sabbath discourse every time. What follows is a specific, spoken question to which Jesus responds. "Lord, will only a few be saved?" (13:23). Jesus takes the question seriously, neither chiding the questioner nor dismissing the question. But he also, as is his custom, really doesn't answer the question directly, turning instead to a Gospel of John-like reflection on what the person really needs to know: focus on what you can be doing, not on speculation about things over which you have no influence. Do not look for the easy way out, or rather in this case, the easy way in. It does not work. Hanging out together on weekends, eating and drinking (bread and cup?), going on retreats is not sufficient. In fact, you can call me "Lord" all you want (a backhand smack at the questioner?), but an evildoer is still an evildoer. Jesus takes the question, and if anything takes it more seriously than the interrogator expected. It is not a direct answer to a theoretical question, but a specific response to the question behind the question, "What must *I* do?"

After a Johannine turn, Luke gets Markan: "At that very hour some Pharisees came . . . " (13:31). Some Pharisees came, but they did not come to test, challenge, or condemn; they came to warn. I have no way to fit this neatly into my Sunday school take on the Pharisees. Pharisees are not supposed to be concerned about Jesus' well-being; they are supposed to do everything they can to endanger it. "Herod's out to get you," they say, and Jesus responds, more or less, "Tell me something I don't know." He goes on, "As long as you are here, go tell that Fox I am doing what I came to do, and will do it in Jerusalem before too long. I'll see him there."

The audience initiates the conversation, but they do not dictate its terms or its conclusion. Jesus does not do what they suggest, any more than he does what James, John, and/or their mother request (Mark 10:35–37/Matt. 20:20–21). You get to ask; you do not also get to dictate the answer. Luke, one suspects, takes over here, with the "Jerusalem, Jerusalem" lament (Luke 13:34; also Matt. 23:27–29), but it is fully in keeping with Jesus' multiple dialogues. He is responding to the situation presented by the Pharisees who seek to warn him away, and also responding to the biblical and traditional idea and ideafication of Jerusalem as cultic center and as "the city that kills the prophets and stones those who are sent to it!" (Luke 13:34).

The dialogical nature of Jesus' proclamation is central to his rhetoric and multiple in its responsiveness. At any given time he is depicted as responding to Scripture, tradition, culture, and audience, to real and manufactured questions, to direct and indirect challenges, to pressing contemporary realities and universal needs and concerns. What would contemporary preaching look like if it shared this commitment to dialogue, conversation, and responsiveness? To that question we now turn.

DIALOGICAL PREACHING

While even Princeton Seminary's Center for Barth Studies admits the lack of a definitive source,[10] most agree it was Karl Barth who admonished us to preach with "The Bible in one hand and the newspaper in the other." A generation or two earlier, in a pamphlet entitled *Bible Study and the Religious Life*, William Rainey Harper argued for much the same posture.[11] How we were, so encumbered, expected to turn the pages of our scintillating sermon manuscript was left to the imagination. The point implied was that our sermons need to be relevant, contemporary, and biblical. It's hard to argue with that. But more than waving the appropriate ancient and current documents seems called for. Truly dialogical preaching is responsive in particular ways, and while models abound,[12] guided by the example of Jesus in the Synoptic Gospels, I argue that the preacher should always try to be in dialogue with Scripture, tradition, culture, and the lives of the listeners. This is not done by accident, nor in a hurried effort to get something together for Sunday. It is always easier to "share a few thoughts" on the day's readings. What we are after is sterner stuff, which requires commitment, intention, and rigorous preparation.

Scripture

When the search committee, ordination council, or Commission on Ministry asks whether the candidate believes the Bible is "the Word of God," the desired response does not begin with "It depends." Not all the nuance we learn in seminary moves seamlessly to the parish. Preachers must learn to be translators in their own native language and work out, with appropriate fear and trembling, the outline of their own hermeneutic in ways that can be clearly shared with listeners. Before we worry about interpreting particular passages, we have some theological work to do.

If one holds, as I do, that the fundamental homiletical question is "What does the Holy Spirit want the people of God to hear from these texts on this occasion?" there is an undeniable privileging of Scripture. Guilty. In my tradition and in my conviction, sermon starts with Scripture. But why? Whimsy, habit, laziness? At times; but over time the practice is grounded in the realization that the conversation people come to church hoping for is not with the preacher, but with God, and in the church's conviction that God's initiative in making this conversation possible starts with Scripture.

The theological turn is next to matters of inspiration and authority, or authority and inspiration, depending on where one begins. This inevitably leads to consideration of issues of transmission, textual criticism, translation, and finally to canon. All of this is background, important as it is. The *homiletical* turn is to concede that a wide range of opinion and conviction is defensible, and to look instead for a normative position on which to ground one's hermeneutic. Our task here is not to argue over matters such as "plenary verbal inspiration," but to make a claim for the primacy—as in the first or starting place—of Scripture in launching the conversation that brings God and people together in worship, of which the sermon is a part. Put differently, one need not hold the belief that the texts of Scripture were "without error in the original autographs" to hold that Scripture is fundamental and normative for the dialogue that the sermon is called to encourage and support. This does not mean that the preacher has responsibility solely for presenting and defending an inoffensive and unremarkable reading of the text, grounded in an equally tepid hermeneutic. It means that the preacher takes clues from Jesus, who is consistently depicted as taking his Bible seriously, regularly bringing it into conversation and proclamation. But, and this is an important qualification, as we saw above, Jesus neither glossed over Scripture's tension nor avoided its demands.

What is the preacher's goal in engaging in dialogue with Scripture? Surely it is first to foster a dialogue between the listeners and Scripture. Where does the preacher stand in that dialogue? With the listeners! Unfortunately, this is often not the case. Claiming the authority of pulpit, education, and position, the preacher is tempted to tell the congregation what Scripture means. The preacher claims the authority of Scripture for the preachments, positioning self with the Book, not with the people. That is not a dialogue, and it is not likely to lead to one either.

What happens when the we preachers realize that our place is with the people in the dialogue with Scripture? Everything changes, and for the better. Among other things, there will likely be less Hebrew and Greek in the pulpit (but not, pray God, in preparation!) because questions about verb tense and noun declension usually do not arise for the listeners when they hear the lesson(s) on Sunday. Nor will there be a discourse on how the text has been received, or its implications for theological reflection on the nature of being. No one in the pew is asking about that either. So what questions do arise? That is *the* question, because the single greatest obstacle to fostering the dialogue with Scripture that the preacher, Jesus, and the congregation seek is this: *the preacher is the only one in the room who has been thinking about the Scripture lesson(s) all week.* Be honest: not only is the preacher the only one who has been thinking about the lessons, half the people in the room only half heard what was just read. Yet the preacher generally launches in as if everybody in the church has shared concern all week for the social location of lepers in first-century Palestine, or the juxtaposition of the Ruth narrative against the prohibition of "foreign wives" in Ezra-Nehemiah.

So, like a native speaker determined to help the visitor who is brave enough to struggle with a foreign language, the preacher's first step is to *slow down*. Then, and only then, do we ask two different sets of questions: (1) What are the real, honest, and thoughtful questions the listeners have in hearing these words from the Bible? (2) How do I provide the listeners with what they need to know without overwhelming them with stuff I think is really cool but is actually just showing off how much I learned in seminary? An example, in this case the lections for Lectionary Year A, Proper 6 (Fifth Sunday after Pentecost) from the Revised Common Lectionary, will help us think about what those questions might be.

Year A provides "the summer of Romans," so a central text for the faithful few in attendance all summer long is the Epistle, Romans 5:1–8, classic Pauline kerygma about Christ dying for us, "while we still were sinners." At the heart of the verses is what in rhetoric is called a "climax," a ladder: "We also boast in our sufferings, knowing that suffering produces endurance, and endurance produces character, and character produces hope, and hope does not disappoint us" (5:3–5).

The Gospel, Matthew 9:35–10:8 (or on to verse 23), is a bit of a hodgepodge, with the naming and then sending of the Twelve as the focus, and a host of interesting, catch-phrasey verses: the people described as "sheep without a shepherd" (10:36), the "harvest is plenti-ful, but the laborers are few" (10:37). It is not all smooth sailing, how-ever, because the Twelve are not to go to Gentiles or Samaritans, they are to shake the dust off when necessary, and those dusted towns will be worse off than Sodom and Gomorrah come judgment day. If you keep reading deep into the optional verses, it gets worse.

The Old Testament gives the preacher a choice. Exodus 19 is a possibility, but Genesis 18 is more compelling: the Lord appears to Abraham by the oaks of Mamre as "three men." The covenant and the promise of a child to Sarah are reiterated, and Sarah is caught laughing, not at the Lord, I think, but at the very idea of these two, "advanced in age" (Gen. 18:11), well, you know. The laughter serves an important narrative function as well—don't think you can dodge your way out of this one with some nonsense about biblical years not lasting as long as years today. Sarah laughed because she and Abraham were old. Really old. And your listeners are going to wonder about that.

Okay preacher. What you gonna do? The first thing to strike me is a cumulative question, born of Sarah's age, the tough road Jesus asks the Twelve to follow, and Paul's ladder: How do you know if your glass is half empty or half full if you don't have clean water to drink, and if you do, the only cup you have is one you make with your hands? My cynical side thinks, frankly, that Paul is nuts—as are James (1:2–4) and Peter (1 Pet. 1:6–7) and every other author, biblical and otherwise, who argues that suffering produces anything other than misery, let alone a hope that does not disappoint us. If our listeners are listening, their question is going to be something along the lines of "What was Paul smoking, and where can I get some?" They know there is a world full of disappointment out there. Shall we start the list? You can start at home and go global, or just begin with Iraq, Darfur, earthquake and typhoon, a veritable apocalypse of, shall we say, *biblical* proportions delivered daily to our door, flat screen, or monitor.

Biblical proportions. Hmm. That is an interesting thought. It is not as if Paul was writing to the Romans while sitting at a Mediterranean villa and sipping something with an umbrella in it, nibbling pistachios, and chatting with Timothy and Luke about rhetorical issues in Galatians. Assuming that Romans was written as a letter of theological introduc-tion to a bunch of people who, as Luke tells us in Acts, had never heard of Paul, then Paul was, once again, writing from prison. And face it: if you believe only a tenth of what he writes in 2 Corinthians, this guy knew something about suffering. He had a doctorate in suffering, and it was not an honorary degree.

We know that suffering produces endurance, endurance produces character, and character produces hope, and hope does not disappoint. Of course there is always the chance that the suffering will kill you. It killed Paul, after all. Then again, here we are talking about him almost two thousand years later, so . . . And what about the verb "produces"? Any English teacher in the congregation is wondering about that. It is only used once, then implied, but it is a Pauline favorite, and interestingly, used only one other time in the New Testament outside writings by or attributed to Paul, in the Letter of James, in his own little ladder: "My brothers and sisters, whenever you face trials of any kind, consider it nothing but joy, because you know that the testing of your faith produces endurance; and let endurance have its full effect, so that you may be mature and complete, lacking in nothing" (1:2–4).

Katergazomai in Greek, to work, produce, act—Paul uses it later in Romans when describing the incomprehensibility of his own actions: "I do not know what I *do*" (7:15 AT). Yet he uses this same verb to describe the creation or production of the hope that is the very opposite of the despair of Romans 7. It may not be perfect, but somehow, Paul is saying, hope is something that we can create. Bingo! The creation of hope! Lord knows this wretched world could use a whole lot more hope than we see right now. But how exactly is one supposed to manufacture it? the listener will rightly ask. Is the church supposed to be some kind of "hope factory"? Well, yes, I think so. Which means the challenge of the sermon will be to bring the listeners to a point where they can imagine that for themselves. How will we do that?

A deductive sermon would start with hope. I don't know where it would end, because given my commitment to let the narrative logic of the passage determine the structure of the sermon, starting with hope is out of the question. I suppose you could preach a deductive sermon, beginning with, "The hope that is ours in Christ Jesus will never disappoint us!" But what happens? As soon as you say that, more than half the audience is thinking, "The hell it doesn't. I've been disappointed plenty of times, and I'm a Christian." By starting with your conclusion, you have lost the ability to define and shape the understanding of hope you wish to share, and when you later do so, it sounds like so much God-defending spin.

The passage itself suggests we start with suffering. Plenty of that around. What we need is a story of suffering, maybe a well-known one,

that shows the same trajectory Paul claims, from suffering to endurance, but we cannot stop at endurance because, well, endurance sounds
hard, so we may need to get to character in our first story, then come
back to endurance. Here I am sure Sarah and Abraham can be of help,
given how long they waited for that particular promise to work out. We
can't use the homiletical "trinity"—Martin King, Mother Teresa, and
Desmond Tutu—because we are only allowed to mention them once
a year, and by June we've already broken that rule a couple of times.
I'm a bicyclist, so Lance Armstrong is always a favorite, but there's the
divorce and the undefined nature of his theological commitments, not
to mention things not working out with what's her name, the singer, so
we'll keep looking. One good place to look is in your own community:
lift up a story everyone knows, of someone's grace in suffering and their
incredible character. I could tell about my late mother and her courage
in confronting breast cancer, but because Jesus was only occasionally
self-referential, I will look elsewhere.

In a way it does not matter because we are trying to get to hope, and
the outrageous claim that hope is something that can be produced and
does not disappoint. After all, where I really want to get to is a shared
reflection on how our own communities can become "hope factories."
The church is a hope factory. And I want to do so in a way that has
my listeners already thinking about what they can do, what we can do
together, not just to be "beacons of hope" but creators of hope.

The dialogue here is largely between Paul, with Sarah as a sidebar,
and the listeners, who are understandably skeptical of Paul's double
claim that hope is producible and does not disappoint, the example of
Sarah notwithstanding. The preacher has to honor their skepticism,
without embracing it, because the biblical side of the dialogue makes
the claim the preacher prays we all may embrace: in Christ, hope does
not disappoint. As this example shows, the dialogue is not simply
between listeners and text; tradition, culture, and personal experience
are constantly intruding. That is a good thing.

Tradition

I love what the biblical tradition did with the Sarah-Abraham story long
before any of us started wrestling with it. Genesis 18 tells us that Sarah
laughed when she overheard the promise made to Abraham, something
Abraham himself did at 17:17. Paul gets ahold of this and writes:

He did not weaken in faith when he considered his own body, which was already as good as dead (for he was about a hundred years old), or when he considered the barrenness of Sarah's womb. No distrust made him waver concerning the promise of God, but he grew strong in his faith as he gave glory to God, being fully convinced that God was able to do what he had promised.

(Rom. 4:19–21)

I guess laughing and pushing Ishmael forward (Gen. 17:18) do not constitute wavering. Earlier, in Galatians 4:21–31, Paul invents a typically tortuous allegory contrasting Sarah/Isaac with Hagar/Ishmael that arguably gets the whole thing backward and at least requires some creative rethinking of the Abrahamic covenant.

Tradition. We have to love it, because it is a part of us. Whether we preach in a tall steeple monument to our Pilgrim ancestors or a storefront start-up in its third week of existence, we and our congregations are not alone. We received the faith we profess and proclaim. We inherited our Scripture, liturgy, anthems, hymns, and songs. We are joined each week not just by the faithful before us, but by hundreds of millions of believers around the world we will never have the privilege to meet, yet are reading, praying, singing, and seeking just like us. So the question is not whether we are part of a tradition, but what part the dialogue with tradition will play in our preaching.

In the brief examination of Jesus' own dialogue with tradition, we saw what we already know: the dialogue is complex and can be a source of great tension. What is the joke about the seven last words of the church? "We've never done it that way before." For many congregations a tradition is something they did two years in a row. Three years in a row and Moses might as well have brought it with the tablets of the law. But that sort of arbitrary, often parochial, and certainly reified understanding of tradition is not really one that can be joined in conversation. Take it or leave it, but do not try to change it. I have in mind something richer and more supple. Real dialogue with tradition takes shape in three ways: history, catechesis, and crisis.

When I was a Baptist, I joked that Baptist history is in three movements: John the, Roger Williams, and Martin King. Certainly part of the appeal of Anglicanism for me is its deep sense of history, although I know cradle Episcopalians who would counter that this deep sense of history is the problem with Anglicanism. Regardless of the tradition, we all have roots. Even the nondenominational church plant in the exurbs has roots, whether it is Azusa Street or Willow Creek. Our stories are not just personal and biblical; they are in part ecclesial, and for better and worse, our history shapes us as Christians and as a community. To ignore it, deny it, or mistell it is a mistake and can have serious consequences. To remember it, celebrating the faithfulness and confessing the failures, strengthens the faith.

Many years ago a pastor took his life in the church building. There was no note, and the conventional wisdom of the congregation was that he had succumbed to depression. The church took care of the widow and children as best they could, and the denomination's pension plan provided for their financial needs. Everyone moved on. But the conventional wisdom was a lie, as the church leaders well knew. The pastor took his life a few days after being told that his involvement in community affairs was harming the reputation of the congregation (honor/shame cultures are not limited to the first century), and he was to resign or be fired in thirty days. The church never came to terms with its role in this tragedy; and it has dwindled in effectiveness and membership.

Remembering the past is not always pleasant, but it is almost always important. After Jesus said, "Jerusalem, Jerusalem," he did not continue by singing its praises, but with "the city that kills the prophets and stones those who are sent to it" (Luke 13:34). Earlier in Luke, when Jesus reminds those in Nazareth that God reached out to non-Israelites through Elijah and Elisha, they tried to kill him (Luke 4:25–29). When Stephen recounts the history of disobedience to God's will and begins his final summary with "You stiff-necked people," they do kill him (Acts 7:51–60). Like many other institutions on both sides of the Mason-Dixon Line, my seminary and the university of which we are a part has a legacy of racism that must be addressed and recounted, not genteelly forgotten. Timothy Tyson's *Blood Done Sign My Name* and Charles Marsh's *God's Long Summer*[13] help us with our memory work and our storytelling.

This is not to say that the dialogue with tradition should come equipped with hair shirt and be accompanied by self-flagellation. There is much in your tradition, and the traditions of your church and congregation, to celebrate. It is to say that the conversation with tradition must include what some wish could be forgotten.

One of the obstacles to a dialogue with tradition is the absence of adequate catechesis. Over the years barriers to church participation and membership have been dropped, and along with the barriers we have also lost the expectations. Arguments in my communion about the place of confirmation, and the appropriate age at which a child may receive the Eucharist, have increasingly substituted for the actual work of catechetical preparation for communion and confirmation. Effective catechesis is crucial for any conversation with tradition, because catechesis provides the grammar and vocabulary necessary for meaningful dialogue.

The challenge for contemporary preaching is to find ways to do the work of catechesis in the sermon, because, sadly, for far too many of our listeners, the sermon is the only opportunity they give us to do this work. Here again we have our model in the rhetoric of Jesus, who is not depicted as neatly distinguishing between "preaching" and "teaching" but as blending them seamlessly. Matthew's "Sermon" on the Mount is a commonplace example, encouraging and challenging as it teaches, but it stands out only for the level of concentrated instruction, and is not unique in the Synoptic Gospels as a depiction of Jesus' style. Fred Craddock is a contemporary master and model of this blending, never patronizing, but not assuming that the listeners already know what is needed for the sermon to proceed. "You will recall," he often begins. Maybe you do, maybe you don't. In either case you are going to hear a concise exposition, biblical, theological, or historical, that not only enables you to follow the flow of the sermon, but adds to your storehouse of Christian information, and to the depth of your Christian formation. Sometimes, in order to preach it, we first have to teach it. Instead of complaining about the lack of biblical and theological literacy in our audience, we should use the dialogue with tradition as an opportunity to do something about it.

Something happened the other day in the Presbyterian Church (U.S.A.). I do not remember what it was, but I do remember thinking, "Thank you for getting the Episcopal Church off the front page." Just kidding—except that I am not. At this point in our denominational histories, and for many others in our nondenominational histories, it is hard to say "tradition" without someone adding "in crisis." The crises are multiple: and while the sex-abuse scandal in the Roman Catholic Church and the splintering of the Anglican Communion over (pick all that apply) biblical authority, human sexuality, women's ordination, and episcopal consecration have received the most attention, we are hardly alone. And crises are not limited to denominations and communions: squabbles can erupt at any judicatory level, from a Methodist district to a Baptist association. And, although this may surprise you, apparently even members of local congregations are known to disagree among themselves.

We could, as we often have, simply ignore the crises in the hope that they will go away. Read sermons from pulpits in the 1960s, and you would have no clue that the Vietnam War and the civil rights movement were taking place. And, as noted in chapter 1, if you went to church in 2002–2003, the only time you heard "Iraq" was if a Southerner was in a car accident. "I wracked my car." But such silence only marginalizes the pulpit further, convincing the listeners of the preacher's timidity and irrelevance. The crises in our communions and in our communities must be brought into our sermons, and we must do so with the same level of research and reflection that we bring to our engagement with Scripture and tradition.

Culture

Count up the amount of time you spend studying the Bible, reading theology, preparing for and teaching education and formation classes, and fashioning your sermons. Add in time on churchy things, both parochial and denominational. Multiply by a factor of three, and you have an approximation of how much time your listeners spent breathing in a culture that could care less about all the things you just added up. Our posteverything first-world culture is not generally hostile to religion, but indifferent. While the usual 75 percent will tell Harris, Gallup, and Pew that they believe in God, the population of the United States has more than doubled since the end of the Second World War; church attendance has declined.[14] As a percentage of the population, the number meaningfully involved in a congregation is beginning to decrease to the low levels of some European countries, at least in some parts of the country.

This means, as Loren Mead has been telling us since the publication of *The Once and Future Church*,[15] that we in the United States live in the midst of the mission field as soon as we step outside the church doors. It also means that the dialogue with culture has the potential to be dangerously one-sided. If the culture beyond the parish is indifferent to the church, but that is the culture in which the congregation's members spend almost all of their time, how does the preacher engage the culture and include the culture in the homiletical dialogue?

The classic, intentionally one-sided approach is to use the culture as a target, treating it as a demon-infested wilderness and wasteland, the source of all that is evil and wrong with the world. While there is enough truth in that view to make it feasible, the trouble with this approach, unless your congregation has withdrawn from the culture, is that it treats their workplaces, schools, neighbors, and so forth as the enemy—which lets *the* enemy off the hook. And because it does not distinguish between the evil and the good, it encourages the listener to dismiss the culture—or dismiss the preacher.

Every now and then, when one is "mad as hell and can't take it anymore," a good old-fashioned culture-bashing sermon probably won't do much harm. But it is not the model Jesus gave us. Jesus engaged the culture, was aware of what was going on in the culture, and preached and taught in ways that encouraged his listeners to live faithfully in the culture. Yes, there was some shaking of the dust off the feet (Mark 6:11), and some towns were told to expect a fate worse than others (Matt. 11:20–24), but fire was not called down on them, as much as James and John might have wished (Luke 9:52–55).

We live in a culture that could be described by whatever term captures what comes after postmodernism. It is postcolonial, postdenominational, post-Christendom, and so on. Some fine works have been written on preaching to the posteverything congregation.[16] The odd semantic problem with all the post-this and post-that talk is that it still privileges what has presumably been left behind, by describing the present in terms of what it has moved beyond. This strikes me as inherently problematic and insufficiently hopeful. Jesus did not proclaim a posttemple, post-Torah, anti-Judaism. Jesus proclaimed a kingdom knocking at the door. His engagement with the culture was hopeful, his proclamation positive. We call it *good* news, do we not?

In our preaching we cannot meaningfully engage a culture we know little about, any more than we can engage by disparaging a culture. There are two keys essential to make this possible. First, get a life. Second, if you do not have a teenager, borrow one. I am quite serious about both. When, dear reader, was the last time you

— Read a book that did not mention Jesus?
— Saw a movie the first week it was in theaters?
— Read a magazine that had more pictures than words?
— Texted instead of called or e-mailed?
— TiVo'd a show on the CW network?

— Tailgated?

— MySpaced your friend?

— Twittered?

— Went to a concert with an audience mostly younger than you?

— Listened to a radio or television opinionator with whom you disagree?

— Spent the afternoon at a museum?

In other words, do you have a life outside the church? Does your world meaningfully overlap with the worlds of your listeners? If not, you have a problem.

Two treasured American values, absolutely unheard of in the biblical world, exacerbate already unhelpful tendencies: privacy and independence. These are not village values, these are suburban values, and when combined with many preachers' tendency toward introversion, lead to isolation and loneliness. Jesus walked with his followers everywhere he went, encountering people at every turn. He ate and slept wherever he was welcomed, and struggled to find time alone for prayer (Mark 1:35–37). We drive, cocoon ourselves with our iPods on train, bus, and plane, and move quickly from one locked door to another. Casual conversation is rare, the idea that someone would ring our doorbell and invite themselves in for coffee and a visit unimaginable. In my last parish I learned always to schedule, never to drop by, and would often be rebuffed by my own parishioners: "You want to come by? Why, is something wrong?" I tried not to take it too personally.

Having a life, getting acquainted, understanding the culture is as much a part of the preacher's job description as reading commentaries, keeping up with theology, and praying. If you would prefer to hide in your study, pounding out sermon drafts on your Mac, or feel that keeping up with what is going on in the world around you may be the devil's work, think of it as a professional obligation. If you do not have a life, which means taking time to live, not just work, how will you help your listeners learn how to have a life? If you do not engage and understand the culture, how will you relate your convictions to your listener's experience? If you have not read, seen, heard, and experienced the richness of the world around you while faithfully living out your call, who will take seriously your calls to do the same?

Early in my preaching life, I would borrow my late father's Daily Study Bible commentaries by William Barclay. Generations of preachers have done the same since they were first published, culling stories and illustrations with abandon. The problem is that we all sounded to our listeners like middle-aged Brits with a public school education and a fascination with the sea. I left the set given to me at ordination in the library of my first parish, in the belated realization that the time spent looking for illustrations in the life and preaching of others would be better spent in having a life of my own.

The world, we know, is a mess. It is sinful, self-destructive, greedy, and corrupt. This is not new nor news, and not worth spending much homiletical time proving. Our listeners know it too. What they do not necessarily know, and certainly would like to hear more about, is how the *good* news relates to all the bad news, and how the hope of the gospel will help them to be transformed and to become agents of transformation.

Listeners

We turn last with more intention to those we have mentioned time and again in thinking how sermon responds to Scripture, tradition, and culture. In many respects the history of the last three generations of homiletics has been the history of the listener, in interesting though generally unconnected parallel to the role of the reader in literary criticism. And the key figure prompting the turn to the listener has been Fred Craddock.

We have already recognized that the fundamental homiletical question is "What does the Holy Spirit want the people of God to hear from these texts on this occasion?" and we conceded a privileging of Scripture in this formation. Now focus turns to the center of the question, the "people of God" and "hear." Who are these people who have invited us to speak of God with and for them, and what will be required for them to hear?

Your listeners are no more the same than my readers are, and we have all changed. A lot. A good question might be whether your listeners are half empty or half full? Hang out with a few Doctor of Ministry students, and you are likely to conclude that the listeners are at least half empty. Parishioners are irregular in attendance, sporadic in focus, biblically illiterate, theologically incurious and uninformed, and to top it off, insufficiently willing to volunteer prolifically and give sacrificially. You might also hear the seminary faculty say the same thing about the students. But the listeners are better educated, more

culturally and politically astute and engaged, professionally accomplished, and socially committed than ever before. On the one hand
they are harder to reach because church is no longer the only game in
town on Sunday, or any day. On the other hand they are much more
interesting, and interested, when you do reach them. Half empty or
half full? The preacher's answer may say more about the preacher than
the listener, and it will surely have a major impact on the preparation
and delivery of the sermon.

Tom Long tells of an elderly woman "with a face like a hatchet dipped
in vinegar" who approached him after he spoke as a guest preacher and
demanded, "You teach preaching at the seminary, don't you?"

"Yes, I do," Long said.

"Well, I have something that I want you to tell your students. Tell
them to take me seriously."[17]

It is easier, frankly, to take the listeners for granted, certainly wel-
coming them along for the ride, but treating the sermon as a sharing
of the preacher's personal encounter with Scripture and the journey of
faith. And so for many the operative homiletical question is "What do
I want to tell the people of God today?" Whatever that is, it is decidedly not dialogical. Recall Mark's summary at the end of his parable
chapter: "With many such parables he spoke the word to them, as they
were able to hear it" (Mark 4:33). Responsive and responsible preaching is focused on what is to be heard; it shapes the speaking to foster
the listening.

Thomas Troeger and Edward Everding have recently and persuasively argued that one important step in taking our listeners seriously is
to recognize that different people have different ways of listening and
learning. Drawing on work in cognitive development, and especially
on Howard Gardner's work in multiple intelligences (MI) theory, the
authors hope to help preachers to

> realize that people do not belong to the same "household" of learn-
> ing and knowing, that our congregations consist of many different
> neighbors, and that our preaching will not erase their differences.
> God calls us to make our preaching neighborly to our listeners' var-
> ied way of knowing and thereby model how they can be neighborly
> to one another. . . .
>
> Howard Gardner . . . has criticized IQ standards because people
> demonstrate intelligence in many other ways than language and
> logic alone.

> Can you imagine a sermon that takes into account "all of us," when each of us is capable of eight intelligences? This does not mean that every person has developed every intelligence to the highest possible degree. But these intelligences are present among "all of us" in the congregation. Clearly, sermons will employ words and some form of logic. But sermons can also tap into people's abilities to experience their lives through spatial imagery or music or action or interpersonal relations or self-reflection or the natural environment. That might initially seem to be more than you as a preacher can or want to handle. But you will discover that the theory of multiple intelligences provides a usable framework for creating and delivering sermons that engage the actual ways your people compose meaning for their lives.[18]

Troeger and Everding point out that the differences in our listeners' ways of hearing and learning require more creativity in our preaching. In some churches and communions, responding to this need leads to skits and sketches, movie clips and musical interludes. Troeger and Everding argue that it can also be done with words. There is much more work to be done here.

Responding to differences in cognitive style and development is one way of taking the listeners seriously, and is certainly in harmony with the model we see in the Synoptic Gospels. There is more, however, and it begins earlier in the sermon creation process than the application of MI theory does. Long gets at this in the chapter cited above as he reflects on what the woman meant in her demand to be taken seriously. "I have been thinking about what she said and what it might mean if those of us who preach genuinely take seriously the people who sit in the pews. I want to think, first, about what it means to take the listener seriously when the listener is not literally present; when we are in our studies doing biblical interpretation in preparation for preaching."[19]

If the greatest advantage and disadvantage the preacher has is in being the only one in the room who has been thinking about the Scripture lessons all week, one way to bridge the gap between the positive and the negative is to develop the discipline of keeping the listeners present throughout the interpretive and sermon-creation process. The ability to do this is why the best preaching, week in and out, is done in communities where the preacher and listeners know each other well. And Long is correct: it starts in the study, the first or second time you read the assigned or chosen lessons. At the beginning of the process, we need to ask an entirely different set of critical questions along with the ones we learned in biblical exegesis classes. Not "instead of" but "along with," for this is not in any way a suggestion to substitute rigorous critical scholarly work for asking what Aunt Sadie thinks about the book of Revelation. It is to insist that the only important questions to ask of a biblical text do not come from commentaries: they also come from the pew.

Return to the lessons considered earlier in the chapter, Year A, Proper 6 (Fifth Sunday after Pentecost) from the Revised Common Lectionary (RCL). In most lectionary-based churches, the congregation will hear Genesis 18:1–15 (the final reiteration of the Abrahamic covenant, laughter and all), Romans 5:1–8 (Paul's ladder of hope), and Matthew 9:35–10:8 (the calling and sending of the Twelve). As the preacher reads those texts, alongside critical questions of language and translation, rhetoric, Synoptic parallels, and so forth should also come critical questions from and for the listeners. How, preachers, do you imagine your listeners hearing these texts? What will likely be their questions, concerns, and points of resistance? What information will they need in order to understand what is going on in the texts? How can you begin to incorporate their likely questions into your preparation?

There is a concrete way to find out: ask them, either through one or another mode of formal collaborative sermon preparation models, lectionary study groups, surveys, feedback sessions, and the like.[20] I have no objection whatsoever to this practice; I hold one form or another of an evaluative process to be a regular requirement for growth in preaching. But this approach is not for everyone, and it is probably never for anyone all the time. When such formal approaches are not possible, does that mean one simply preaches for oneself? Of course not. But if you will lift your head up from this book, picture yourself in the pulpit or at whatever spot you regularly preach, and take a moment to visualize your audience. Look around the room, focus on someone, and ask yourself, "How will she hear the lessons this week? What might it mean to her? And if it means nothing, what gaps does my sermon need to fill so that it will mean something?" Move around the room in your mind's eye and ask the questions again and again. Sometimes it helps to get up, grab your Bible, and go sit in one spot or another where you worship and read the lessons *for* and *from* your listeners' perspectives. Do not jazz it up, water it down, or pretend. You know these people, you love these people, so learn how to read *for* and *with* these people.

What will their questions be? Are they going to wonder about Sarah and Abraham's age thing? Or maybe wonder what took God so long to get around to fulfilling that particular promise: was God showing off, or was there a technical glitch somewhere in the communication process? I have already tipped my hand on the questions that interested my imagined audience, whose lived experience thoroughly challenges Paul's claim that "hope does not disappoint." They may view Paul's ladder—suffering produces endurance, then character, and finally hope—as sadistic, masochistic, or both. They may also wonder about the disciples' job description in Matthew 10, especially if the preacher chooses the RCL option to read through 10:23. Sure, being given authority to perform exorcisms, teach, and heal sounds good; but being handed over, flogged, and promised family enmity are definite drawbacks. Are you sure Jesus found twelve to sign on?

I do not know what questions your listeners will ask. You do. And if you take *them* seriously, you will take their questions seriously and do your best to incorporate those questions into your sermon. Every now and then there is another way to take your listeners seriously, and that is to step back from the demands of weekly sermon preparation and ask what their larger questions might be. Not the questions that may arise from any given week's Scripture lessons, but the questions of life and death, faith and doubt, meaning and purpose, questions that bring them to church in the first place. This can and should sometimes be done over coffee, one on one, and in a small group. It is a reality check, and it is also an opportunity to transcend the "tyranny of the immediate" and explore how one's preaching is and is not connecting with the larger questions of the congregation. One can, I suppose, avoid and ignore those questions. They are difficult, after all, and do not submit themselves to easy answers. But if our preaching is not at least occasionally responding to our listeners' most pressing questions, why bother?

The preaching of Jesus was responsive to Scripture, tradition, culture, and the lives of his listeners. We surely do not want to settle for any less. Now we will look at a sermon that models what contemporary preaching that is intentionally responsive to these four strains looks like.

A SERMON BY FRED B. CRADDOCK

What is the fundamental longing of the human heart? This profoundly dialogical question is at the heart of the following sermon. Notice the opening two images and the ease with which the preacher draws us in while gently chiding us for our substitution of "chatter" for conversation, and for our discomfort with our own questions. Observe also the preacher's consideration of the sufficiency of natural theology and even Scripture in response to our questions. Finally, pay attention to the use of images that capture the interest and honor the experience of every person in the church.

More Than Anything in the World

John 14:1–9

"Lord, show us the Father, and we will be satisfied." We do not know, of course, whether Philip whispered these words, hoping no one else would hear, or shouted them above the noise of many conversations. We do not know if he spoke in a tear-filled voice or blurted out his request. We do not even know if he realized the importance of what he asked. What we do know is that he spoke for all of us: to know God is a fundamental human longing, so deeply imbedded, in fact, as to rise very seldom to our lips. Why?

Perhaps it is pride. One has to swallow pride of self-sufficiency in order to form the words of this request. A man paces back and forth outside a church door before entering. This is strange territory. Inside a friendly face wearing an usher badge hands the visitor a worship bulletin and with a smile says, "Welcome; we know you are here in search of God." "Well, no, I just had an hour to kill and thought I would drop in."

Perhaps the difficulty in expressing a desire to know God lies in the fear of exposing one's emotion. After all, the desire is not solely cerebral; it is visceral as well. A patient lies in a hospital bed awaiting surgery early the next morning. Through a partially open door he sees his pastor coming down the hallway toward his door. "Pastor, what are you doing here? You should be visiting other patients who are really sick. Of course, I have a little surgery tomorrow to remove my kidneys and liver, but no big deal. A piece of cake. But some folks in here are nervous and could use a good visit by a reverend." What's with the frivolous chatter? What's going on? The patient doesn't want the minister to come over to his bed, take his hand, and pray. What he really wants is for the minister to come over to his bed, take his hand, and pray. But he doesn't want to cry.

Or perhaps the request "Show us God" sticks in the throat because of a suspicion that the request will go unanswered. Maybe the preacher in

Ecclesiastes is right: "God has set eternity in our hearts, but we can't know the beginning or ending of anything" (cf. 3:11). After all, just because you're hungry doesn't prove there is bread. I recall hearing Professor James Crenshaw of Duke describe this grim view of life as being similar to a huge Easter egg hunt. In the morning all go out with baskets and full of anticipation. During the day, now and then, someone yells, "I found one!" but in the evening most go home with empty baskets. Maybe that eloquent agnostic of another generation, Robert Ingersoll, had it right: "Life is a narrow vale between the cold, barren peaks of two eternities. We know not whence we come or whither we go."

But suppose a kind fellow traveler wished to give some answer to my request, to what or to whom would I be pointed? After all, the author of our text has already acknowledged, "No one has ever seen God" (John 1:18). The answer most readily available is creation. "The heavens are telling the glory of God; and the firmament proclaims his handiwork" (Ps. 19:1). Even Paul, in his own way, holds that all humanity, including those beyond access to Scripture, is without excuse. "For what can be known about God is plain to them, because God has shown it to them. Ever since the creation of the world his eternal power and divine nature, invisible though they are, have been understood and seen through the things he has made" (Rom. 1:19–20). Luke agrees: "[God] has not left himself without a witness in doing good—giving you rains from heaven and fruitful seasons, and filling you with food and your hearts with joy" (Acts 14:17). Even John, who raises the question of knowing God, at least implies the Godward pointing of creation (1:1–5).

And our own experience of nature offers a strong Amen. It is so in the spring, when the world is a poem of light and color, when "butterflies all flutter up and kiss each little buttercup" (Howard Dietz, "Carolina in the Morning"). It is so in the summer, when trees and vines hang heavy with fruit, provisions for all God's creatures. It is so in the fall, when a chill nips the air and autumn weather turns the leaves to flame. And it is so in winter, when the long fingers of barren trees welcome a blanket of snow. There is hardly a square inch of earth as barren and desolate but what one can see in the lower right-hand corner the initials of the artist—G.O.D. Take a walk "down the back roads and along the river of your memory" (cf. Chas Ryder, "Back Roads of My Mind") and among your thoughts—God. Sit alone on the back steps with your fingers cupped around your early morning coffee and see how long it takes for God to enter your thoughts.

Then why is this not enough? Why is Philip still standing there, waiting for an answer? He has eyes and ears and heart; he has the same access to creation as we do. So why is he still asking, "Lord, show us the Father, and we will be satisfied?" Probably because it is not satisfying simply to have witnesses in creation that there is a God. There is nothing saving, nothing redeeming, in believing there is a God. Our desire is to know God, to know what God is like, what is God's relationship to us. Show us that; no cloud, no bird, no leaf, no sunset can tell me.

Philip's question was not only poignant, it was urgent. His only hope for an answer had just announced to his followers that he was going away. "Do not let your hearts be troubled. . . . In my Father's house there are many dwelling places. . . . I go to prepare a place for you . . . so that where I am, there you may be also." His followers are confused. They are children playing on the floor, only to look up and see Mom and Dad putting on their coats. The children have three questions, always three questions: "Where are you going? Can we go? Then who will stay with us?" Jesus responds, "I am going to my Father and your Father. You cannot come now; you can come later. But I will not leave you orphans. I will send another friend, another helper who will never leave, but who will stay with you forever."

Hearts heavy with the news of the approaching death of their leader and friend cannot grasp these words. It is too much. Questions tumble upon questions, until finally Philip speaks, not only for himself, not only for the Twelve, but for all of us. We are all full of questions about life, death, and what we do next. But our minds and hearts will find satisfaction if we can know God. Show us God.

Show us God? Is that your question, Philip? Where have you been? All this time together, and you don't know? He turned to Philip, to the Twelve, and to all of us, and said, "Whoever has seen me has seen God." Were you there when the lame man at the pool stood and walked? Were you there when the blind man saw his family for the first time? Were you there when the centurion's son left his sick bed? Were you there when the hungry crowd was fed? Were you there when Lazarus was restored to his grieving sisters? Yes, I was there and I believe in miracles, but I want something more; I want to experience God. And so Jesus took a towel, tied it around his waist, and in a basin of water washed their feet. Oh no, not this; show us God. And so Jesus took up a cross and he walked up to Golgotha. Jesus healing, feeding, caring, serving, dying: this is the portrait of God.

But is that the end of it? The class in theology is over, students dismissed? By no means! Jesus has shown us God in order to show us ourselves as believers. To be a believer in the God revealed in Jesus is to heal, feed, care, serve, die. Whether or not Philip understood it, we do: knowing God carries the assignment to live out the character of God.

"And we will be satisfied." Are we? I must confess I did not realize that in knowing I would be known, in finding I would be found.

When I was a child I played hide-and-seek with my brothers and sister. You remember the game, don't you? One of the group is "It," which means hiding one's eyes, counting to one hundred, then announcing, "Coming, ready or not." Now It goes in search of the others, now well hidden. The first one found is now It. When my sister was It, she cheated. "One, two, three, four, five, ninety-seven, ninety-eight, ninety-nine, one hundred; coming, ready or not." But I didn't care that she cheated because I was well hidden under the porch and under the steps of the porch. Behind trees, in the barn, in the corncrib, round and round she searched. She passed by me again and again. I was confident; she will never find me here. But after awhile it hit me—she will never find me here! So I stuck out a toe; she saw it, "You're It, you're It!" I crawled out muttering, "Aw, phooey, you found me."

What did I want? to be hidden? Well, yes, but what did I really want? To be found, just as every person in this room.

And then we will be satisfied.

Analysis

Fred Craddock's preaching is inherently and timelessly dialogical because he takes the listener as seriously as any preacher this side of Jesus.

> It is so vital to our task that we be aware that the experience of listening is not a secondary consideration after we have done our exegesis of the texts and theological exploration. The listener is present from the beginning. The Christian tradition, biblical and extra-biblical, came to us from those who *heard* it, and we *hear* it and pass it on to other *hearers*. The stamp of listening and the listenability of the message is on it when we get it, and in telling it, we confirm that it is listenable. To give such attention to the listener is not a concession to "what they want to hear" . . . ; it is no more or less than to describe the shape of the subject matter (it came to listeners) and the nature of the occasion (to effect a hearing).[21]

The impact of this interplay of listener, text, and occasion is a sermon about something that matters, and matters profoundly: a vision of God. "Our desire is to know God, to know what God is like, what is God's relationship to us." Exactly. We stammer otherwise, chatter, as

Craddock calls it—an hour to kill, someone who really needs a pastor, but we are not fooling anyone. Show us God!

Students have long noted the masterful way Craddock moves from the biblical to the contemporary. This sermon displays two things we all can do with a little careful attention. First, everything is in the present tense—biblical, historical, personal: it is all here and now. Second, Scripture is honored not by being privileged, but by being made real. The psalmist's glory-crying heavens are a piece with our fingers wrapped around a steaming cup of coffee. And just as real. We also note the sheer volume of passages and allusions in this brief homily: John, of course, but also quotations from Ecclesiastes, Psalms, Acts, and Romans; and references to the healing at the pool of Beth-zatha, of the man born blind, and the centurion's son; the feeding of the multitude, the raising of Lazarus, the footwashing, and the crucifixion. "Jesus healing, feeding, caring, serving, dying: this is the portrait of God." It is also excellent catechesis in the midst of preaching.

What Craddock is best known for are the stories, and this sermon is shot through with them. There is also the persistent use of figurative language necessary for compelling preaching. We feel the hospital patient's anxiety, smell the coffee, and see the beauty of nature, just as we recognize Philip in ways we have not before, and come to share his calling to "heal, feed, care, serve, die."

And we play hide-and-seek, remembering the times we cheated, and I suspect, remembering when we had also hid ourselves too long. Here Craddock shows his ultimate respect for the listener, leaving a considerable, and critical, piece of work for us to do. How tempting it is to want to tell our hearers what to think of our stories, to draw the conclusions for them, to make sure they get it. How mistaken we are when we do so. We want, in the game, to be found, yes, and he says as much. It is what he does not say that may matter most. "And so, my friends, if you find yourself feeling cut off and hidden from God, you too need only stick your toe out, and God will do the rest." Phooey.

3

Proclamatory Preaching

There are only two things wrong with the phrase "proclamatory preaching." It sounds awkward *and* redundant. Does not all preaching involve proclamation? No, this chapter argues, it does not, but it should and it can. A driving conviction is that for a variety of reasons defensible and not, much preaching has lost its edge, more afraid of offending listeners than of failing to proclaim good news. Whether this has come to pass is a post-9/11, lectionary-based, triumph of the therapeutic mystery that does not finally matter. While many preachers may have lost their sense of why it should be otherwise, this chapter focuses on *how* it can be.

Among the terms considered and rejected to describe this characteristic of the preaching of Jesus were *provocative* and *prophetic*. Not because the preaching of Jesus we encounter in the Synoptic Gospels is not regularly provocative and deeply prophetic, but because the terms have come to suggest something negative, verbal missiles fired from the pulpit upon unprepared listeners. To be provocative seems always to come with the unspoken adverb "needlessly." To be provocative is to stir things up for the fun of it, jabbing rhetorical fingers while perhaps waving and pointing physical ones. Prophetic is even worse. When someone claims to be a "prophetic preacher," we take it that they are making people mad in the name of Jesus, for the sake of a cause that may or may not be dear to the preacher's (and God's) heart. Prophetic preaching fosters guilt; it may or may not induce change. Sadly, when we speak of prophetic preaching, we assume that the guilt may be more important to the preacher than the change.

THE PROCLAMATION OF JESUS

So proclamatory it is, staking a claim and taking a stand, with clarity and conviction. Yet with a difference, that difference being a passionate desire to connect and communicate, because change is more important than guilt, and because if the preacher is not truly heard, it doesn't matter how important are the things one has to say. Jesus' preaching was proclamatory from the start, Mark tells us, and if it caused some to feel guilty, well, a part of the proclamation was the good news of forgiveness, was it not? Jesus was interested in changed lives, not guilty consciences. In this chapter we will consider the proclamation of Jesus in three ways and develop the implications for our preaching. I understand Jesus' preaching to be proclamatory because in it Jesus (1) announced the kingdom, (2) resisted the Powers, and (3) shared and shaped the faith. "Well and good for the Son of God," some may think, "but look where that got him." Whatever the historical argument about a correlation between Jesus' preaching and teaching and his execution, there is still a biblical argument about taking up one's cross and *following*, right?

Announcing the Kingdom

Matthew and Mark agree in describing Jesus' opening message as the announcement of the coming of "the kingdom," then differ in the noun used in defining the prepositional phrase that follows, "of heaven" (Matt. 4:17), "of God" (Mark 1:15), a difference that likely says more about Matthew and Mark than about Jesus. They also agree, significantly, on the verb used to characterize Jesus' action: *kēryssō* in Greek, "preach" or "proclaim" in English. Whether or not we call it a sermon, the evangelists called it preaching. That much is fairly simple. Preaching, after all, comes in a variety of forms and dynamics, in and out of the pulpit. It is the second half of the equation that is tricky, what Jesus is described as preaching: the coming of "the kingdom." Whether "of heaven" (Matthew) or "of God" (Mark and Luke) is secondary. Jesus is shown so consistently proclaiming the kingdom that it was undeniably central to his message. But what did Jesus mean by announcing "the kingdom"?

We saw two things in chapter 1 that must be recalled. First, despite the patriarchal, political, and perhaps even militaristic senses the word "kingdom" may have for us, attempts to substitute "reign" or "rule" or "hegemony" miss the point. Jesus was using a somewhat stable image as the ground for his central metaphor. This leads us to the second thing to remember: "kingdom" is a metaphor, taking that somewhat stable image, a territory ruled by a sovereign, and juxtaposing it with a prepositional phrase, "of heaven/God," to create a dynamic image. The complicating factor, we also saw, is that the metaphor of the kingdom of God is then frequently paired with another metaphor, parable, allegory, or aphorism, leading to all sorts of interpretive fun to be explored in chapter 5.

There are many ways to understand what Jesus meant in announcing the nearness or coming of the kingdom. It is a metaphor hardly chosen at random. I take Jesus to be after something all-encompassing, not peripheral; though "citizenship" seems to be a more Pauline metaphor ("Our citizenship is in heaven," Phil. 3:20), it is one way of approaching and appreciating what Jesus may have intended. Globalization has certainly softened some of the sharpness with which we identify and distinguish ourselves based on nationality and political affiliation, until, say, the Olympics, or much worse, armed international conflict; but when we answer, "I am a Canadian" or "Soy de Méjico," we are not simply talking about our residence or birthplace. The claim we stake is much larger, about identity, self-understanding, customs, and expectations. And as also noted in chapter 1, when Jesus says the kingdom is "near" or "at hand," he simply means "now." To the extent that "kingdom" is a spatial metaphor, "near" is temporal; taken together, Jesus is saying, "This is it! Right here! Right now!" In announcing the coming, if not arrival, of the kingdom, Jesus was inviting hearers to consider where their loyalties should be truly and rightly given, and challenging them to place their loyalty with the God of Israel. So where is the problem? The problem is that as far as the Romans, Herodians, and religious elite in Jerusalem were concerned, there already was a kingdom in place. By using this particular metaphor, Jesus was not just announcing the arrival of God's kingdom; Jesus was implicitly challenging the kingdoms of his and every day.

When Jesus said, "The kingdom of God is near," I wonder if it was only the Twelve who said, "Huh?" While the image of God as

king was common, and the word "kingdom" is used hundreds of times
in the Old Testament; the juxtaposition of "God" and "kingdom" is
rare outside of Daniel (e.g.,"For he is the living God, enduring forever.
His kingdom shall never be destroyed, and his dominion has no end";
6:26), and the specific phrase "the kingdom of God" (*hēbasileia tou
theou*) not found except in the apocryphal Wisdom of Solomon.[1] But
Jesus made repeated glimpses of his understanding of the kingdom of
God central to his proclamation not because the "kingdom of God/
heaven" was an unfamiliar phrasing. Jesus did so because his vision of
God's reign and his listeners' experience of kingly rule were so different. "You know that among the Gentiles those whom they recognize
as their rulers lord it over them, and their great ones are tyrants over
them. But it is not so among you; but whoever wishes to become great
among you must be your servant, and whoever wishes to be first among
you must be slave of all" (Mark 10:42–44). Jesus had some explaining
to do, and he used every rhetorical tool at his disposal, especially parable, allegory, and aphorism, but also healing, exorcism, and riposte,
to show what the kingdom of God looks like, what Wink calls "God's
domination-free order."[2]

Resisting the Powers

"There are bad people in this world, and sometimes bad people stay
bad. Sometimes you have to stand up to them," says Amir to the orphan
Sohrab after the climactic confrontation in the novel *The Kite Runner*.[3] There are bad, evil people, evil institutions, and finally, evil itself.
Jesus clearly knew this, and in the memorable work of Walter Wink
these *Powers*, the Powers that will collude to execute him, were often
the focus of Jesus' proclamation. The Powers are manifest in multiple
ways, most clearly in the Gospels as empire, temple, and adversary. As
one who knew how to read the signs of the times, Jesus is not depicted
as having any illusions about Pax Romana, or about the intentions of
the religious elite. And he knew devil and demons as well as they knew
him. And so he resisted them, in exorcism, prophetic act, and above all,
in preaching and teaching.

"Woe to you, Herod, Pilate, and Caesar, tyrants! You fashion peace
on the broken backs of slaves, laborers, and conscripts, and your prosperity comes from taxes, bribes, and extortion. History will judge you
as harshly as you have judged all who stand up to you, and God will

judge you more harshly still!" I know Jesus said this somewhere, didn't he? I just cannot seem to find the citation. Of course if Jesus had stood in the courtyard of the temple and said something like this, his ministry would have lasted three minutes, not three years.

What we do find in the Synoptic Gospels is an indirect resistance to empire, coupled with and complicated by a much more direct approach toward the temple and the religious elite. Here our contemporary division between church and state confuses my neat distinction between empire and temple, a distinction quite unbiblical and ahistorical. So while "Render unto Caesar" lacks the impact of a good prophetic "Woe unto Caesar," the woes to scribes and Pharisees and the Lukan woes to the rich, the full, and those spoken well of (Luke 6:24–26) may be read as a challenge to empire and not just to temple.

This does not mean we should discount the resistance to empire because it is offered obliquely. Direct assault often sounds better than it is effective. In the somewhat parallel stories about tax paying, one unique to Matthew the other common to the Synoptic Gospels, first Peter (Matt. 17:24) and then Jesus (22:17) is asked about paying a tax. Peter is asked whether Jesus pays the "temple tax," generally understood to be an annual half-shekel tax required of all Jewish adult males. Jesus is later asked, "Is it lawful to pay taxes to the emperor or not?" Jesus' answers are indirect and artful. He asks Peter, "From whom do kings of the earth take toll or tribute? From their children or others?" (17:25), collapsing the empire/temple distinction in his question. And in response to the Pharisees and Herodians (another collapse of our modern church-state division), Jesus neatly avoids the trap of their question by pointing out that if the coin has the emperor's image and inscription, the coin must be his anyway, so go ahead and pay it—while never forgetting to give God what is God's (22:18–22).

At times Jesus is shown using a strategy of indirection when confronting the power of empire, although we recognized that the first words of proclamation out of his mouth in Mark, "The kingdom of God has come near" (1:15), was anything but a subtle beginning. Herod is a "fox" (Luke 13:32), and in the Synoptic Gospels' trial scenes before his execution, Herod, Pilate, and the Sanhedrin are resisted with silence rather than defiance. This does not mean that Jesus lacked some choice and telling words for the religious elite and the temple authorities, not to mention the temple itself.

In Matthew, Jesus denounces the scribes and the Pharisees in two long and highly charged passages, 15:1–20 and 23:1–36, calling them "hypocrites" (15:7; 23:13), yes, but also "blind guides" (15:14; 23:16), "white-washed tombs" (23:27), "snakes" and a "brood of vipers" (23:33). It is much more than name-calling. Jesus denounces a long list of specific religious behaviors that in his opinion contradict the "weightier matters of the law": burdening others, seeking honor, locking others out of heaven, misplacing priorities, tithing herbs while ignoring mercy and justice, and so on. All this is direct and sure to provoke a response, but not nearly as well known or as polarizing as what may best be termed the "temple action."

All four Gospels include the temple action, John placing it at the beginning of Jesus' ministry, the Synoptic evangelists at the beginning of the final week. Even here there is a crucial difference: Matthew (21:23–27) and Luke (19:45–48) place it on the day of the "triumphal entry" into Jerusalem, but Mark (11:15–19) places it on the day after. Mark, I believe, understood some things the others did not, and to fully understand Jesus' proclamation in this event, we do best to look at Mark.

Two problems with the changing of Mark's chronology stand out. In Mark, Jesus enters the temple precincts, looks around, and then leaves without doing or saying anything (11:11); in Matthew and Luke, his reaction to what he sees in the temple is immediate, so that Mark's implicit suggestion that Jesus' action is a planned response after reflection on what he saw is lost. Second, Mark's sequence relating the action in the temple to the "cursing" of the fig tree is ignored. By separating the fig tree incident from the action in the temple, Jesus' response to the lack of fruit on the tree seems petulant at best. Why would Jesus "curse" a fig tree for not having fruit when it was not *supposed* to have fruit? Look at the sequence in Mark:

1. Entry into Jerusalem and initial visit to temple (11:1–11)
2. "Cursing" of the fig tree (11:12–14)
3. Temple action (11:15–19)
4. Withered fig tree (11:20–24)
5. Promised destruction of the temple (13:1–2)

The reader has to wait a while for the completion of the sequence, but it is found in Mark 13, when Jesus pronounces the coming destruction of Jerusalem (13:1–2) and another fig tree enters the discussion (13:28–29).

The reader of Mark is thus led to see that the temple is not "cleansed"; it too is "cursed." As surely as the fig tree "withered away to its roots" (11:20), so also "not one stone will be left here upon another" (13:2). The clearest forerunners to the temple action are the symbolic actions of the prophets: Isaiah, walking around naked for three years to depict Israel's fate (Isa. 20); Jeremiah, burying the loincloth (Jer. 13), at the potter's wheel (Jer. 18), and smashing the potter's vessel (Jer. 19). Jesus does not act out of seething anger, but from prophetic courage.

Jesus' action in the temple contains a sequence itself: (1) physical action interrupting business as usual; (2) Scripture citation; (3) condemning pronouncement. Actions speak louder than words, we say. But without the words, and the biblical justification for the action, the proclamation would not be complete, and the target of Jesus' resistance would be unclear. He was not just mad at the money changers; he was condemning the entire enterprise for what it had become and for forgetting what it had been called to be.

The combination of actions and words in resistance to the Powers is also powerfully depicted in Jesus' initial encounter with the adversary. Here Matthew and Luke profoundly alter Mark's simple story with three challenges to Jesus' self-understanding. You can call him what you will. Matthew uses "tempter" (4:3) and "devil" (4:5, 8, 11), while Jesus says "Satan" (4:10). Luke sticks with "devil" throughout the temptation scene, and later the Synoptics will mention "Beelzebul" (Mark 3:22 and par.). Old Scratch and Screwtape have yet to be found in any ancient manuscripts, but it is the power, not the name, that matters. Jesus resisted the power of evil in all its names; the temptation scene is only the opening confrontation. More common were confrontations with demons, with Mark 1:21–27 being a classic example:

> They went to Capernaum; and when the sabbath came, he entered the synagogue and taught. They were astounded at his teaching, for he taught them as one having authority, and not as the scribes. Just then there was in their synagogue a man with an unclean spirit, and he cried out, "What have you to do with us, Jesus of Nazareth? Have you come to destroy us? I know who you are, the Holy One of God." But Jesus rebuked him, saying, "Be silent, and come out of him!" And the unclean spirit, convulsing him and crying with a loud voice, came out of him. They were all amazed, and they kept on asking one another, "What is this? A new teaching—with authority! He commands even the unclean spirits, and they obey him."

As throughout Mark, the demon, or unclean spirit, recognizes Jesus and calls him by name; Jesus silences and exorcises the demon; the crowd reacts favorably, their reaction to both Jesus' teaching and healing power conflated because they did not distinguish teaching and action.

The adversary is most recognizable in the temptation scene, in exorcisms, and other explicit references—"Get behind me, Satan!" (Mark 8:33). But Jesus' resistance to the Powers is not limited to the explicit. Indeed, the most important examples may be much more mundane calls to repentance. Recall the scene in Levi's house in Luke 5:29–32.

> Then Levi gave a great banquet for him in his house; and there was a large crowd of tax collectors and others sitting at the table with them. The Pharisees and their scribes were complaining to his disciples, saying, "Why do you eat and drink with tax collectors and sinners?" Jesus answered, "Those who are well have no need of a physician, but those who are sick; I have come to call not the righteous but sinners to repentance."

It is easy to read the Powers as represented by the Pharisees and scribes, and to focus on the ongoing struggle between Jesus and his religious opponents. But it is not just those who complain; it is also the attitude and understanding that they represent, the separation, which Jesus rejects. Jesus recognizes that the power of the adversary is equally represented in the sins of the "crowd of tax collectors and others," and not just the dismissal of such people. By sharing fellowship with those whom others reject, Jesus resists the power they represent. Every call to repentance, every invitation to discipleship, resisted the adversary and encouraged faith.

> Resisting the Powers is central to the proclamation of Jesus. For Jesus, preaching offered a distinct alternative to the means employed by the Powers, the means of violent domination. Preaching, in contrast to the way of the Domination System, was the *means* that was ethically consistent with the *end* of God's shalom. The very act of preaching—the choice of preaching as a means—represented a rejection of and alternative to the 'myth of redemptive violence.' Preaching itself was a practice of nonviolent resistance to the values and means of the Domination System.[4]

Sharing and Shaping the Faith

Jesus announced the coming of the kingdom in his ministry, and challenged the Powers that resisted his ministry and the kingdom he announced. But there was more to his proclamation than decisive announcement and dramatic encounter. Jesus was also a teacher of life in the kingdom. In his proclamation, Jesus shared and shaped the faith, first by showing what the kingdom of God/heaven "looks" like, and then by teaching what living in, or perhaps *into* the kingdom looks like.

Summarizing this aspect of Jesus' proclamation is challenging, because in many important ways *all* of Jesus' proclamation shared and shaped the faith. While not all the parables, allegories, and aphorisms begin as helpfully as the Mustard Seed, "With what can we compare the kingdom of God, or what parable will we use for it?" (Mark 4:30), many of them do, and many more make clear that life in the kingdom is the point of comparison. Nor are all Jesus' straightforward teachings about life in the kingdom as helpfully gathered as Mathew does for us in the Sermon on the Mount (Matt. 5–7), but the sermon, whether we consider it an epitome or some other summarizing genre, is a very useful guide.

— The Beatitudes (5:3–12) offer an ironic opening, inviting us to a fresh and surprising way of seeing.

— The proclamations that we *are* salt and light, that Jesus has come to fulfill the law, and that our righteousness must exceed that of the religious elite (5:13–20) invite us to look at Jesus, and ourselves, in a new way.

— The six antitheses (5:21–48) show us what fulfillment of the law and exceeding righteousness looks like in our daily lives.

— The instruction on practicing the faith in giving, praying, and fasting (6:1–18) begins to shape our worship lives.

— The instruction on our attitude toward money and possessions (6:19–21, 24–34), with the enigmatic saying about the eye adding emphasis to the importance of how we look at things (6:22–23), challenge us to see as God sees.

— The proverbial instructions not to judge (7:1–5), to ask, seek and knock (7:7–11), how to "do to others" (7:12), to seek the narrow way (7:13–14), and to be very careful whom we trust (7:6, 15–20), pass on a mixture Jesus' conventional and unconventional wisdom for daily living.

— The closing warning (7:21–23) and parable (7:24–27) stress that the kingdom is for "the one who does the will of my Father in heaven" and not for those who have the liturgy down pat.

What is compelling and engaging about Jesus' proclamation of kingdom living is the combination of showing, challenging, and inviting.

Look at that crazy sower over there! (Mark 4:3–9). Did I tell you about the man who had two sons? (Luke 15:11–32). It was hot in the vineyard that day, and you will not believe what the owner did! (Matt. 20:1–16). These glimpses of the kingdom capture our interest in ways no didactic exhortation really can. But there is such exhortation in Jesus' proclamation. There are dos and don'ts, challenges to live as citizens of the kingdom, and instructions on what that living looks like: Don't engage in wishful thinking; ask! Don't plot revenge, thinking you can fight violence with violence, but turn and face another blow. I didn't say it was easy; I said it was blessed. Above all, Jesus' proclamation of life in the kingdom was inviting. The listener is not coerced, but welcomed.

Jesus announced the arrival of that which has always been there, the presence and reign of God. The announcement itself was an act of resistance, but Jesus was also more direct, challenging the powers of empire, temple, and adversary with a message of peace, justice, and forgiveness. Aware that his listeners needed both remedial and advanced instruction in the blessed life of the kingdom of God, he showed them what that life looks like and challenged them to practice the faith he proclaimed.

PREACHING AS PROCLAMATION

I listen to a lot of preaching. Since leaving full-time parish ministry for full-time seminary teaching, with a wonderful transition period at the Louisville Institute, I have found myself sitting in the pew more frequently than standing in the pulpit, and in the classroom I hear a few hundred sermons each year. If there is a homiletical sin I have come to hold more damning than any other, it is the absence of clarity. Boring is bad, exegetical error egregious, and excessive length an indication of a lack of preparation; but all these I will forgive. Not deciding what you want to preach about, and not making your proclamation clear? Well, perhaps that is why I still sort of believe in purgatory—a year for every sermon that didn't go anywhere. If the two basic rules of preaching are *having something to say that is worth hearing* and *saying it well enough to be truly heard,* the rules are in that order for a reason.

Whether he spoke in parables, aphorisms, or direct exhortation, Jesus' message, give or take the parable of the Dishonest Steward, was invariably clear at its heart, even if open to interpretation at the edges.

Sometimes we act as if we are not sure what Jesus was getting at, but this usually has more to do with the fact we do not want to *do* what Jesus says, so we pretend the whole thing is an enigma. The problem with Luke 14:33, "None of you can become my disciple if you do not give up all your possessions," is not a lack of clarity. We know what the words mean; the complete absence of a lack of clarity is the problem.

When moving from critical to homiletical exegesis, the preacher is required to do something most preachers hate: focus. The lectionary preacher may be faced with two or three wonderful passages and even a favorite psalm, yet realize that it is impossible to begin to do justice to all of the rich biblical material to be heard by the congregation that week. The energy and effort of sermon development mandates that the preacher set aside one or more passages for at best fleeting reference, because after the preacher chooses where to focus, there is another step: really, really focus. We hate that even more. A study at the Massachusetts Institute of Technology may explain why people do not like to focus and show that those who refuse to do so are in good company. Using a game that involved opening and closing doors on a computer screen, participants were rewarded with a small but varying amount of money each time they clicked open a door on the screen. One could quickly learn which doors provided the greatest reward, but most failed to use this strategy. Why? Because after a while an unclicked door would begin to fade from the screen and disappear. Players returned time and again to click on the fading doors to keep them from disappearing, even when a variation in the game caused them not only to lose turns but also to lose money when they did so. For some reason, even in a simulation, participants could not bear to let go of any option; they hated the idea of watching options disappear.[5] Good preachers make difficult choices every week. Poor preachers hope the listeners will find a sermon in their jumble of unfocused stories, musings, and exegesis that they have not taken the time or effort to focus.

Preachers want to bring clarity and focus when following the example of Jesus in announcing the kingdom, resisting the Powers, and sharing and shaping the faith. And they also need to bring conviction and compassion to the task. Balance is required, a balance that may seem at odds with the passion implicit in the phrase "proclamatory preaching." How to bring focus, conviction, and compassion to announcing the kingdom, resisting the Powers, and sharing and shaping the faith is a crucial question.

Announcing the Kingdom Jesus Announced

If the kingdom of God was "at hand" two millennia ago when Jesus first made his proclamation, just exactly what is the preacher announcing today? Is the kingdom of God now closer than close? Has it come and gone? Is it coming again, with complete eschatological fulfillment? These and other choices depend on how the preacher understands Jesus' own proclamation. In other words, our clarity and focus are grounded in our own convictions. The preacher must come to some conclusions about the nature of God's kingdom—or rule, reign, or hegemony—and fashion the proclamation accordingly. This is a considerable exegetical, theological, and hermeneutical task before it is a homiletical one, but the basic choices are few.

One may decide that the kingdom of God means "heaven," and heaven means a hard-to-describe temporal/spatial place of abiding for all the resurrected faithful—"whether in the body or out of the body I do not know" (2 Cor. 12:2–3), be it after death (Luke 23:43) or after the end of the age (Rev. 21–22). In any case, the kingdom of God, while always as near as it can be, is always yet to come. It is not here yet, but we shouldn't have to wait *too* much longer.

One may also hold a variation of the above, popularized in dispensationalism (see the Left Behind series), which posits the kingdom of God as yet to come, but thinks of it in millennialist terms and likens it to the "thousand-year reign" of those "beheaded for their testimony to Jesus" between the first and second defeats of Satan (Rev. 20:1–10). The kingdom is thus earthly, not heavenly, and those who rule over it will be resurrected saints. "This is the first resurrection" (20:5b).

The advantage of either of these views is that they provide an answer to the obvious question of what is taking so long if Jesus said the kingdom was "at hand." This may make the preacher look good, but it leaves Jesus looking a bit like he didn't know what he was talking about. And it also undermines the force of the metaphor in its Gospel setting, the contrast of kingdoms—God's and the empire's—now replaced by heaven and earth. I know, I know, Jesus said, "My kingdom is not from this world," but that was in the Fourth Gospel (18:36). In the Synoptic Gospels, Jesus said, "In fact, the kingdom of God is among you" (Luke 17:21), and said it in response to a question about "when the kingdom of God was coming."

To return to an earlier claim, I take Jesus to mean "here" and "now" when he announces that we should repent and believe because "the time is fulfilled and the kingdom of God has come near" (Mark 1:15). This is it, sisters and brothers. Stop waiting and start living. Don't expect everyone to agree, and watch out for those who really don't want you to live in/into the kingdom. That is their issue, not yours. Yours is to look at the signs and symbols of the kingdom all around you, and to live in the way I am showing and teaching you. The moment is here. God is here. Be present to the moment. Be present to God.

You do not have to agree with my understanding. But you do have to clarify your own convictions about the meaning of Jesus' announcement of the kingdom in the Gospels for your announcement of that kingdom today. And then, because your preaching is proclamatory, you proclaim it in a focused, convincing, and compassionate way. If yours is a premillennial dispensationalist theology, then you proclaim that, and you proclaim it in a focused, convincing, and compassionate way. Whatever your understanding of the kingdom of God, the homiletical task requires focus, conviction, and compassion.

It is hard to have focus without conviction. What you have instead are qualifications, reservations, and footnotes. It is dangerous to have conviction without compassion, for then you are tempted to have no reservations and make no qualifications. "Whoever is not with me is against me" (Matt. 12:30) is a perilous mind-set to bring to the pulpit. So our proclamation must have all three: focus, conviction, and compassion.

When Jesus said, "The kingdom of God has come near," listeners said, "Huh?" not just because they needed time to work out the metaphor, but because the available evidence suggested otherwise. It was the kingdom of Caesar that was not just near: it was everywhere. When you paid your taxes, passed by the soldiers that joined the pilgrims in coming to Jerusalem for the festivals, you knew: Caesar is lord. If you didn't believe it, look at the coin in your hand. It was not just the image, but also the inscription. "A coin of Julius Caesar shows his spirit ascending cometlike to take its place among the eternal deities. A coin of Augustus Caesar calls him *divi filius*, son of a divine one, son of a god, son of the aforesaid comet. A coin of Tiberius Caesar hails him as *pontifex maximus*, supreme bridge-builder between heaven and earth, high priest of an imperial people."[6]

Jesus knew all this, and he did not care. He announced the kingdom of God not just to resist the kingdom of Caesar, but to recall his listeners to their true identity as children of God. The signs and symbols around us today are certainly no less corrupting than those of first-century Palestine. And they are more omnipresent, leaving our listeners as much in need of being reminded of their true identity as beloved of God, as those oppressed by Augustus and Tiberius. Caesar still lives.

Resisting the Powers

Which is it going to be? Will we quiver in the pulpit like so many patriotic sheep, or rise up and denounce the evils of neocolonialist aggression emanating from our nation's capitol, be it Washington, London, Moscow, or Beijing?

Well, when you put it that way, how about a nice sermon on the psalm for the day?

The choice cannot be between cowardly acquiescence and indiscriminate denunciation. Neither is faithful to the gospel or to the listener. We noted above that Jesus is not recorded to have said, "Woe to you, Caesar, Herod, and Pilate, tyrants!" When he was warned because "Herod wants to kill you," he called Herod a fox and offered a poignant lament over Jerusalem (Luke 13:31–35), not a curse. Proclamatory preaching does not mean direct assault, Sunday after Sunday. The emphasis on focus, conviction, and compassion is just as important for resisting the Powers as it is for announcing the kingdom. Proclamatory preaching does mean that our commitment to the gospel is deeper than our fear that someone might be offended, but it does not delight in giving offense.

A popular television news network built its image on the idea that there was a distinct "liberal" bias in the media, and that it would instead offer reporting that was "fair and balanced." Many observers now consider it to be the most biased network on the airwaves. The same is true of every medium of communication, including the pulpit. We are all biased, every preacher, every parishioner. So abandon the idea of neutral sermons unless you do not want to stand for anything; in which case, just abandon the idea of sermons altogether.

The challenge is not to preach sermons that are "fair and balanced"; the challenge is to preach focused, faithful sermons that come out of your convictions and are shared with true compassion. The listeners do not always have to agree with you, but they do need to know, to feel, that you respect them. Which pretty much leaves "Woe to you, hypocrites" out of the question. Or as Arthur Boers memorably titled his helpful book on dealing with difficult people in the parish, *Never Call Them Jerks.*[7]

We have eliminated the obvious. How then does one preach in resistance to empire, temple, and adversary? First, by recognizing the Powers for what they are, how they act, and not pretending that they no longer pose a threat to the faith and the faithful. Caesar is not the only power still alive. Ecclesial corruption and distortion, and abusive and destructive religion, abound. And the last time I checked, the adversary is very much with us as well. The first step, like the first volume in Walter Wink's trilogy, is naming the Powers.[8] The problem is that many congregations have long tried to teach their preachers that there are three things it is impolite to talk about in the pulpit: politics, sex, and religion. Expect some resistance to your resistance, one more reason to refer to the third power as the adversary. After all, if most candidates for high national office begin their stump speeches with "The problem with Washington today is . . . ," why can't the preacher?

There are times, more times than most of us ever address, when direct resistance from the pulpit is what the gospel calls for. But even proclamatory preaching begins with what the Gospel calls for—or the Epistle or the Old Testament lesson. It does not begin with what ticks the preacher off about the current administration. The question remains, no matter how mad the preacher might be: *What does the Holy Spirit want the people of God to hear from these texts on this occasion?*

Pick a Proper, any Proper. Okay, how about the one for this Sunday? As I write, that happens to be Proper 15 Year A, the fourteenth Sunday after Pentecost. And the Gospel is Matthew's version of the Canaanite (Syro-Phoenician) woman and her sick child (Matt. 15:21–28). Jesus is on vacation, and the woman challenges Jesus to help her. He and his entourage seem to hope she will just go away. She doesn't, and the metaphors begin to fly:

> "I was sent only to the lost sheep of the house of Israel."
>   "Lord, help me!"
>   "It is not fair to take the children's food and throw it to the dogs."

Whoa! Stop right there. Did you hear that? Jesus just called that woman's daughter a dog! And that right after he says in Matthew 15:11 (which can be included in the RCL reading), "It is what comes out of the mouth that defiles."

Except that is not what happened, and such an interpretation ignores the rhetorical context. Jesus and the woman are not in a shouting match, but they are in a contest, a rhetorical contest known as "challenge-riposte." The woman has presented an honor challenge to Jesus by asking him in front of the disciples to heal her daughter. Jesus tries to deflect her, and she will not be deterred. Jesus ups the rhetorical ante with a commonplace, a bit of proverbial wisdom. It is a *metaphor*, for crying out loud, not name-calling. And the woman responds to Jesus' riposte with a deft answer of her own, in the spirit of the rhetorical contest she, if not contemporary readers, realizes she is in. "Yes, Lord, yet even the dogs eat the crumbs that fall from their masters' table." Bingo! For the first and only time in the Gospels, Jesus is bested in an argument. And he knows it. "Woman, great is your faith! Let it be done for you as you wish."

A couple of years ago a student approached this text with the boldness and skill of a seasoned preacher, and in a way that *in*directly challenged the Powers. The story was no longer about Jesus and a woman from another country and culture. It was about a doctor at an urban medical center, an immigrant woman with a sick child, and a system that forced the mother to decide whether to risk deportation by seeking medical care for which she had no insurance, no *right*. It was amazing, it was proclamatory, and it was effective because it was indirect. Just like the dialogue between Jesus and the woman! If the preacher had begun the sermon by describing and denouncing the problems with the American immigration situation, then moved on to attack health care policy, she may have been right, and lots of folks may have agreed with her. Others—say, a physician, an insurance executive, and Lou Dobbs—might never come back to hear her again. Because the sermon grew, in content and form, out of a faithful reading of the text, shaped by the preacher's deep convictions, and was offered with a compassionate awareness of differing opinions on complex subjects, it was effective. It was focused, even though figurative, and powerfully proclamatory.

Institutional evil abounds, and is not limited to policy-making and makers. It is corporate, civic, educational, medical. It is real. And when the lessons point to it, the preacher must too. And sometimes, *sometimes*, even when the lessons do not.

You may have heard that certain communions, like, well, mine, are having their problems. Since Wycliffe, Luther, and Coverdale translated Scripture into the language of the people and the printing press made it available, folks have been reading the Bible and making their own decisions about its meaning and message. Not that they all agreed before, but since then? God help us! Which is why the people who count these things say there are approximately forty thousand Christian denominations worldwide. The question has never been whether or not we will disagree about matters of biblical authority and interpretation, human sexuality, peace and justice, and so forth, but how we will handle our disagreements.

We could close our eyes and hope they will go away, but they do not. Some of the people hoping to have a chance to hear, pray, and reflect on what they hear, see, and read in the media might go away, but the problems will not. At least one Episcopal parish took the ostrich approach to topics of human sexuality following the election and consecration of Eugene Robinson as bishop of New Hampshire, declaring that it was not to be talked about from the pulpit or in the classroom, and going so far as to try to censor the choices of an adult reading and discussion group. Those who wanted to learn, discuss, read, and grow, left. In droves.

We have to preach about it, whatever the "it" this time around may be. Not in platitudes or evasive language, but in focused sermons that offer our best reflections growing out of our deepest convictions, with compassion and respect for those who disagree and agree. And not in ways that make controversy central, but in ways that bring the heart of the gospel, Jesus Christ, into meaningful dialogue with the controversy that is troubling the parish. The pulpit is a place to proclaim the gospel, not to propagandize, coerce, politic, or demean.

Here's a topic for you: Sin. Temptation, after all, is the adversary's core skill, and while it is probably more fun to point to corporate malfeasance and politicians' peccadilloes, there is sin closer to home on most Sundays. One of the Powers that needs to be named is the power of sin, and its ever-willing helpmate, temptation, because the corrupting, destructive nature of the Powers is not only institutional. It is damnably personal as well. The rules still apply: focus, conviction, and here especially, compassion. It is a safe assumption that every person in the congregation is at some level or another struggling with their own sinfulness. Jokes about Sunday worship following Saturday night excess are not helpful, nor is "sin in haste, repent at leisure." A much better place to start is Barbara Taylor's *Speaking of Sin* and Martin Smith's *Reconciliation.*[9]

And here's a surprise: the lessons on most Sundays are going to require that, like it or not, we talk about sin. It seems the ancients struggled with it as much as we do today. Struggle is the right word, too, one the preacher should pay attention to. If you ask yourself—or even better, ask your congregation—what topics they would like to hear addressed from the pulpit, do not be surprised if not every matter is abstract, theological, and safe. People struggle with right and wrong, at home and work and school and play. Preachers do too, but we have trained ourselves to act like we do not. We are not fooling anyone. Every now and then we should try to preach a sermon about something really troubling our listeners. Like sin.

Sharing and Shaping the Faith

Sunday morning, worship over, handshake line in the narthex. Parishioner says to the preacher, "When are you gonna preach about sinn-uh?"

"Why, I preached about sin just last week. The parable of the Prodigal Son."

"That wasn't about sinn-uh. That was about fuh-giiivvee-ness!"

Some people are hard to please, and it is hard to preach about sin in a Christian pulpit without at least a passing reference to forgiveness and salvation. To do otherwise would be distortion, not proclamation.

Just as preachers may safely assume that most everyone listening to them are at some level struggling with sin, they may also assume that they would like help with their struggle. They would like to hear words of hope, and also of instruction. They want to understand the faith more fully, and probably would like to live it more faith-fully. Unless their parents or habit dragged them there—and let's face it, there is not much of that going on anymore—they came to church for some reason. Forgiveness, sacrament, help, hope, yes, and thanks, silence, mystery, and desperation are also represented. What are you going to do?

You are going to teach. I do not mean get out the PowerPoint, unless that is customary, nor does it require handouts, outlines, and note-taking. Jesus managed to teach quite effectively without visual aids except what all could see or imagine. More important, separating Jesus' teaching from his preaching is impossible. *That* is something to emulate. Proclamatory preaching does not mean an absence of instruction; it means, surprise! instruction that is focused, compassionate, and arising out of the preacher's deepest convictions. Paul and the author of Hebrews seemed to get irritated when they needed to pause to offer instruction, the milk-versus-meat metaphor (1 Cor. 3:2; Heb. 5:12–13). Jesus did not seem to mind.

My faculty colleagues and I would often sit around the room, over coffee or at meetings, and bemoan—yea, verily I say, bewail—the absence of formation, catechesis, and basic theological and biblical knowledge among our entering students. Two things finally dawned on us. First, if they already knew everything we wanted them to know, why did they need to come to seminary? Second, was it not our job to teach them what they did not know? Point taken.

It is just as tempting, and I have also sat in those circles, to bemoan the biblical and theological illiteracy of parishioners. You have seen the surveys. What is the percentage of professing Christians who can name at least two of the four Gospels? Low. Higher than those who can name four of the Twelve, but still low. Hand them a Bible and ask them to look up the book of Ezekiel, and you might as well have asked them to translate a cuneiform tablet. Here's the question for the preacher: What are *you* going to do about it? You are going to teach, patiently, lovingly, respectfully. They will love you for it.

I have already noted that the contemporary master at this kind of teaching is Fred Craddock. He knows full well that many, if not most, of his listeners do not know enough Scripture and theology to make the most of his sermons. So Craddock teaches. When he can, he leads an hour of Bible study in Sunday school before the service, on the passages that will be read in worship. When he is a guest and that opportunity is not possible (although why you would invite Fred Craddock and not have him teach Sunday school when he wanted to do so is a mystery to me), he still teaches, but in the sermon. Two things are especially noteworthy. First, everything is in the present tense. The Bible is not viewed as of and about long ago and far away, to which the preacher must painfully, desperately ask, "And what does this mean for us today?" Everything is in the present tense: Sarah, David, Isaiah, Deborah, and most especially Jesus. They say and do, not said and did. This allows the preacher to move seamlessly between Scripture and listener; it invites the listener to see Scripture the same way.

Second, when Fred Craddock is about to explain and interpret, he speaks as if he assumes the listeners already know what he is about to say, and that this is just a little reminder. "Now you will recall," he begins before unraveling a biblical conundrum even the host pastor has wondered about. Or, "Of course you do not need me to tell you," before he summarizes the doctrine of the Trinity from the Council of

Nicaea to the Second Vatican Council. It is not just a nice touch; it is also rhetorically effective in its respect for listeners. Another personal favorite is Michael Curry, bishop of the Episcopal Diocese of North Carolina, whose sermon comes at the end of this chapter. Bishop Curry often segues to the instructional by saying, "Now I'm going to tell you this so you know I went to seminary." And then he teaches. He doesn't teach down, nor should any preacher. Those listening are just as well informed and competent in their vocations as we are in ours, and the preacher should never forget it.

How we teach should be as informed by the preaching of Jesus as the fact that we should teach. It is an old canard, but your eighth-grade English teacher was correct: show, don't tell. The best teaching allows the listeners to see for themselves, and it does so by being concrete and vivid. We all put extraordinary effort into how we begin our sermons, hoping to capture our listeners in the couple of minutes they offer before deciding if we are going to talk about something that matters to them. And so we are usually vivid and concrete, telling a story that connects and invites, be it biblical, topical, or off the front page. It is hard work, isn't it? But it's worth the effort, and the same effort should be given to our teaching. Instead, we often say, in our demeanor if not our words, "Hang in there through this boring teaching part, and then I will tell you a really great story." The clicking sound you hear is everyone under the age of forty text-messaging how bored they are.

Jesus used stories to teach, not just to inspire. As we will see in chapter 5, almost every discourse in the Synoptic Gospels is shot through with figurative language, language that intrigues even as it calls on the listeners to reflect and ponder deeper meanings. It was figurative, which made it vivid, but it was also concrete. Real people, real scenes, real ideas. For example, to go back to the readings for Proper 15, Year A, the Old Testament reading in the RCL is the climactic scene between Joseph and his brothers, Genesis 45:1–15. In the reading from the previous week, the brothers sold him into slavery, so a lot has happened biblically. What is the preacher going to do? You could forget the whole thing: it is not as if the Joseph Cycle is important to the tradition or anything. And never mind that the whole foreigner/immigrant theme bumps right into the Gospel reading about the Canaanite woman. Okay, forgetting Joseph is not going to work. You have four minutes. Tell them about Joseph in Egypt. Tell them about the power of dreams. Tell them about famine and desperation. Tell them about a dysfunctional family. Don't drag it out, telling them everything you know. You have four minutes before you must move on, so discipline yourself to tell them what they need to know to see that there is more to Joseph than his "technicolor dreamcoat."

It is like this every week, whether you are a lectionary preacher or select your own texts. If you are a biblical preacher, the abundant riches of the material are overwhelming. Which is why you need to focus, really, really focus.

A SERMON BY THE RIGHT REVEREND MICHAEL B. CURRY

This sermon, famous in the Episcopal Church, USA, was preached at the 74th General Convention of the church in August 2003, a few days before the House of Bishops and the House of Deputies consented to the election of Gene Robinson as Bishop of New Hampshire. It was the first time I had the privilege to hear Bishop Curry preach. Every sermon has a text, a context, and a subtext, and listeners are aware of each to a greater and lesser extent. When I heard it, still new to the Episcopal Church, the extent was decidedly lesser. I knew that the Archbishop of Nigeria, Peter Akinola, had preached the day before, and the woman who was then Bishop of Nevada, now Presiding Bishop Katharine Jefferts Schori, was celebrant, but I did not know what that meant. Live and learn. Bishop Curry obviously knew what all that meant, and he carefully built his way to "And all means *all*," with "all that" in view. And I have to concede, if you have not heard the bishop preach, you will have missed a good bit of the sermon's power. The bishop can preach. Period.

The Mountain

Isaiah 2:1–5
> "Come, let us go up to the mountain of the LORD,
>   to the house of the God of Jacob;
> that he may teach us his ways
>   and that we may walk in his paths."
> For out of Zion shall go forth instruction,
>   and the word of the LORD from Jerusalem.
> He shall judge between the nations,
>   and shall arbitrate for many peoples;

they shall beat their swords into plowshares,
and their spears into pruning hooks;
nation shall not lift up sword against nation,
neither shall they learn war any more.

The late Robert Kennedy, quoting George Bernard Shaw, was fond of saying, "Some men see things as they are and ask, Why? I dream things that never were and ask, Why not?" Isaiah of Jerusalem was someone who understood things as they are. This prophet understood the world as it very often is. And yet he was someone who dreamed the dream of God and asked, "Why not?" The Bible says that he began his ministry "in the year that King Uzziah died" (6:1). That death, for the people of this biblical era, had much the same impact on them as the death of President Kennedy or Dr. Martin Luther King Jr. did on us. Isaiah knew the world as it is. Much of his mature preaching occurred during the reign of King Hezekiah, when the city of Jerusalem itself was under siege from the armies of Assyria. Isaiah knew the world as it often is. His prophecies frequently speak of the need to end nightmares of violence and plagues of injustice, suggesting a realistic understanding of the world as it often is.

The later sections of the book of Isaiah reflect the writings of his disciples who applied Isaiah's thought to the period of the Babylonian exile, when for the people of God the whole world fell apart; when as the poet said, "The center cannot hold." Babylonian armies destroyed Jerusalem and then carted the leading citizens off like cargo to Babylon. There they lived in virtual slavery. There they languished as people without hope. There one of their poets would speak these words: "By the waters of Babylon we sat down and wept when we remembered thee, O Zion. . . . How shall we sing the Lord's song in a strange land." Isaiah and the literature of the book of Isaiah spoke to such a time. Isaiah understood the world as it is.

And yet, this same Isaiah was able to speak as one who dared to dream the dream of God in the midst of the nightmare that often is the world. He dreamed it and he asked, "Why not?" Why not a world where children do not go to bed hungry? Why not a world where justice does roll down like a mighty stream and righteousness like an ever-flowing brook? Why not a world where we lay down our swords and shields by the riverside to study war no more? Why not, O Lord, why not?

Old Testament scholar Walter Brueggemann spoke of this text as a "bold and daring act of imagination." Isaiah looked into the nightmare that is often the world and was able to behold the dream of God for this world. And that sanctified act of the imagination became possible because Isaiah had been to the mountain. Come, let us go to the mountain.

In the Bible, the mountain is frequently a way of talking about those ways and places, those moments and memories, when God gets real, when we meet and are met by God. Sometimes it is those moments when we go apart to rest for a while. Sometimes it is in that "still, small voice." That is a sound in silence if you listen. Sometimes it is as we look deeply into the face of each other to behold the imago dei, the image of God, the face of Jesus etched on us. "When did we see you hungry, Lord?" "When you did it to the least of these you did it to me," says Jesus. When Dr. Martin Luther King Jr. was murdered, he was in Memphis to stand with garbage workers who were striking for human dignity and freedom. He was looking in the face of the other when he said, "I've been to the mountaintop, and I've seen the promised land."

The mountain is a way of talking about those moments when God gets real. The mountain is a way of talking about what the Celtic tradition calls "thin places." One of the Negro spirituals says it this way:

Upon the mountain, my Lord spoke,
Out of his mouth came fire and smoke.
Every time I feel the Spirit,
Moving in my heart, I could pray.

You've got to come to the mountain! Hearts get changed on the mountain. Lives get changed on the mountain. Worlds get changed on the mountain. The mountain is the place of messianic metamorphoses.

If you don't believe me, ask Abraham. Abraham went to the mountain on a mission. He thought he was engaging God's mission by sacrificing his son Isaac. But on the mountain he discovered that when it comes to God's mission, grace and mercy, and compassion and faith, are closer to the heart of God than either stern sacrifice or blind obedience. You've got to come to the mountain!

Think about Moses. Moses went up the mountain one way, and went down another. "Go down, Moses, way down in Egypt's land; tell ol' Pharaoh, let my people go." You've got to come to the mountain!

And in the writings of Isaiah, it is that reality on the mountain that transforms lives and can transform a world. In chapter 2 (v. 4), on the mountain, "They shall beat their swords into plowshares, and their spears into pruning hooks; nation shall not rise up against nation, neither shall they learn war any more." In chapter 11 (v. 6 alt.), on the mountain, "The wolf shall lie down with the lamb." Wolves and lambs don't share the same self-interest. Dick Gregory used to say the wolf may lie down with the lamb, but the lamb won't get much sleep that night. But on the mountain the wolf and the lamb lie down together. They dwell together. Now there are some wolves in this convention. There are some lambs here. And if you're like me, you've got some wolf and lamb in you. But on the mountain the wolf and lamb dwell together in peace. "They shall not hurt or destroy in all my holy mountain, for the earth will be filled with the glory of God as the waters cover the sea" (11:9 alt.). You've got to come to the mountain!

So when you get to the New Testament, it is not an accident that there is a Sermon on the Mount. It's not an accident that Jesus must go to the mountain of transfiguration before he can enter the valley of the shadow of death. It's not an accident that Jesus sends the disciples on the mission to make disciples and make a difference in the world from a mountain. It is on the mountain that folks get transformed. On the mountain that enemies can become friends. On the mountain that worlds get changed. The mountain is the key to the mission. Come, let us go to the mountain.

A few weeks ago, when I was working on this message, I found myself stuck at this point. I knew the mountain represents the context of Gospel transformation, but I was stuck on the question Why? What is it about the mountain that can so incredibly change us all? Then I went to church.

While on vacation, I was visiting a church when we stood to sing number 686 in *Hymnal 1982*, "Come, Thou Fount of Every Blessing." I've been singing that hymn all my life, but I never paid attention to the entire first verse until that day. It goes like this:

Come thou fount of every blessing, tune my heart to sing thy grace!
Streams of mercy, never ceasing, call for songs of loudest praise.
Teach me some melodious sonnet, sung by flaming tongues above.
Praise the mount! O fix me on it, mount of God's unchanging love.
(Robert Robinson)

There it is. The mount of God's unchanging love.

The key to living the ways and teaching of God that Isaiah speaks about is living in and out of the love of God. And that unchanging love can change the world. I think that's what Jesus was teaching us when He said, "You shall love the Lord your God with all your heart, soul, mind, and strength. And you shall love your neighbor as yourself. On these two hang all the law and the prophets" (Matt. 22:37–40 alt.). This is the gospel. This is the good news! This is the message of the mountain and the motive of the mission. And it can change the world.

God didn't create us because God needed us. God didn't make me because God needed me. God will be God without me. God was doing just fine before I came along. And God will be doing fine when I've gone on to glory. And if the truth is told, I'm one of God's biggest headaches. And I'll let you in on a secret: you're the other one. No, no, no. God is God.

When I was the new rector at St. James Church in Baltimore, I went into the sacristy of the church before service to get vested. Several people involved in the service were there, and we introduced ourselves to each other. One gentleman in particular introduced himself with the words, "Hello, I'm so and so, and I'm a member of the B Group." I didn't understand what he meant by the B Group, so I asked him what that was. He said, "I be here before you. I'll be here while you're here. I'll be here when you're gone." And I have to admit that nearly twelve years later, at my consecration as Bishop of North Carolina, he stood at the end of the aisle of Duke University Chapel, put out his hands, and said, "I'm still in the B Group."

God is the ultimate B group. God didn't create this world or any of us because of God's need or anything external to God. The Bible says that God is the alpha and the omega, the beginning and the end. God is the one who was and is and is to come. God is God. God doesn't need us. God said, "Let there be . . . ," for one reason and one reason alone. First John says, "God is love" (4:8). The book of Deuteronomy says that the reason God set the Hebrews free was love (7:7–8). Psalm 33 says that the reason for creation is love (v. 5). The reason for redemption, the reason God came in Jesus, was love. "God so loved the world that he gave his only Son" (John 3:16). And the way to discipleship is living in the power of God's love. "By this everyone will know that you are my disciples, if you have love for one another" (John 13:34–35). The love of God will change our hearts. Love will change our minds. Love will change our lives, our country, our world, our church. Come to the mount of God's unchanging, steadfast love. Come, let us go to the mountain. . . .

And let us not think of this love of God as weak and anemic. Three years ago, when I was blessed to be elected Bishop of North Carolina, I found myself trying to explain to our then six-year-old daughter what a bishop did. She had some sense of what I did as a parish priest. She could see it. But a bishop wasn't quite as clear. One day, while we were eating dinner, the UPS truck pulled up to the house. The delivery guy rang the bell, and my wife answered the door. It was a gift from the late Bishop Walter Dennis. It was a beautiful white linen miter. From that point on, she began to identify the miter with being a bishop.[10]

After we had moved to Raleigh, she was watching a video with a friend. It was a cartoon version of the story of Dr. Martin Luther King Jr. I happened to be walking through the den, where they were watching the video. As I passed through the room, I noticed that in the story they were watching a scene of a cross burning, with hooded knights of the Ku Klux Klan present. As I walked through the room, Elizabeth asked me, "Why are all those Episcopal bishops standing by that burning cross?"

After I told them what it was, they understood. But it was not an automatic reflex. Thirty years ago or so, it would not have been possible for any black child in America not to automatically have a reflex reaction of terror at that sight. Those two children, one black and one white, did not react automatically because something did change in this country and this culture. And I'm here to tell you that it changed not by sword, not by might, but by the power of God's love translated into our social situation. America is a different place because some people decided, of all colors and kinds, that we're going to live by love, not by hatred. Disciplined love changed that. Love works!

Don't be afraid of it. Don't be ashamed of it. Don't underestimate the power of God's love lived out. This is the gospel. This is the good news. Here is our greatest strength. Here we can find healing, courage, and grace. Here we find life for us and for the world. So come to the mountain. Come to the mountain of God's unchanging love. Come, there's room for us all. And all means all.

And remember, God loves you maybe more than any of us will ever know, and that love will never ever let us go, so

Go, tell it on the mountain,
Over the hills and everywhere.
Go, tell it on the mountain,
That Jesus Christ is born.
            (John W. Work Jr.)

Amen.

Analysis

I admit it. The bishop did raise his voice a time or two. And he may have made a few gestures. So did the audience, however many thousand of us there were, our last gesture coming in the shape of five minutes of standing, cheering, shouting, and clapping. It was the most excited I had yet seen Episcopalians, and it scared me to death. I know it may not read that way, but believe me, it preached that way. But the proclamation was not in the shouting, it was in the truth-telling.

Excellent sermons frequently share one thing in common: a transparent structure, whether the preacher planned it or not. The really good ones do not seem to need to plan it; they think that way. My later experience with sermons by Bishop Curry suggests that the clear structure of this sermon was no accident, or more precisely, it was the accident of design. To use David Buttrick's terms,[11] the sermon was structured around four moves:

> Move 1—Isaiah the prophet, who sees the world as it is and asks, "Why not?"
>
> Move 2—Come to the mountain, with Martin, Abraham, Moses, Isaiah, and Jesus.
>
> Move 3—The mount of God's unchanging love, the love that changes everything.
>
> Move 4—The transforming love of Jesus, love that works for all.

Move 1—Why not? Like Dr. Craddock, Bishop Curry speaks of biblical material in the present tense. Isaiah knew the world "as it is," not "as it was." He handles the material skillfully, mentioning Assyria, Hezekiah, and topics important to Isaiah 1–39, then Isaiah's "disciples" and the pain of exile to Babylon generations later, all without tedious explanations of multiple authors, the post-Solomon division of the kingdom, and other matters not important to the sermon, nor to the world "as it is." He does not want us to focus on the prophet, but on the mountain, so that is where he focuses. Far too often preachers fail to do this, more concerned with demonstrating knowledge and erudition than advancing the purposes of the sermon. He then depicts the world both as it was, the Babylonian exile, and as it is, our own sufferings. Next he comes to his transition and the central question of the sermon, asking, "Why not?" Isaiah dreamed God's dream, and we could too, asking, "Why not a world where children do not go to bed hungry? Where justice does roll down, . . . where we lay down our swords and study war no more? Why not, O Lord, why not?"

Move 2—Visitors to the mountain. The preacher next takes us on a mountaintop tour, from Abraham to the Sermon on the Mount, with an emphasis on Isaiah, and on epiphany, what is revealed to us on the mountain. There is teaching here, and also reminder—if the listeners happen to think of their own experiences, or the experiences of others, more the better. Bishop Curry uses humor, something he does with great skill, not only to lighten the mood, but also to bridge easily from the biblical to the contemporary. And he uses humor to slip in something particular to the setting: "There are some wolves here." Again, the listener has work to do, identifying the wolves, and the wolf-spirit within. Along the way he also reaches to the tradition, in particular the tradition of the spirituals: "Every time I feel the Spirit" and "Go down, Moses," the spirituals, like the humor, changing the pace, and in the last reference, providing the transition to the next move.

Move 3—God's transforming love. This move begins with a rhetorical pause. The pause gives everyone a chance to relax, catch up, and refocus. The preacher pauses by inviting the listener into the sermon development process. You may not believe a word of it, and I am not sure that I do because it is hard to imagine Bishop Curry not knowing where he wants a sermon to go, but that does not matter. It "works" rhetorically, bringing the audience together again, and building a little suspense. "I wonder what the key will be? I wonder where he will go next?"

This bit of indirection also recalls Dr. Craddock. When the preacher mentions the hymn, and begins the quotation, many listeners beat him to the last line of the verse, to the "mount of God's unchanging love," and are nodding in agreement, mouthing the words along with the preacher. What the preacher wants the listener to remember about God's love has yet to be developed. But he has predisposed the listener to a posture of agreement in the way he brings us there.

God's love may be unchanging, but for Bishop Curry it is always transforming. "The love of God will change our hearts. Love will change our minds. Love will change our lives, our country, our world, our church. Come to the mount of God's unchanging, steadfast love." God does not change; we do. God does not even need us; God chooses us, and we are along for the ride. Again the preacher turns to humor, and to the personal, with the self-deprecating story about the B group. But it is much more than self-reference, particularly given the context of this denominational convention. It is a reminder to all the priests, preachers, and parishioners in the convention hall that it is not about us. God, and by extension God's church, was there before we were, and will be after we are gone. So don't mess it up!

Move 4—A picture of transformation. In writing, this is the weakest move, beginning with the transitional reference to the mountain. But the mountain has been left behind, and to tell you the truth, I don't think that in the preached sermon it was mentioned at this point.

Once the love of God has been described and developed, the mountain recedes into the background. What we need, and what we get, is a concrete depiction of how love transforms.

Looking at the written sermon, I find the message a little unclear: God's love in Christ has so transformed the landscape that the bishop's daughter and her friend could mistake a KKK cross-burning for the House of Bishops. The preached sermon was altogether different. Everyone knew what the bishop was getting at, and also knew the way we were meant to apply the lesson learned. What unimaginable thing does God have in store for us, and for the church, today? "And I'm here to tell you that it changed not by sword, not by might, but by the power of God's love translated into our social situation. America is a different place because some people decided, of all colors and kinds, that we're going to live by love, not by hatred."

The closing was more powerful than the printed word can ever do justice. In Minneapolis that week, hate groups were lined up outside the convention center, proclaiming God's hatred for "fags" and "queers." Signs proclaimed that 9/11 was God's judgment on all who accepted gays and lesbians as equal under the law, and the collapse of the church was certain if they were accepted as brothers and sisters in Christ. In the sermon the day before, the archbishop of Nigeria offered what felt to many like a baptized version of a similar denunciation, emphasizing God's demand for purity and righteousness. Bishop Curry made an exquisitely clear response. There is room for us all. *And all means all.* There are no barriers on God's love, and no boundaries on what God's transforming love can do.

Were some offended? No doubt! Nobody likes to be called a wolf, and some surely were aware, and disagreed, with the indirect way Bishop Curry responded to Archbishop Akinola. Proclamatory preaching always risks giving offense. So be it.

4

Self-Reference in Preaching

The combination is toxic, a perfect homiletical storm. A recent seminary graduate comes to her first parish, moving halfway across the country, her fiancé soon to follow. Sermon after sermon includes a story about a seminary classmate, where she used to live, and the differences here in her new community, and inevitably, how the wedding plans remind her of something in the Epistle. It could be worse, and it often is. Another preacher, closing in on retirement, has discovered that while he cannot show you pictures of his grandkids from the pulpit, he can tell you about them. So he does, week after week after week. "A funny thing happened to me on the way to the pulpit today," is as familiar in some churches as "It was a quiet week in Lake Wobegone" is on Saturday night radio. But have you noticed how rarely Garrison Keillor talks about himself in his weekly monologue? There is a lesson here, to which we will return.

What, exactly, is *wrong* with sharing one's life and experience from the pulpit? Nothing. And everything. Isn't it important to let the members of the congregation know the preacher does not think she is better, or more spiritual, or more whatever, than they are? Yes, it is, but why is that best done by talking about oneself every Sunday? Would it not be more rhetorically effective to send that message by *not* talking about oneself? But, others object, if I don't share my faith with them, how will they know what I believe? How can I witness to the gospel if I do not tell my story? Now we're getting somewhere.

The issue, the real issue, is our witness to the gospel. No argument there. The point of dispute is the extent to which self-reference in preaching strengthens the preacher's witness. I maintain, based on the example of Jesus in the Synoptic Gospels and my own experience as a preacher and a listener, that self-reference is vastly overrated, and in fact undermines the effectiveness of preaching for a number of important, and avoidable, reasons.

Every high school English teacher in history has told the students, "Write what you know." That is why every first novel is about a fascinating woman or man coming of age as they write their first novel. No problem there, but what happens when the author tries a second novel about a fascinating author struggling to write his second novel? It can work, as Philip Roth certainly proved over the years. But for every Philip Roth, there are a dozen Jay McInerneys. *Bright Lights, Big City* was a best seller, but that, pretty much, was that. More to the point, the preacher is not writing a novel every two or three years; the preacher is before the people every Sunday. Tiresome gets here quickly on a weekly basis.

There are practical reasons, then, not to indulge in self-reference each Sunday. But there are more important theological, rhetorical, and homiletical reasons, not to mention the example of Jesus in the Synoptic Gospels.

WHO DO YOU SAY THAT I AM? JESUS AND SELF-REFERENCE IN THE SYNOPTIC GOSPELS

While the reader cannot turn a page in the Gospel of John without finding Jesus saying, "I am this" or "I am that," one of the reasons the experience of reading Matthew, Mark, and Luke is so different than the experience of reading the Fourth Gospel is the almost complete absence of "I am" sayings in the Synoptic Gospels. There are theological and christological explanations for this difference, but that is not our focus. Instead, we want to explore the rhetorical basis for the difference, in order to understand the homiletical implications the difference has for our preaching today. What difference, we should ask, does it make that Jesus rarely speaks about himself in the Synoptic Gospels, and when he does, it is usually in metaphor and in the third person? The claim of this chapter is that the difference is great.

This is not to claim that Jesus is not depicted speaking in the first-person singular in Matthew, Mark, and Luke, nor to claim that, like a host of professional athletes and at least one presidential candidate (remember Bob Dole?), preachers should refer to themselves in the third person, by name. Fire up your BibleWorks program, do a search on *egō*/I, and you will find about the same distribution in Gospels one through three as in the Fourth Gospel. The difference is that in the Synoptic Gospels, Jesus rarely speaks about himself, while in the Fourth Gospel one is forgiven for thinking that Jesus rarely speaks about anything else, and the difference in rhetorical impact is great.

The Sermon on the Mount is a good case in point. In the NRSV we see Jesus using the first-person singular eighteen times in 111 verses, an impressive usage even by Johannine standards. Yet in every case save two, in 5:17, Jesus is not referring to himself but is using one variation or another of "I say to you." And when we recall 5:17, we see that the focus is as much on the tradition as it is on the speaker: "Do not think that I have come to abolish the law or the prophets; I have come not to abolish but to fulfill." The point? Even when Jesus speaks in the first-person singular, he is not necessarily talking about himself; hence, when he says, as in the antitheses, "You have heard it said to those of ancient times . . . , but I say to you . . . ," the focus is on the topic—anger, adultery, oaths, and so forth—not the speaker. Think of all those "amen" sayings—"Truly I say to you [*amēn legō hymin*]" (such as 5:18; 6:2 AT)—as an ancient, more solemn version of "Let me tell you." What then of the times when Jesus both speaks in the first-person singular and is referring to himself? They are significant.

> [Jesus said,] "Everyone therefore who acknowledges me before others, I also will acknowledge before my Father in heaven; but whoever denies me before others, I also will deny before my Father in heaven."
>
> (Matt. 10:32–33)

But notice the parallel in Luke:

> [Jesus said,] "And I tell you, everyone who acknowledges me before others, the Son of Man also will acknowledge before the angels of God; but whoever denies me before others will be denied before the angels of God."
>
> (Luke 12:8–9)

There is a similar intensification by Matthew in his account of the challenge of the Pharisees over the disciples' grain plucking on the Sabbath (Matt. 12:1–8/Mark 2:23–28/Luke 6:1–5). Mark and Luke follow the same pattern: challenge, response recalling David and the "bread of the Presence," and a dominical saying in the third person, "The Son of Man is lord of the sabbath" (Luke 6:5), with Mark adding, "The sabbath was made for humankind, not humankind for the sabbath" (2:27). Matthew adds, "Or have you not read in the law that on the sabbath the priests in the temple break the sabbath and yet are guiltless? I tell you, something greater than the temple is here" (Matt. 12:5–6). Why does Matthew depict Jesus more frequently using self-reference in his proclamation than Mark and Luke do? Different Christologies, perhaps, but clearly different rhetorics. Matthew and Luke share the John-like prayer:

> At that time Jesus said, "I thank you, Father, Lord of heaven and earth, because you have hidden these things from the wise and the intelligent and have revealed them to infants; yes, Father, for such was your gracious will. All things have been handed over to me by my Father; and no one knows the Son except the Father, and no one knows the Father except the Son and anyone to whom the Son chooses to reveal him."
>
> (Matt. 11:25–27/Luke 10:21–22)

Matthew alone adds the powerful, beloved invitation:

> "Come to me, all you that are weary and are carrying heavy burdens, and I will give you rest. Take my yoke upon you, and learn from me; for I am gentle and humble in heart, and you will find rest for your souls. For my yoke is easy, and my burden is light."
>
> (11:28–30)

What finally stands out about such memorable verses is their relative scarcity in the Synoptic Gospels, and in most instances the presence, even in the verses cited above, of a reversion to the third person, with the "Son of Man" formula.

> In the Synoptic Gospels, Jesus is depicted as avoiding designation as messiah, son of God, or God, though his disciples gave these titles to him after his death and resurrection. But the Gospels repeatedly depict Jesus using the expression, "the son of the man," as virtually his only form of self-reference. Not once in the Gospels does he call himself by his own name. Not once does anyone else call him the son of the man. The expression appears only on his lips.[1]

The theological and christological basis for this pattern is not our concern, however, and the interested reader may turn to Walter Wink's book *The Human Being*, quoted above, and the rich bibliography one will find in its endnotes. Our interest is in the rhetorical and homiletical impact and implications.

Jesus is only occasionally self-referential in the Synoptic Gospels. In the first chapter we saw this as a reflection of an understanding of Jesus within history as one who "proclaimed a kingdom and resisted a crown." The focus of Jesus' proclamation in Matthew, Mark, and Luke is thus on the kingdom of God/heaven as a present reality, and not on himself as a royal aspirant. Indeed, the evangelists' handling of Jesus and kingship is entirely ironic. In Matthew the magi come to Herod in Jerusalem, seeking "the child who has been born king of the Jews" (2:2); Herod, after checking with his advisers, sends them to Bethlehem, whereupon the "royal family" flees to Egypt in a reverse exodus, since Herod surely is a pharaoh who knows not Joseph. At the "trial" before Pilate in Mark 15 and parallels, the question is whether Jesus considers himself "king of the Jews." The soldiers mock, torture, and "hail" Jesus as "king," as do the passersby, and the inscription bearing the charge for which he is crucified reads, "The King of the Jews." Jesus answers in half-sentences ("You say so," Mark 15:2) and silence.

The biblical foundation for this chapter, then, is that in the Synoptic Gospels, Jesus speaks about himself only occasionally, most often indirectly when he does so, and that on those rare occasions when he did speak about himself in the first person, it was to great effect. Nowhere is this more true than at the "trial" before the council. "Again the high priest asked him, 'Are you the Messiah, the Son of the Blessed One?' Jesus said, 'I am [*egō eimi*]; and "you will see the Son of Man seated at the right hand of the Power," and "coming with the clouds of heaven"'" (Mark 14:61–62). Even here, though, the shift to the third person and the reference to Daniel 7:13 underscore my claim, exceptions that prove the rule.

SELF-REFERENCE AND SELF-DISCLOSURE IN PREACHING

How does the old line go? "Well, that is enough about me. Now why don't you tell me what you think about me?" Between the homiletical narcissism born of low self-esteem and Philips Brooks's dictum that preaching is "truth through personality,"[2] I am, like John the Baptist, a voice crying in the wilderness. See how easy it is to slip into the first-person singular, not only when preaching, but just when writing about preaching? What is the big deal? Where is the harm? And what about Aristotle's advice on ethos?

In *The Art of Rhetoric*, Aristotle wrote that there are three primary forms of proof (*pistoi*, interestingly) in rhetoric. "The first depends upon the moral character [*ēthei*] of the speaker, the second upon putting the hearer into a certain frame of mind, the third upon the speech itself, in so far as it proves or seems to prove."[3] These three are conventionally referred to as *ethos*, *pathos*, and *logos*. *Ethos* focuses on the character of the speaker, but for Aristotle this was confined to the speech itself.

> The orator persuades by moral character when his speech is delivered in such a manner as to render him worthy of confidence; for we feel confidence in a greater degree and more readily in persons of worth in regard to everything in general, but where there is no certainty and there is room for doubt, our confidence is absolute. But this confidence must be due to the speech itself, not to any preconceived idea of the speaker's character; for it is not the case, as some writers of rhetorical treatises lay down in their "Art," that the worth of the orator in no way contributes to his powers of persuasion; on the contrary, moral character, so to say, constitutes the most effective means of proof.[4]

The issue for Aristotle is credibility, primarily within the speech itself, but also as a matter of reputation. Yet Aristotle is often casually applied as if he was speaking of *likability*, not credibility, so that the speaker's ethical task is to endear himself to the audience. As near as I can tell, endearment is not a rhetorical term. The result of such standard-issue applications of Aristotle are opening jokes, prattle, and patter, with a tendency toward self-deprecation and an excess of cute stories about the speaker's family or pets.

There are a host of problems when applying a *Toastmaster's Guide* to the proclamation of the Gospel, but these will have to do: (1) Patter is not the purpose of an introduction; it only delays the introduction. An introduction is offered with the goal of leading the audience into the sermon, not into the preacher's family room. (2) The preacher is not there to be liked, admired, or praised. The preacher is there to proclaim the gospel. (3) From the perspective of pastoral leadership, ethos is not primarily earned in the pulpit; it is brought to the pulpit from the other corners and crossroads of pastoral practice. Ethos is important, but in its Aristotelian sense, not from some watered-down *Public Speaking for Absolute Idiots.*

As for the big deal around self-reference in preaching, it is only a big deal if the preacher makes it one. The argument of this chapter is that we should not, and not just because of the example of Jesus in the Synoptic Gospels, as important as that is. We should also limit self-reference because it is subject to at least as many negative as positive possibilities. Consider the following don'ts and dos.

Don'ts

Four things to avoid: (1) the unintended consequences that come from casual self-reference; (2) compounding legitimate problems about pulpit authority by too frequently filtering theological and spiritual truth through the preacher's own experience; (3) cultivating an unhealthy focus on the person and persona of the preacher through persistent self-reference; and (4) dulling the ears of the listeners by self-reference so that true self-disclosure loses its power.

1. That is not what I meant: The law of unintended consequences. The preacher began the sermon by telling the gathered faithful how much her family disliked her uncle's wife. Using a level of detail captured in the initials "TMI" (too much information), the congregation learned of every foible and flaw that had grated on the familial psyche from the first time the pastor's family met the uncle's then fiancée. After a few minutes of biting critique, one learned that upon the birth of the uncle and aunt's first child, feelings softened. But by then it was too late. The congregation had long since stopped really listening and started to wonder about the preacher's family and her own disposition. To tell the truth, they wondered, "How does she talk about me when I am not around?"

Once the words leave the preacher's lips, they are no longer his. The listeners are the ones who decide what the words finally mean, how they will be understood, and in what context they will be applied. This is neither good nor bad: it just is. And woe to the preacher who does not take into account the possibility that some words will be misunderstood and misapplied.

Fond of travel, a preacher frequently prefaced a story or comment with reference to one of the countries or cities he had visited. "Last year, when we were in Lucerne, we marveled at the warm hospitality of the Swiss. Their reputation, of course, is quite otherwise, cool and calculating, with their secret bank accounts and military neutrality." Let's count the ways this offhand reference came back to haunt the preacher: (1) I wish I could afford to travel as much as he does. Exactly how much are we paying him? (2) Switzerland? Why would anyone go to Switzerland when they could visit the Rockies? "See America first" is what I say! (3) "Cool and calculating," is that what he said? What does he have against the Swiss? My mother's family is Swiss. Jerk! (4) How dare he scoff at military neutrality. Hasn't he seen *The Sound of Music*? That wasn't Germany the von Trapps fled to for safety. If we had more real neutrality, we would have a lot less war! On the way to making an unimportant point about the surprising places where one encounters hospitality, the preacher inadvertently raised questions about his spending habits, his patriotism, his attitude toward the people of a foreign land, and his stance on national aggression.

Mention the last movie you saw, and half the congregation questions your taste while the other half wonders why you don't use Netflix like they do. The same with music, television, and sports teams. Every sentence that begins with "I" invites someone in the congregation to identify, or misidentify, the point you are trying to make with what you did, said, saw, or heard, shifting the focus to the preacher's judgment, competence, preferences, or experience. You know that is not what you meant, but it does not matter. By placing yourself at the start of the story, you invite the congregation to wonder about you. It is simply not worth it.

2. Pedestal problems, or, "I hate to have to tell you, preacher, but not everybody likes you." The pulpit is an inherent problem. High and lifted up or a clear Plexiglas podium, the preacher stands behind it. If you set the pulpit aside and stride purposely up and down the aisle, you only call attention to the fact that you alone can stand and walk about. Many preachers struggle with the authority of the pulpit, as do many in the congregation. For every preacher asking, "Who am I to speak to these people?" there are at least a dozen within the sound of the preacher's voice asking, "Who does she think she is to tell me what to do/feel/believe?" The problem is not really in the pulpit, or in the truth that not everyone in every church we serve will consider us their favorite preacher. The problem is in the preposition. Best understood, the challenge is not to speak *to* the faithful but to speak *for* them. A judicious reduction in the number of times one says "I" in the sermon is almost guaranteed to help.

If we are honest, in our best moments we do not hope to inspire the congregation to see things our way, but to help all of us see things God's way. It is problem enough that we may come off sounding like we think we speak *for* God *to* them. We compound the problem by doing so in the first-person singular. "I believe the most serious issue confronting the church today is _____." For some it will not matter how the preacher fills in the blank. You lost them at "I." Turn it around and ask, "What do you consider to be the most serious issue confronting the church today?" Offer them multiple choices, with real, serious, perhaps painful possibilities, and allow the congregation as a whole to consider the question before sharing your thoughts by saying, "A strong case can be made that . . . ," and then making the strong case.

3. A loss of focus, or, "What exactly were we talking about a minute ago?" The Buddha liked to remind his students that when he pointed to the moon, they were not supposed to focus on his finger. Preachers can learn a lot from the Buddha. Put most simply, the argument of this chapter is that preachers need to do everything in their power to get out of the way. It is not about us. It has never been about us. And when it begins to seem like it is about us, we must remember, it is not about us.

Preachers are aware that there is considerable evidence to the contrary. The apostle Paul, to take the first Christian example, fills his writing with personal narrative and first-person-singular discourse. Personal correspondence, however, even from *apostolos* to *ekklēsia*, is not preaching. Closer to our time and closer to home is the example of megachurch and other pastors whose congregations seem to thrive on personality-centered preaching. We know more about Bill Hybels, Joel Osteen, and Rick Warren than we do about our next-door neighbors. That is their choice. It is not mine. And I will argue below that it is not necessary.

How the listeners feel about the preacher at any given moment should not be the basis for their receptivity to the preacher's proclamation of the gospel. Intentional and inadvertent use of the first-person singular may make this difficult. It is not necessary, for example, to relate the key plot points of a movie by prefacing your comments with "I saw this incredible movie the other day." Preachers' repeated reference to themselves when seeking to introduce listeners to important information from other sources—"As my good friend Tom once told me" or "When I saw the riveting performance by _____ in the definitive production of _____, I was reminded that _____." If what matters is what the preacher was once told or had been reminded of, the rest is distracting detail. When preachers lead instead with what they really want the listeners to focus on, nobody loses focus.

4. Something very important happened to me, or, "The preacher who cried wolf." Habituation, famously described in the example of the frog in the kettle, happens in church every Sunday. People sit in the same pew, prefer familiar hymns, and fidget if the sermon is longer than usual. Listeners also accustom themselves to moments of interest and times to tune out. They become accustomed to the rise and fall in the preacher's voice, a familiar gesture, and what to expect if the preacher steps out from behind the pulpit. This, among other reasons, is why it is important to be able to preach with equal effectiveness with or without notes, from a manuscript or from memory, in or out of the pulpit.

More to the point of this chapter, habituation is the practical reason why it is important for preachers to avoid unnecessary self-reference. Like the boy who cried wolf, the preacher who prefaces every story with a touch of autobiography dulls the ears of the listener. When the time comes to share something personal and important that can only be shared autobiographically, what I call self-disclosure, the preacher may well have trained the listener to pay little attention, having learned that the important material always comes after the self-reference.

So yes, by all means share your faith with your listeners, and when the occasion calls for it, share your story, your *witness*. But do not do so in every sermon, and do not clutter each sermon with who you saw, what you watched, where you shopped, and how you did whatever it is you do on Saturday. If you saw someone the congregation would like to know about, tell them about her, and get yourself out of the way. If there was a movie or show that helps to illustrate the move you are developing, tell them about it, but get yourself out of the way. And so on.

Then, when it is time to talk about something that can only be shared autobiographically, they are ready, even eager, for the self-disclosure you offer in humility and trust. Caution must be the rule here as well. Self-disclosure loses its power as surely as Jimmy Swaggert's tears. And there are some things, no, many things, that simply have no place in the pulpit, even with the permission of family or friend. Talking about your marriage, your children's struggles, or your difficult relations with parents or siblings is not *self*-disclosure, but *family*-disclosure. While I can imagine a situation when it might be appropriate—a panel discussion moderated by a counselor or therapist during which you and the family member(s) share your story, doing so unilaterally from the pulpit is not that place. There are other ways, as we will see below, to share your truth without violating confidences or putting relationships on display. And those ways are in fact homiletically more powerful.

Dos

Where there are "Thou shalt nots," it is only right to look for positive alternatives. Here are four: (1) learn how to share the truth of your experience without putting yourself in the story; (2) share what you know, not what you did, or thought, or felt; (3) don't let the story get in the way of the sermon; (4) limit self-reference so that there is room for genuine self-disclosure at the appropriate time.

1. The story is told, or, the power of the personal can be general and universal (and not autobiographical). A hard but important lesson to learn is that while regularly talking about ourselves in our preaching has more drawbacks than benefits, we still must draw on our own experiences if our sermons are to have a ring of authenticity. Googling for stories from the lives of others may be better than recycling an old volume of somebody's *Sermon Illustrations for Every Occasion*, but not by much. So how have I not created a competing, and mutually excluding, demand—don't talk about yourself all the time but share from your experience for the sake of authenticity? No, because it is more than possible to share your truth without telling every story as your own. You make them up, just like Jesus did.

Unless you share the view that the parables of Jesus were simply commentary on the behavior of those around him, you understand the parables to be fabrications. We tend to use the word "fabrication" as a four-syllable synonym for the word "lie." But that is not the root meaning. The root meaning of "fabricate" is to make, form, fashion, or create. This does not mean that Jesus, and contemporary preachers, do not include in their stories something they learned in observing others. But it does mean that Jesus did not have to overhear the Pharisee and Tax Collector (Luke 18:9–14) for their story to have meaning, and truth.

Our text is Matthew 5:23–24: "So when you are offering your gift at the altar, if you remember that your brother or sister has something against you, leave your gift there before the altar and go; first be reconciled to your brother or sister, and then come and offer your gift." Imagine a preacher who had an up-and-down relationship with his brother. Each had learned over the years how to creatively push the other's buttons to great effect, guaranteeing at least a verbal brawl almost every time they were together. When their mother became seriously ill, they found they could not continue the bickering and put-downs; something deeper about their relationship, and the possibility that the one who brought them into this world might be leaving it, called the two grown men to grow up. The preacher wanted to share the story of this growing up, but he did not want to invite the congregation into his living room, or into his late mother's hospice unit. So instead he told of three sisters and their father, and while some may have thought of Chekhov or Shakespeare, none thought the preacher was sharing from his own truth, or wondered why he was such a jerk when he was younger.

Preachers can and should do this every Sunday. They should also screen their sermons for unneeded self-reference. The story about the man you met at the barbershop need simply be a man at a barbershop, or could become a woman at a salon. Every time we get ourselves out of the way, we make it easier for the listener to get into the story, we leave aside a host of unintended consequences, and we keep the space clear for times of genuine self-disclosure.

2. A healthy humility and an appropriate self-regard go a long way. Why did the congregation hire you, or the district superintendent or bishop send you? Or take it back a step: Why did God call you to preach, and the church affirm this call through ordination or licensing or inviting you to the pulpit? Somewhere in the answer may be the idea that you were called in part because you have something to say that is worth hearing. They may have sent you to seminary and supported you through a long (and likely frustrating) process of ordination. All, in part, to hear what you have to say. But that does not mean that they want to hear you talk about yourself. They want to hear what you *know*.

In the last chapter I reported that seminary faculty spend more time than they should bemoaning how poorly prepared entering students are (conversations paralleled by search committees bemoaning how poorly the faculty have prepared their graduates, but that is another topic). Preachers bemoan how little biblical and theological background they can rely on, so that quick references to the Assyrian exile, the Maccabean Revolt, or the Corinthian church are impossible, but must be spelled out in enough detail to connect with what they might vaguely recall from a long-ago education class. These problems are intertwined, certainly, because the seminarians come from the congregations with inadequate educational and catechetical training, and then go back to them thinking that their listeners do not know about the Corinthians because they do not want or need to know, and so the preachers rarely provide the necessary background. Not teaching breeds not teaching, so that—well, you've seen the polls—the churchgoing public could not name the four evangelists if you spotted them Matthew and Mark.

That is why you the preacher must tell the congregation what you *know*, what they sent you to seminary to learn. You have gained an impressive amount of foundational wisdom: biblical, theological, historical, liturgical, and practical. The congregation trusts you to share it with them in ways that they can understand, and relate it to what they remember, how they understand themselves, and how they are called to live. There is no such thing as wisdom too sophisticated or controversial for any congregation. There are preachers who do not know how to explain things in ways their listeners can understand. You are not that preacher. So you tell them, confident in your training and preparation, without needing to convince anyone that you have all the answers.

3. Keep your eyes upon Jesus: the problem with Philippians 4:9. This is not the best translation of Philippians 4:9, but it is the one I grew up with, from the RSV. "What you have learned and received and heard and seen in me, do; and the God of peace will be with you." Apparently we have to do it like Paul, or the peace of God will not only pass our understanding, it will also pass us by. Paul did not shy away from urging his readers to "be imitators of me, as I am of Christ" (1 Cor. 11:1; cf. 4:16; 1 Thess. 1:6; 2 Thess. 3:7, 9). Here, however, I think the preacher does best by *not* imitating Paul. While congruity between our preaching and our practice is vital, pointing at ourselves rather than at Jesus is multiply problematic (note the difficulties Paul had with the Christians in Corinth and Thessalonica!).

Since this is a book about Jesus and preaching, we recall that in the Synoptic Gospels what Jesus says sounds nothing like what Paul says in the passage above. "I am the way" is from the Fourth Gospel. In the Synoptic Gospels it is the evangelists who are pointing to Jesus, not Jesus pointing to himself. Jesus points to God. There is a related issue having to do with the use and abuse of illustrative material. When you consider a story so good you just have to use it this week, the example from wherever, or the film clip your colleague used last week at his church and then reported that it went over so well—along with other things, be sure to ask yourself what the story, example, or film clip will do to the focus of your sermon. Will it help the listeners to focus more clearly on Jesus?

It is tempting to talk about sports to keep the jocks interested, and to throw in a little Harry Potter for the kids and *Lord of the Rings* for the Tolkeinites. *Desperate Housewives* is good for a laugh, and *American Idol* shows that we are trying to stay relevant. But this must not be at the expense of losing our focus.

4. I don't quite know how to say this: self-disclosure in preaching. Just for fun, let's pretend that you agree with every word in this chapter and have faithfully avoided all the don'ts and done the dos (Mark 10:20). This puts you in the rhetorically powerful but pastorally frightening position of being able to truly share yourself in your sermons. When and how you should do so are important questions, but not nearly as important as *why*. Why do you want to share, in the first-person singular, a portion of your autobiography in the middle of your sermon?

We've agreed that we do not want to do this simply because it is easy to talk about ourselves, baptizing our experiences and preferences before the listeners' trusting ears. The law of unintended consequences encourages us to find other ways to share our truth: fashioning a story or anecdote that keeps the preacher out of the picture is almost always preferable. And we've agreed that issues of authority, role, and focus are all aided by sharing what we know, and not just who we are. It may not get us on television, but is that why we were called to preach?

Why, then, would a preacher ever want to self-disclose? It is potentially as scintillating as it sounds, an emotional striptease inviting the homiletical voyeurs in the congregation to feast on the preacher's vulnerability. I do not put it this way to encourage you, obviously. So why would a preacher want to self-disclose? Only, and I do mean "only," because there is no other way to share what you feel called and inspired to share. You self-disclose because you must, not because you want to or find it easier. That is self-reference, which I have argued should be discouraged so that self-disclosure is possible.

Return to the example of Jesus. "Jerusalem, Jerusalem, the city that kills the prophets and stones those who are sent to it! How often have I desired to gather your children together as a hen gathers her brood under her wings, and you were not willing!" (Matt. 23:37/Luke 13:34). Jesus recalls the psalmist's fondness for describing God's protection as a hiding under the wings. "How precious is your steadfast love, O God! All people may take refuge in the shadow of your wings" (Ps. 36:7). And Jesus claims the divine role for himself; the pathos at its rejection resonates throughout the Gospels. But if Jesus were depicted as regularly crying out in love and sorrow, this verse would melt away, not shine forth as it does. The primary reason to avoid the tendency to too-frequent, often-inappropriate self-disclosure is that Jesus resisted it himself.

When the time comes, then, you and the church will be ready. This is not the time for announcements—the birth of a child, your divorce, an impending IRS investigation, next week's surgery, your call to another parish, receiving a contract for a book of your best sermons—any and all "announcements" belong where you put the other announcements. Just because they are about you does not mean that you interrupt the sermon to tell the faithful, any more than tonight's potluck should find its way into your sermon. Announcements are not self-disclosure, no matter how personal or painful.

Self-disclosure is sharing something that has happened to you, in your walk of faith, which can be shared in no other way. If you can faithfully imagine another way, use it. If you cannot, if it is too personal, too specific to who you are and how the congregation understands you, or you realize they will come to understand you, then God be with you. One of my own cases in point may serve as example.

We noted in the chapter on dialogical preaching that in matters of human sexuality, the topic on which Jesus is recorded as having something to say is divorce, not abortion, GLBTs, or other topics du jour. And whether we like it or not, Mark 10:1–12 comes around in the Revised Common Lectionary every three years. In most of our churches, the topic of divorce has blown from hot to cold. What once disqualified one from table, office, and ordination is now politely ignored. Though in the wedding homily the occasional misguided preacher will congratulate the couple for daring to buck the 50/50 odds that their marriage will endure, for the most part divorce is not much discussed, except perhaps in a list of unpleasant things that "happen." Divorces, however, do not happen. Divorces are made. Made badly, painfully, and sinfully, but they are made. They are made by abuse, neglect, and infidelity; made by change, challenge, and loss. I know because I helped to make one.

So the question is obvious: does the preacher talk about one's own divorce when the lectionary rolls around to Mark 10? No and yes, I think, based on my experience. And I have a lot of experience, because my divorce happened a long time ago, a few years after my first marriage, and a few years before my second, which is more than twenty-five years strong and counting, thank the Lord (and Christine!). But the in-between years were awful, and the best thing I could do in the pulpit was either change the subject or put on my academic blinders and focus on marriage in Scripture and antiquity. Anything personal was much too painful, and way too close to the surface, to belong in a sermon. More to the point, I learned not to let my own experience of divorce become my one, and constant, touchstone for talking about pain, loss, guilt, and so forth. Whenever the preacher's experience becomes the touchstone for anything, *caveat* congregation.

There are clear limits, of a variety of sorts, to self-disclosure in the pulpit. Though we do not want to hide or deny our personal investment in the topic or matter before us, we need to be aware that at times our personal stake overwhelms our ability to speak biblically, faithfully, and well. There are times when we are too qualified to speak, or too invested or engaged to trust ourselves to speak. Step aside, or set the issue aside, and let another preacher, or another topic, speak.

But there are other times, and for me this came more than a decade after my divorce, when our experience, what we have to share in faith, humility, and love, is essential. It hurts; it really, really hurts; but it must be shared. We do not do it because we want to, but because we cannot do anything else. I did not say it was easy. If it is easy, don't do it.

A SERMON BY THOMAS G. LONG

Tom Long, who holds the Bandy Distinguished Chair in Preaching at the Candler School of Theology, Emory University, is a person of many gifts. A scholar, author, teacher, and administrator, he is first and foremost a preacher and is well known in his own right as a master storyteller. In this sermon, which begins as a sermon much concerned about the preaching moment, Long shares a few stories from others and one powerfully his own. In this chapter on self-reference in preaching, observe how Long, even in the first person, slips out of the way so that the listener may fully enter into the stories he tells.

Astonished and Silent

Matthew 7:21–29

You have very graciously invited me here this morning to preach a sermon. Now, a sermon, as we all know, is made out of words, and I have brought some words with me today. But even though sermons are crafted out of words, I think it is important for us to remember that in sermons there are two powerful moments of silence.

The first of these comes at the very beginning of the sermon. You may not have noticed it a minute ago. It was brief and fleeting, but it was there. The Scripture lesson is read, the congregation sinks back into their seats, the preacher takes a deep and anxious breath, and there it is. It is so routine we hardly even notice this silence, but down at its depth it is an electric silence full of anticipation and expectation. What is going on in this silence? I think the African American church has it right when it says, in effect, "In that moment of silence for everyone, for preacher, for choir, for congregation, there is the wondering, 'Is there a word from the Lord?'" Amidst all the words of our culture that besiege us, is there a word that can cut through the clutter, a word that can make a difference, a word from beyond that can touch us and heal us; is there a word from the Lord? This question shouts in that silence.

I love the way that novelist and essayist Frederick Buechner has described this moment of silence. He writes:

> The preacher climbs the steps to the pulpit with his sermon in his hand. He hikes his black robe up at the knee so he will not trip over it on the way up the steps. He feels as if he has swallowed an anchor. . . .
>   The preacher . . . deals out his sermon note cards like a riverboat gambler. The stakes have never been higher. Two minutes from now he may have lost his listeners completely to their own thoughts, but at this minute he has them in the palm of his hand. The silence in the . . . church is deafening because everybody is listening to it. Everybody is listening, even [the preacher].[5]

The theologian Karl Barth also talked about this moment of silence at the beginning of a sermon when he noted that when the bells in the church ring and the congregation gathers, we do not come to hear about the cherry tree or the symphony or everyday life. In fact, our gathering is a sign that "cherry tree and symphony and everyday life are possibilities somehow already exhausted."[6] What hangs in the air is one question: Is it true? Is it true that God is present? Is it true that there is a word from the Lord today?

Now I know, I know, we preachers frequently squander the promise of this first urgent moment of silence. Two sentences into the sermon, and the air of expectation has been let out of the room. This moment of silence anticipates a word from beyond, and we often fill it with a word from the all-too-familiar; this moment of silence cries out for a word that brings life, a word that changes everything, and we focus on the trivial. I think of Terry Waite, the Anglican clergyman who, in the mid-1980s, was assigned by the Archbishop of Canterbury as an envoy to Beirut to negotiate for the release of hostages. However, events went badly, and Waite himself was captured and made a hostage. For four years he was confined to a tiny cell in a Beirut prison, cut off from everything he loved—from church, family, civilization, homeland—isolated and alone. Over the years, though, he developed a relationship of trust with his guards. So much so that one of them was willing to do something very risky. He surreptitiously placed in Terry Waite's cell a transistor radio with one precious battery. For the first time in four years, Waite had the means for contact with the outside world. Careful to save the battery, Waite had to choose when to use the radio. He decided that the most urgent need he had was not for news or music, but for the gospel. Is there a word from the Lord? So he waited until Sunday morning to turn it on. He tuned in the BBC to get a worship service, hungry for a word from God, hungry for the gospel, hungry for comfort. Imagine how he felt when the preacher began, "My theme for this morning is spiritual lessons from Winnie the Pooh." Waite said of this experience, "All I could do was laugh out loud, so he did me a good service!"[7]

I think also of one of my students who was invited to preach a sermon at a worship service at the nursing home where she was serving as a student chaplain. This nursing home had worship in the big entrance lobby, and for the service it was crowded with elderly people, some with oxygen tanks, some in wheelchairs. One of the gifts that God gives to people of great age is the freedom to say and do exactly what they want, and sure enough, my student got a paragraph into the sermon when suddenly one of the elderly women present pulled the joystick on her electric wheelchair, turned it around, went back down the hall to her room shouting, "Blah, blah, blah!"

We preachers can squander the promise of that first silence, but it is amazing to me: even congregations that have been numbed into submission decade after decade come back the next Sunday, and it's there: the silence of expectation—maybe this time.

But there is also a second moment of profound silence in preaching. If the first one comes at the beginning of the sermon, the second one comes at the end of the sermon. It is much rarer; in fact, some people wonder if they have ever experienced this moment of silence at all. If the first moment of silence in preaching is the wondering, "Is there a word from the Lord?" the second moment of silence comes when the Holy Spirit has taken the fragile human words of the preacher and turned them, in fact, into the word of God. When a word penetrates our existence; when a word separates life from death, wisdom from foolishness, blessing from curse, and our lives are touched and transformed; when the room in which the preached word has happened is breathless and still, and when there is the sudden awareness that the world has been drastically changed; when that happens, you can't simply pick up the hymnal and casually go into the next hymn. This is a moment like Easter, a moment when the light of the future is yet so bright, so full of promise and fear at the same time, we shield our eyes and close our mouths. This moment provokes astonished silence.

Matthew wants us to know this is the kind of silence that occurred at the end of Jesus' Sermon on the Mount. What Matthews says is, "When Jesus had finished speaking all these words, the crowds who heard him were astonished" (7:28 AT). The word "astonished" is, in Greek, even stronger. It's more like dumbstruck, flabbergasted, speechless. At the end of the Sermon on the Mount, there was the silence of astonishment, dumbstruckness, flabbergasted, speechlessness.

And Matthew wants us to know that this is not the only time this happened in the preaching of Jesus. In fact, it happened all the way through his ministry. It happened at the end of his ministry when he preached to the crowds in Jerusalem; they were dumbstruck by his words. It happened in the middle of his ministry when he was preaching to his hometown synagogue in Nazareth. They were flabbergasted at his wisdom. It happens here at the beginning of his ministry when he preaches the Sermon on the Mount: they were left astonished and silent. Matthew tells us the reason that this dumbstruck silence occurred was that Jesus did not preach like other preachers. He did not preach like the scribes; he preached with authority. The hungry desire for a word from beyond was fulfilled in their hearing, and Jesus' preaching precipitated a crisis. If the first moment of silence is a wondering if there is a word from the Lord, the second moment of silence occurs when, in fact, there is a word from the Lord, a word that turns the world over and creates a crisis.

Several years ago during the Sunday morning service in a church in Charlotte, North Carolina, the time came for the sermon. The prayer for illumination had been uttered, the Scripture had been read, and the preacher was standing in the pulpit and about to open his mouth and preach, when suddenly a man in the balcony, a stranger nobody knew, stood up and said in a loud clear voice, "I have a word from the Lord." Heads swiveled around to see who this was who had intruded on worship. Whatever the man intended to say, whatever this word from the Lord was, no one ever got to hear it because two bouncers, disguised as ushers, bounded up the balcony steps like gazelles and muscled this guy out of the sanctuary and into the street.

I don't blame them; I fully understand the ushers' actions. The apostle Paul said we ought to do things in worship decently and in order. This was out of order, and, who knows? It could have turned out to be indecent as well. Who knew what this fellow had in mind? I don't blame the ushers at all for escorting this man to the street. But it does cause me to wonder a bit, because I am a preacher, and almost every week I stand in a pulpit saying, in effect, "I have a word from the Lord." No ushers have ever bolted into alarmed action at my announcement; no one has ever muscled me out of the church. I wonder if it is because I, and many other preachers like me, have so often turned the silence of expectation into the sacrament of disappointment. I wonder if here, among the stained-glass windows and the robes and the liturgy and the way we have preached, we have domesticated and tamed the gospel so that it can no longer provoke a crisis, so that the words "I have a word from the Lord" do not prompt the ushers to tense but instead tempt the congregation to relax and yawn.

Jesus did not preach like that. He did not preach like the scribes or the Presbyterians or the Methodists, the Lutherans or the Episcopalians. He preached, says Matthew, "As one with authority," which means his word generated a crisis. His preaching cleared the space of clutter and chatter, leaving a dumbstruck silence filled only with the largest of all human questions. What do we do now? How do we live? Who shall we be? That is the second silence in a sermon.

Now if we listen to the end of the Sermon on the Mount, we might not like what we hear because what provokes this second silence are hard and demanding words. Jesus does not come across as the cuddly, warm, inclusive Jesus we have come to love. He says instead at the end of the sermon: "Not everybody who says 'Lord, Lord,' will enter the kingdom of heaven, only those who hear these words and do them, only those who build their lives around them. There will be a lot of people who say, 'Lord, look at me. I did wonderful things in your name. I was a very powerful person in terms of communicating what you wanted us to communicate. Look at me, Lord.' And I will say to you, 'I don't recognize you. I recognize only those who have built their lives around the words that I have given, who have built their lives on solid rock. If you build it on sand, the winds will come and the storms will come and blow you away'" (Matt. 7:21–27 AT).

No way around it: these are words of judgment. I don't want to take the sting out of them, but I don't want us to misunderstand them either. While we often think of judgment as the mark of a punitive God and the playground of fundamentalists, in the gospel the judgment of God is actually a good thing, a promise that God will bring justice, will set things right. One day I was walking across the seminary campus where I teach. One of my students hailed me.

"Dr. Long, could I speak to you for a minute?"

I said, "I'm going to get a cup of coffee; you want to go?" She did, and in the cafeteria she told me what was on her mind. She said she was serving as a field education student in a local church and that her supervising pastor was requiring her to preach next Sunday.

"Good." I said, putting down my coffee cup.

"No, it's not good," she said, shaking her head. "He is making me preach on the lectionary texts for Sunday."

"Good," I said again.

"No," she repeated, "it is not good. Have you read the lectionary texts for next week? They're all about judgment. I don't believe in judgment. I believe in grace, I believe in mercy. It took me three years of therapy to get over judgment. I am not going to preach judgment."

We talked about this for a while, with no resolution, and then we moved on to other topics. She began telling me about her family life. She and her husband have several children; only the youngest, a teenage boy, was still at home, and he was giving them hell. He was into drugs, maybe dealing them, and in trouble with the police.

"Like last night," she said, "we were sitting at the supper table, my husband and I, and we had no idea where our son was. In the middle of supper, he comes banging in the back door, and I said to him, 'Would you like some supper?' He practically spit at us. He then stomped down the hall to his room and slammed the door. "My husband got up and turned on ESPN," she said. "That is always his response to this."

Now it was her turn to put down her coffee cup. She looked at me with firmness in her eye. "I don't know, . . . something got into me right at that moment. I'm afraid of my son, physically afraid of my own son. But something got into me and I got up from the table and I went down to his room and I pushed open the door and I said to him, 'You listen to me. I love you so much I am not going to put up with this anymore.'"

"Marilyn," I said, "I think you just preached a sermon on judgment."

God loves us so much, God will not put up with the foolishness in our lives. We have hungered for success and power and status, and Jesus says in this sermon that this is foolish and that God loves us so much God will not put up with this anymore. "Blessed are those that hunger and thirst for righteousness and justice." That is what makes life free and good. We Americans have been those who have trusted in military might and made war on others, and Jesus says that this is foolish and that God loves us so much that God is not going to put up with this anymore. "Blessed are the merciful. . . . Blessed are the meek. . . . Blessed are the peacemakers." The judgment of God is nothing more and nothing less than God's intention to set things right, in the world and in our lives. The judgment of God is the love of God. As one theologian put it, "Do not fear the wrath of God; fear the love of God, for the love of God will strip away everything that stands between you and God."

One of the ways we domesticate the Sermon on the Mount, one of the ways we diminish its power to render us speechless, is to think of it as a collection of religious rules and advice. "When you pray, do this; when you give alms, do that. . . . Do not worry about your life, turn the other cheek, do not judge others." Good sage advice, rules for living. But Jesus is not talking about rules for coping in this world; Jesus is announcing the destruction of this world and the coming of God's reign.

To misunderstand the Sermon on the Mount as a series of rules is, by the way, the same thing we often do to the Ten Commandments. We tend to think of the Ten Commandments as ten things we'd really like to do, but that God doesn't want us to do. So to please God, we should not do them. But that misses the point, misses the way the commandments begin: "I am the LORD your God. I brought you out of slavery into the land of freedom, and this is the shape of freedom. I love you so much I am not putting up with your enslavement any more. I, the LORD your God, am setting things right. I am setting you so free you don't even have to have any other gods. You have been given so much you are free not to covet what is your neighbor's. You are free to have the joyous rest of the Sabbath day and to keep it holy." This is not a list of rules; it is the shape of freedom; it is the quality of life in a world remade by the judgment of God.

So it is with the Sermon on the Mount. These are not words of advice; they are words of life and death, words that create a crisis, words that stun us into speechlessness as we contemplate the world we have so carefully built, the world in which we have invested, the world we have so dearly cherished falling into the sea like a plywood shack in a flood.

As the theologian Paul Tillich put it many years ago:

> We can be cynical . . . only so long as we feel safety in the place in which our cynicism can be exercised. But if the foundations of this place and all places begin to crumble, cynicism itself crumbles with them. And only two alternatives remain—despair, which is the certainty of eternal destruction, or faith, which is the certainty of eternal salvation. "The world itself shall crumble, but . . . my salvation knows no end," says the Lord.[8]

To cling to the old structures of death, war, and greed is to live in a world that is passing away, to occupy a house with no foundation, a dwelling slated for condemnation. This is not God's world, and as Jesus says, even the pious who still cling to this world will be unrecognizable: "I never knew you." "I recognize," said Jesus, "those who are shaped by this freedom, who belong to God's new world."

And there is astonished silence as we imagine the collapse of a world that once seemed so stable, a house so compelling and attractive. But then, even as we stand speechless, the silence is broken by the first words of Easter: "Do not be afraid." Do not be afraid because even as our foolish house stands in watery ruins, there stands a house built on the solid rock of Jesus' own word, and the door is open, and the voice of Jesus is beckoning, "Come to me, all you that are weary and are carrying heavy burdens, and I will give you rest" (Matt. 11:28).

When my wife and I moved to Atlanta eight years ago, we shopped around for a church. We finally decided we would join a congregation in downtown Atlanta. We liked the worship, we liked the commitment to mission, and we decided to join. The minister invited us, and all the others who were joining that particular season, to come and meet with the church officers on a Wednesday night for dinner. So we did. We were gathered in the fellowship hall around a square table, and when dinner was done, the pastor said, "I would like to go around the table and ask each person joining the church to say why you are joining this church."

We did, and each of us said the kind of things one would expect. One person said, "I'm a musician; this church has one of the finest music programs in the city, and therefore I'm joining." Another one said, "We've got two teenage daughters, and the youth program here is fantastic. That is why we're joining." Still another person said, "I didn't like the minister in the church I belonged to, and I like the minister here a lot. I'm going to join."

Then it got around to a man I'll call Samuel. His story was that he was high on crack cocaine on the streets, stumbled into the church's outreach center, and begged to be helped. The director of the center said, "We've spent our budget for this month. I can't get you into a treatment program until next month. But if you will stay with us, we will stay with you." She then took his hand; they knelt on the carpet of her office and prayed together. He stayed and got into the treatment program.

"I've been sober for three years now, and the reason I'm joining this church is that God saved me in this church!" he exclaimed. The rest of us looked at each other sheepishly. We were there for the music and the parking; he was there for the salvation.

A few weeks later, there was a little squib in our church newsletter that said Samuel was now an inmate in one of the local county jails. I thought to myself, "Samuel and I joined the church together; we were brothers in Christ." So I went to see him. After going through three metal detectors, I found myself on the opposite side of a thick plate-glass window, holding a telephone and looking at Samuel in an orange jail jumpsuit. He was holding the other phone.

"Samuel," I said, "how are you?"

"By the grace of God," he said, "I'm doing all right."

"What happened?"

"I was working in the outreach center," he replied, "counseling people, people like myself, people off the streets, telling them they could do right. But then I realized I hadn't done right myself. I had a warrant for my arrest out here. It was an old warrant, years old; it would have never caught up with me, but I knew about it. So on Christmas Eve I turned myself in." But then Samuel's face brightened, "I will be out by Easter! I cannot wait to worship at church on Easter. But in the meantime I've got an outreach center going here in the jail. A lot of these people can't read or write, so I write letters to their sweethearts and wives, telling them that they miss them and love them. Every night we have a prayer meeting in my cell. Not many come, but we pray for the other prisoners and the guards."

I looked through the plate glass at my brother-in-Christ Samuel in the jumpsuit of a county prisoner, and I saw one of the freest human beings in the world, a man who is building his life not on sand, but on the rock of the gospel.

In the presence of such a free and joyful life, so filled with the promise of God's new world, I was astonished and silent.

Analysis

Dr. Long's Reformed tradition expects sermons of greater length than my own, allowing more time for development, illustration, and reflection. And when he is the one doing the preaching, the listener does not mind one bit. Despite greater length, in this sermon there is not a greater number of basic moves than in the other sermons presented in this book. While your analysis may differ, I see four, the same as in Bishop Curry's sermon:

> Move 1—The silence at the beginning, in and out of the pulpit; Buechner and Barth quotes, Terry Waite story.
>
> Move 2—The silence at the end: is there a word from the Lord? Jesus in Matthew, the shout from the balcony.
>
> Move 3—Judgment, at the end of the Sermon on the Mount and in a student's life.
>
> Move 4—Freedom, the promise of new life, Tillich quote, closing story of true freedom.

Simple enough, but it is not the structure, nor the quotations, that give shape, direction, and movement to the sermon; it is the stories. It would not be a Tom Long sermon without a couple of quotations from theological titans, but no one went home that day telling others about Barth and Tillich, and they may not remember Terry Waite's name. But they will remember his story, and they will never forget Samuel.

It was an interesting decision to spend so much time at the beginning of the sermon reflecting on preaching, and words, especially in juxtaposition to the emphasis on silence. Who dislikes silence more than speakers? There were two challenges in the first part of the sermon for all preachers, one implicit the other explicit. The first was to tend differently to silence, to listen to it carefully and use it wisely. The second was to take with absolute seriousness the silence of expectation, so that our words are up to the significance of the occasion. Yes, they are listening to us, but they are hoping for nothing less than a word from the Lord. Will there be one?

By my count, aside from the kind of in-passing first-person-singular uses I have discouraged above (e.g., "I love the way Frederick Buechner describes . . . " and "I think of Terry Waite") the preacher references himself three times in the 3,900 or so words of this sermon: (1) the contrast between his own standing in the pulpit and the man shouting from the balcony; (2) the story of his student who does not want to preach about judgment; and (3) the story of his fellow new member, Samuel. Three times. And in each instance, Dr. Long essentially plays straight man to the story's real protagonist. Recall these lines:

She said she was serving as a field education student in a local church and that her supervising pastor was requiring her to preach next Sunday.

"Good." I said, putting down my coffee cup.
"No, it's *not* good," she said, shaking her head. "He is making me preach on the lectionary texts for Sunday."
"Good" I said again.
"No," she repeated, "it is not good. Have you read the lectionary texts for next week? They're all about judgment. I don't believe in judgment. I believe in grace, I believe in mercy."

The preacher was there, said "Good" two times, but it was not his story, and he did not get in the way of the listeners' making it their own.

This is even more true of the closing story, which includes one of the five best lines I have ever heard in any sermon: "We were there for the music and the parking; he was there for the salvation." Notice the shift to the first-person plural. Like Luke in Acts 16:11 and following, the preacher is there, but it is not his story. Even when he visits Samuel in jail, it is only a vehicle to bring the narrative to climax and conclusion, not to say, "Look at me: I am visiting those in prison, just like Jesus said we should!" Instead the "we" subtly includes the listeners, and not just the new members of Central Presbyterian Church in Atlanta.

The conclusion invites us all to rethink what it means to be free, and to be free in Christ. The silence spoken of earlier in the sermon, the silence of recognizing a word from the Lord truly spoken, is very much present.

5

Persistently Figurative Preaching

Jesus is consistently depicted in all four Gospels as speaking in a manner I characterize as "persistently figurative." This is not a difficult case to make. Just open a Bible.

> Consider the lilies of the field, how they grow; they neither toil nor spin, yet I tell you, even Solomon in all his glory was not clothed like one of these. But if God so clothes the grass of the field, which is alive today and tomorrow is thrown into the oven, will he not much more clothe you—you of little faith?
>
> (Matt. 6:28–30)

Vivid description and sharply made analogy. Check.

> The kingdom of God is as if someone would scatter seed on the ground, and would sleep and rise night and day, and the seed would sprout and grow, he does not know how. The earth produces of itself, first the stalk, then the head, then the full grain in the head.
>
> (Mark 4:26–28)

Simple parable with keen observation and exaggeration for effect. Check.

> While he was speaking, a Pharisee invited him to dine with him; so he went in and took his place at the table. The Pharisee was amazed to see that he did not first wash before dinner. Then the Lord said to

him, "Now you Pharisees clean the outside of the cup and of the dish, but inside you are full of greed and wickedness. You fools! Did not the one who made the outside make the inside also? . . . But woe to you Pharisees! For you tithe mint and rue and herbs of all kinds, and neglect justice and the love of God; it is these you ought to have practiced, without neglecting the others. . . .Woe to you! For you are like unmarked graves, and people walk over them without realizing it."

One of the lawyers answered him, "Teacher, when you say these things, you insult us too." And he said, "Woe also to you lawyers!"

(Luke 11:37–46)

Diatribe with invective, sarcasm, and insult. Check. (Not that this will be recommended for regular implementation in our pulpits.)

That Jesus used lively, creative, vivid language in his proclamation is beyond dispute. Why he did so is obvious: to capture and hold the attention of his listeners. How he did so, and how contemporary preachers may do so also, is the topic of this chapter.

JESUS AND FIGURATIVE LANGUAGE:
THE LOST ART OF FABRICATION

While students of rhetoric may rightly disapprove, this study groups a variety of tropes, genres, and figures of speech into the catchall phrase "figurative language." In the appendix one sees that the letter "F" used in the typology to describe this characteristic of Jesus' rhetoric appears more frequently than any other letter. But it does not characterize a single, simple use of language. Jesus was much more rhetorically sophisticated than that. Without belaboring what I have already claimed is obvious, it will still be helpful to recall and describe the most important figures of speech and rhetoric prominent in the Synoptic Gospels. Jesus excelled at rhetorical fabrication. He made stuff up. In the next section I will argue, and demonstrate, how contemporary preachers may apply the lessons learned from Jesus. But first, the lessons.

Parable

The land of a rich man produced abundantly. And he thought to himself, "What should I do, for I have no place to store my crops?"

Then he said, "I will do this: I will pull down my barns and build larger ones, and there I will store all my grain and my goods. And I will say to my soul, 'Soul, you have ample goods laid up for many years; relax, eat, drink, be merry.'" But God said to him, "You fool! This very night your life is being demanded of you. And the things you have prepared, whose will they be?"

(Luke 12:16–20)

The parable of the "rich fool" is among the most compact and challenging of the narrative parables of Jesus, and an excellent example for our purposes. Jesus was speaking to "the crowd gathered by the thousands" (Luke 12:1; a bit of Lukan hyperbole?) when someone asked him to resolve a family dispute (12:13). Jesus declined, and then read to the crowd from the obituaries in that day's *Galilee Times* about the death of a prosperous local farmer, who died just as he finished an expansion of his holdings. Or so goes one thankfully forgotten school of parable interpretation, which imagined Jesus overhearing prayers in the temple, watching farmers at work, and telling about a Samaritan he once knew. While Jesus did comment on current events, for example at Luke 13:1–5, the parables, allegories, metaphors, and analogies of Jesus were fabricated. He made stuff up, apparently all the time. And he did it very well.

I prefer the word fabricate to "create" because it suggests a craft, a skill we can learn and develop, rather than a gifted ability we may or may not have. Current usage has unfortunately reduced the meaning of "fabrication" to "lie," which is accurate only to the extent that a fabricated story did not happen—a videographer could not have captured it. But an evangelist could, and that is the point.

Interested readers are welcome to delve deeply into the abundant literature on the parables of Jesus, and invited to begin with my own short book.[1] Interpretation is not the issue here, though, but imitation. Jesus made up stories to amplify, illustrate, and create meaning. He could have simply settled for saying to his petitioner in Luke 12, "One's life does not consist in the abundance of possessions" (v. 15). He could have even slathered on a cliché about owning your possessions, not letting your possessions own you. But instead he told a story, a pointed story about a man who was apparently a skilled farmer, who wisely reused and recycled, quoted Scripture, and yet was called "Fool" by God. Go figure. Which is exactly what the listener/reader is expected to do.

Metaphor/Simile

Is a lamp brought in to be put under the bushel basket, or under the bed, and not on the lampstand? . . .

With what can we compare the kingdom of God, or what parable will we use for it? It is like a mustard seed, which, when sown upon the ground, is the smallest of all the seeds on earth; yet when it is sown it grows up and becomes the greatest of all shrubs, and puts forth large branches, so that the birds of the air can make nests in its shade.

(Mark 4:21, 30–32)

Oops. Jesus made a grammatical boo-boo. Did you catch it? Your eighth-grade English teacher did. Right there in verses 30–31, Jesus asks what "parable" we could use for the kingdom of God and then launches into a simile. Or he did not, because the Greek *parabolē* draws on the Hebrew *māshāl*, which functions biblically like my phrase "figurative language," covering a multitude of tropes. What is the difference? It is a matter of degree, not of kind, because the principle at work in every case is what Paul Ricoeur notably described as a "metaphorical process."[2] The kingdom is not a seed; it is "like" the entire process of the seed's growing and becoming a plant large enough for nesting birds and, more to the point, like the meaning generated in the very process of comparison. The "kingdom of God" is itself a metaphor, which is then elaborated in the simile.

The homiletical point is twofold. First, Jesus did not always need or use full narrative parables or allegories to fully develop his ideas. Sometimes a simpler, but vivid, metaphor—this is that—or simile—this is like that—would do. Second, to extend our reading of Mark 4 a verse or two further, Jesus used figurative language to "[speak] the word to them, as they were able to hear it." It was Jesus' rhetoric that gave them ears to hear. I know, I know, earlier in Mark 4 Jesus quotes Isaiah 6 to suggest that he uses figurative language so that people would not understand, "so that they may not turn again and be forgiven" (Mark 4:12). But if Jesus' appropriation of Isaiah 6 is not itself metaphorical, then I do not know a metaphor when I read one.

Jesus uses another form of comparison better termed analogy or comparison, a distinction that is more important for homiletics than rhetoric. In Matthew 12:43–45/Luke 11:24–26, Jesus compares "this evil generation" with a person exorcised of an unclean spirit: the spirit wanders in search of a new home, and finding none, returns to discover things more hospitable than ever, and brings "seven other spirits more evil than itself." The analogy is imprecise in its application, allowing the interpreter and preacher room to play. The evangelists actually serve as our example, placing this, and many other stories, analogies, and so forth, in different contexts. Matthew precedes the wandering spirit analogy with the sign-of-Jonah saying, and follows it with Jesus' saying that the members of his family are those who do the will of his Father, then launches into the parable chapter, Matthew 13. Luke precedes the saying with an exorcism and the Beelzebul controversy, and follows it with a saying on true blessedness unique to Luke (but parallel to the saying on family, found in Luke 8:21), then with the Jonah sign, lamp and lampstand, and a diatribe against the Pharisees. The sayings, in other words, are not in fixed position and are used in analogy in different ways. So too in our sermons, not only with the metaphors, similes, and analogies of Jesus, but also in the ones we must learn to develop ourselves.

Hyperbole

> Then Peter came and said to him, "Lord, if another member of the church sins against me, how often should I forgive? As many as seven times?" Jesus said to him, "Not seven times, but, I tell you, seventy-seven times."
>
> (Matt. 18:21–22)

Not to mention the perfectly good convention that understands the Greek to mean seventy *times* seven. Is 490 too much? Well, that could be hyperbole. But Jesus is just getting warmed up. In the parable of the unforgiving servant that follows, the debt described, ten thousand talents, is a staggering amount, Bill Gates before the stock market crash kind of money, $30 billion at minimum wage. In other words, a debt impossible to pay, but Jesus did not choose other words: he chose hyperbole.

Jesus loved to exaggerate: one hundred sheep (Matt. 18:12); thirty, sixty, one hundredfold (Mark 4:8); one hundred jugs of olive oil (Luke 16:6) and not just big numbers. "If your hand causes you to stumble, cut if off. . . . If your eye causes you to stumble, tear it out" (Mark 9:43, 47). Hating one's family, lacking *one* thing, like lopping off limbs, are plausibly interpreted as exaggerations for effect, vivid, colorful, and memorable. That is what hyperbole is for, grabbing our attention, surprising us by size or scope or dimension. Why we would want to toss "this mountain" (Mt. Zion?) into the sea is not obvious (Mark 11:23). That we could is the outrageous claim, outrageousness being the purpose of hyperbole.

Irony and Sarcasm

While it may come as a surprise to television devotees, David Letterman and Jon Stewart did not invent irony and sarcasm. Sarcasm and irony have been around for a while. Their interrelationship is complex; sarcasm is often understood to be a more biting, angry version of irony. We will see in the next section that though irony and sarcasm have their place in the pulpit, there are limits, limits that did not necessarily apply to Jesus.

> As they went away, Jesus began to speak to the crowds about John: "What did you go out into the wilderness to look at? A reed shaken by the wind? What then did you go out to see? Someone dressed in soft robes? Look, those who wear soft robes are in royal palaces. What then did you go out to see? A prophet? Yes, I tell you and more than a prophet."
>
> (Matt. 11:7–9)

Jesus' tone is not gentle. It is almost mocking and dismissive. What exactly did you expect to see in the Judean desert? A soft, fragile princess? Then why are you complaining about what you found? And he is not done, comparing the inconsistent reactions to John the Baptist and Jesus to the petulant nonplay of children in the marketplace, before concluding with outright sarcasm—John has a demon! Jesus is a glutton and drunkard!—and a wisdom saying.

The deeper the sarcasm bites, the more problematic it becomes. Gentle irony is one thing, a sometimes humorous way to point out inconsistencies and foibles. Sarcasm can at times seem mean-spirited, and we know that cannot possibly be attributed to Jesus. Jesus was always sweetness and light, as nice as he could be. He would never go into someone's home and insult them. Yes, there is the verse from the triptych of verses at the beginning of the chapter, "One of the lawyers answered him, 'Teacher, when you say these things, you insult us too.'

And he said, 'Woe also to you lawyers!'" And that time at Simon's house (Luke 7:36–50). But my personal favorite is the long-distance healing of the centurion's servant, at the beginning of Luke 7 (vv. 1–10). The narrative is well-studied for its insight into how the honor/shame culture worked in first-century Israel. The centurion sends "some Jewish elders" to Jesus, then heads Jesus off by sending "friends" to say, "I am not worthy to have you come under my roof." What he probably means is "I do not want to be in a situation where I have to honor you in my own home." The punch line, though, for "elders" and "friends" is Jesus' caustic, "I tell you, not even in Israel have I found such faith." So yes, Jesus is depicted as using biting sarcasm, and as we will see, invective.

Invective

The rhetoric of the Letter of Jude is about as nasty as it gets.[3] Jude calls people names we are not certain we know the meaning of, and refers to sins and errors whose lineage is equally unclear. By my count there are more than twenty-five insults in this one-page missive. But we do not have to look far to find where Jude may have learned the art of invective. Assuming Mark knew what he was up to (6:3), the tradition argues that Jude learned it from his brother, Jesus.

Turn in your Bibles to Matthew 23. The scribes and/or Pharisees

— do not practice what they teach (v. 3)
— tie heavy burdens on others and do nothing to help (v. 4)
— do everything for show and demand signs of respect (vv. 5–7)
— are hypocrites (six times over: vv. 13, 15, 23, 25, 27, 29)
— lock people out of heaven (v. 13)
— turn converts into children of hell (v. 15)
— are blind guides (vv. 16, 24), blind fools (v. 17), and just plain blind (v. 24)
— neglect justice, mercy, and faith (v. 23)
— are "whitewashed tombs" (v. 27)
— are descendants of murderers (v. 31)
— are snakes and vipers who cannot escape "being sentenced to hell" (v. 33).

It is an exhausting list, filled with figurative language that for some reason we have tended to take literally, resulting in some incredibly anti-Semitic and anti-Jewish preaching. Since Jesus was a Jew, that does not make a lot of sense. So what was he up to? There is arguably no issue more current in New Testament studies than how best to understand Judaism's relationship to emerging Christianity. Matthew 23 is front and center in the discussion. How do we understand Jesus, the Galilean Jewish Jesus, in relationship to Judaism, which is inevitably Judean—Jerusalem—Judaism? Very carefully, the joke goes, but after the limited laughter, what? Rhetoric.

I am not arguing that Jesus spent an undocumented semester abroad in Athens. But granting this study's decision not to distinguish the rhetoric of Jesus from the rhetoric attributed to him by the evangelists, he knew what he was talking about. So what was this rhetoric about? Anger. Forget about the one time an evangelist attributes anger to Jesus (Mark 3:5). Jesus is really ticked off, and his rhetoric reflects it. This diatribe is real anger. And the problem is that we do not know how to handle the anger of Jesus. Is it "real" or "rhetorical"? And is there a meaningful hermeneutical and homiletical difference? We suppose that Jesus would never "pretend" to be angry. Why? Because it would be lying? Or because we do not understand the role of invective in rhetoric?

Somehow we need to figure out how to balance our understanding of how the Jesus of our contemporary piety acts ("Not my Jesus!") and the way Jesus is depicted as acting in the Gospels. It appears he gets angry, or, and this is more the point, it appears that he is depicted as acting angry. "Woe to you" is classic, commonplace, prophetic diatribe. Jesus uses it. Was Jesus *really* angry? Wrong, unanswerable question. The real question is what we should make of the evangelists' presentation of Jesus' diatribe? We should learn from it. There are times, and they are few, when we should be willing to move way out of our comfort zone and say what we have come to believe God really thinks.

Is there a place for invective in contemporary preaching? Good question for the next section.

Scripture and Proverb

Jesus must have gone to Sunday school, because he really knew his Bible. And he may have gone to a good seminary, because he knew how to use it. Matthew soon follows the Beatitudes with the "antitheses" in the Sermon on the Mount: "You have heard that it was said," followed by a quotation, then by, "But I say to you." And there is a whole lot more where that came from, not just in Matthew.

> He said to them, "Isaiah prophesied rightly about you hypocrites, as it is written,
>
>> 'This people honors me with their lips,
>>   but their hearts are far from me;
>> in vain do they worship me,
>>   teaching human precepts as doctrines.'"
>>   (Mark 7:6–7)

> But he looked at them and said, "What then does this text mean:
>
>> 'The stone that the builders rejected
>>   has become the cornerstone'?"
>>   (Luke 20:17–18)

> [He answered,] "The reason I speak to them in parables is that 'seeing they do not perceive, and hearing they do not listen, nor do they understand.' With them indeed is fulfilled the prophecy of Isaiah that says:
>
>> 'You will indeed listen, but never understand,
>>   and you will indeed look, but never perceive.
>> For this people's heart has grown dull,
>>   and their ears are hard of hearing,
>> and they have shut their eyes;
>>   so that they might not look with their eyes,
>> and listen with their ears,
>>   and understand with their heart and turn—
>> and I would heal them.'"
>>   (Matt 13:13–15)

It is not all bad news. Jesus quotes Scripture positively—the Decalogue, for example—and in celebration. The point is that Jesus quoted Scripture, period. And as we will see in the next section, he quoted it from memory, not from BibleWorks.

> [Jesus taught them,] "Do not store up for yourselves treasures on earth, where moth and rust consume and where thieves break in and steal; but store up for yourselves treasures in heaven, where neither moth nor rust consumes and where thieves do not break in and steal. For where your treasure is, there your heart will be also."
>   (Matt. 6:19–21)

"So I say to you, Ask, and it will be given you; search, and you will find; knock, and the door will be opened for you. For everyone who asks receives, and everyone who searches finds, and for everyone who knocks, the door will be opened."

(Luke 11:9–10)

Then Jesus said to them, "Prophets are not without honor, except in their hometown, and among their own kin, and in their own house."

(Mark 6:4)

Proverbs come in many shapes and sizes. They are not all from the Old Testament or the Apocrypha, and there are proverbs on the lips of Jesus in the New Testament for which we have no earlier source. It is okay. Proverbial and conventional wisdom is in the public domain. We saw in chapter 1 (above) that though Jesus is frequently depicted as using conventional wisdom, Marcus Borg and Ben Witherington III have rightly argued that Jesus is best understood as a teacher of *un*conventional, or alternative, wisdom. For that to be effective, one must know and reference the commonplace. You have to know "Doctor, cure yourself!" before you accuse your audience of thinking it themselves: "Doubtless you will quote me this proverb" (Luke 4:23) a fine example of dialogical preaching, by the way.

The use of proverbial wisdom was, and perhaps still is, a mark of an accomplished and well-trained teacher. If all the sources available did not agree in depicting Jesus as frequently using proverbs, it would be tempting to conclude that it was the well-trained evangelist at work, not the Galilean *tektōn*—but that is an argument we agreed in chapter 1 not to worry about. Still, just as Scripture was part of Jesus' background, so was proverb. The passage from Luke 4 mentioned above shows the interplay. After baptism and temptation, Jesus, "filled with the power of the Spirit," makes the preaching circuit in Galilee "in their synagogues," and finally comes to Nazareth, where he "stood up to read." No one remarks, "Wow, I didn't know Jesus could read." That surprises no one, we presume, because they all could. What surprises them, and then outrages them, is the way Jesus uses Scripture and proverb.

Jesus made stuff up, a fabulous fabricator, giving his rhetoric a persistently figurative character that drew and held the interest of his audience. He drew on powers of observation, knowledge of Scripture and tradition, and a storyteller's craft to give us a powerful model of how we can do a better job of drawing and holding the interest of our audiences.

FABRICATION: THE CRAFT OF PREACHING

Is it possible the reason people are not very interested in our sermons is that our sermons are often not very interesting? I know it is not feasible to be good every week, and I often point out that if we batted one for three every game, we would make the Hall of Fame. But is that an excuse to plan to be boring? Yet we are, week in and week out. We plan to be boring, sometimes because of the way we structure our sermons, beginning with our conclusion and hoping folks will hang on to the end anyway. More likely, we plan to be boring because we have planned our sermon preparation time to focus almost exclusively on exegesis, theological analysis, reflection, and shaping and developing our thoughts. We leave almost no time to shape and develop our words in order to bring our thoughts to life.

Good preaching can be fairly defined as having something to say that is worth hearing and saying it well enough to be truly heard. Hence, it is more important to have something to say than to say it well; but *good* preaching is both.

Thesis: it takes more time and work to be an interesting preacher than to be a boring preacher. What, you thought Craddock, Curry, Long, and Taylor just roll out of bed on Sunday morning, pop into the pulpit, and say whatever comes first to mind? Hardly. They, like Jesus, are master fabricators, making meaning and interest where it was not there before— not making it out of nothing, creatio ex nihilo, but out of everything around them and within them: their experience. While this may sound a little Buddhist of me, the best preachers are the ones most present to their experience. Because they live their lives with focused attention, they see and hear, taste and smell, what the rest of us pass by as if it were not there. Then they tell us about it. This skill, fabrication, is the preacher's ultimate craft. For Jesus it was an art, but for us it is a learnable skill.

Name your favorite preacher, famous or not, and when you begin to describe why you like, say, one of the preachers whose sermons grace this volume, or the preacher who changed and shaped your life years ago, I would be very surprised if you did not get to "stories" by the second sentence. Where, students often ask, do you "get" your material? I once received a request for the title of the book I used for my "illustrations." I had no idea what the point of reference was until the inquirer mentioned that one of my students had said I always began class with a short reading and a prayer, and he wanted to know what the title of the book was. The Bible, most of the time, but also everything and everyone else I have been reading. How we bring to our sermons what we learn from paying attention to life is the focus of this section.

Better Descriptions, Fewer Words

Two senior pastors of large, successful churches are among the best read and most eloquent preachers I know. But they were terrible at doing the morning announcements, going on endlessly about what we could all easily read in the bulletin. In one case the leadership finally did an intervention, and the rector learned to write down, word for word, everything that truly needed to be said. The other pastor continues to add five boring minutes to every service. You may have the gift of gab. Preaching is not gabbing.

One of the simplest ways to add interest to our sermons is to pay more attention to how we describe and phrase things. Sharp, vivid, active words and phrasing beat tortured, adjective-laden, convoluted ones every time. The sermon is a time to channel our inner Hemingway, not our inner Proust. Here is a confession, by way of example, from a sermon preached at Christ Church Cathedral in Nashville.

> We are removed from the origin of things. Richard Lischer, who teaches preaching at Duke Divinity School, might remind us of just how far removed we are by asking us to compare a kitchen table in our country, say the one Senator Biden and Governor Palin wanted us to imagine them sitting around Thursday night, with the table of a Central American family. Ask most Tennessee ten-year-olds where their chicken fingers came from, and they will point to the KFC bag on the kitchen counter. If you press them, they might mention the take-out window, or even the teenager who took your order. The Guatemalan ten-year-old chased the chicken around the yard, watched as its neck was broken, then helped pluck off the feathers. Forty-five minutes later, dinner.

What's wrong with this paragraph? Lots. First, I included an "oral footnote" by mentioning Professor Lischer, from whom I "borrowed" the idea. We need to give credit where it is due, but while it must be in our manuscript, it often should not be on our lips.[4] The seminary students and retired clergy who know of Professor Lischer did not need to be told who he was, and the others did not find the information helpful. Second, the reference to the 2008 vice-presidential debate was distracting, a detour on which more than a few listeners likely got lost. Third, the details about tables, take-out window, and order-taker added no meaning, just words; the point was the KFC bag. Finally, I needlessly used the past tense. So if I had a homiletical do-over, I would say:

> We are removed from the origin of things. Ask a Tennessee ten-year-old where his chicken comes from, and he will point to the KFC bag on the kitchen counter. Ask a Guatemalan ten-year-old, and she will describe chasing the chicken around the yard, watching as its neck is broken, then helping pluck off the feathers. Forty-five minutes later, dinner. We are removed from the origin of things.

The time saved could be used later to further develop this or another idea.

Using better descriptions, with fewer but livelier words, is a discipline. Many preachers will feel they do not have time, and are fortunate to get something coherent banged out by Saturday night. You are not that preacher. You are a good preacher who wants to be a better preacher. And like most disciplines, this one gets easier over time. There is a school for learning how to do this, too. It is called a library. Reading good writers is part of the discipline of becoming a better preacher. Over time the good habits of these good writers seep into our preaching.

Should we use contemporary references, jargon, even slang? Yes. While my reference to the debate is not a good example, letting listeners know you have some idea what is going on in the world around you is a good idea. And not every reference should be to *The New York Times*, *Foreign Affairs*, PBS, and *The Christian Century*, wonderful as they may be. As Tom Troeger argues, multiple-intelligences theory teaches that we have a responsibility to develop sermon material for all the various ways people "know," and not just catering to our own ways of knowing.[5] It helps to have a teenager, and if you do not, for heaven's sake get to know the ones in your church. How else will you keep MySpace and FaceBook, music, movies, and celebrities straight? This is not to argue for sloppy or profane prose. But it helps to let them know that you have a life. You do have a life, don't you?

Quotations

When sermons needed "three points and a poem," preachers kept the *Oxford Book of English Verse* or the *Norton Anthology of Poetry*, with their subject indexes, ready to hand. Few seminarians now own one or have any idea why they would want to. This is a good thing. Not because poetry is a bad thing, but because all citations and quotations need to be organic to the sermon, not tacked on to demonstrate a measure of literary acumen. Many homileticians teach us to avoid poetry altogether and warn that quotations, "as Churchill once said," are so subject to the law of unintended consequences as to be not worth the bother.

The real problem is when we transfer from academic research and term papers the need to have supporting references for our own thoughts. Out come Karl Rahner and Edward Farley, the Niebuhrs, and Elisabeth Schüssler Fiorenza, Rowan Williams, Ellen Davis, and Cornell West. The problem is exacerbated by the need to dust off our diplomas in the pulpit, making references more to tell them how hard we study than to share with them what we learned. Sermons are not term papers, footnotes are not an oral tradition, and names only confuse. You do not write a sermon, then pass out the manuscript for everyone to read during the break between the Scripture Lesson and the Creed or Passing of the Peace. You craft and fashion a sermon that people will *hear*—if you keep their interest. If someone says something clearly and persuasively that helps to clarify what you are trying to say, use it. But do not use it because you think someone might be impressed by the name of the person you are quoting.

There are dangers from overquotation, inept citation ("It says in the Bible somewhere"), and pedantic references to books you read half a lifetime ago. But there is also power in quotation, especially when we are quoting from the heart. When a psalm, a song, or a poem is a part of you, comes to mind not from a Google search but because of who you are and what you care about, then sharing that verse or stanza, from memory, can be homiletically powerful. This is not to call for ending every sermon by getting out your guitar and singing your favorite song from your youth, or with a poem or any other device. Quotation, song, and so forth as homiletical devices flop, every time. But the right reference, accurately shared but nevertheless shared from the heart, adds character and interest.

Example

Every book on preaching should quote Aristotle's *Art of Rhetoric* more than once: "There are two kinds of examples, namely, one which consists in relating things that have happened before, and another in inventing them oneself. The latter are subdivided into comparisons [*parabolē*] or fables [*logoi*]."[6] We will modify Aristotle slightly, saving "example [*paradeigma*]" for "relating things that have happened before" and using "story" for that which we, or others, invent—sheer fabrication, I suppose.

If it were not for the explosion of television channels devoted in one way or another to matters historical, it would be much easier to negotiate our way through the list on our cable boxes and satellite dishes—not just the History Channels, but the Discovery Channels, National Geographic channels, PBS, and channels I have never heard of. While I have no proof, I presume the channels have proliferated because someone is watching them. These someones come to our churches. We can use that.

The quotation from Aristotle comes at the beginning of the longest section of the *Rhetoric*, the chapters devoted to "proof [*pistis*]." Every now and then it is a good idea to remember that on a certain level a sermon is an argument, and one the preacher wants to win. We are not arguing with the congregation—if we are, we are in a lot of trouble; we are arguing before them, and they are the judges deciding whether not we have been persuasive. That makes us truly *hypokritai*, but I have now far exceeded the number of Greek references I would ever allow in a sermon. We are doing our best to persuade our audience of something, and one of the ways we do this is by historical analogy and example. If their television-viewing habits are any indication, argument by historical example, biblical and otherwise, will be helpful. But our strategy for the nonbiblical is different from the biblical.

When we talk about something being impossible, we may reference Napoleon's march on Russia, just as we may have our Waterloos and our small-man complex. We might reference courage by way of Washington at Valley Forge, or the Episcopal nuns who died caring for yellow fever victims in 1878, the Martyrs of Memphis. What we are generally after is support for our argument by analogy, and the better and more widely known the historical example, the better it forwards our argument. It is far easier to talk about the Martyrs of Memphis to Episcopalians in Tennessee, especially where I teach, because Sewanee is home to the Sisters of St. Mary, the religious order of Constance and her companions. If you do not know your saints, you will not enjoy the wonderful English movie *Millions* nearly as much: St. Clare of Assisi smoking a joint, Joseph of Nazareth, "dates uncertain," and the Martyrs of Uganda will pass by as a young boy's hallucination, not his informed grieving for his late mother, who he hopes will be canonized herself one day. And if you have not seen the movie, you do not know what I am talking about.

That is the point. Our use of historical references, general and ecclesial, must have enough currency to make contact with a wide swath of our audience. If you are a history buff of one era, conflict, or another, watch out: unless you want a congregation of Civil War reenactors, you need to space out your references to Chickamauga, Antietam, and Shelby Foote. Intentionally making our historical references broad is the best strategy for peaking interest around the congregation.

An even better strategy is to talk about the congregants themselves, because most everybody likes to talk about themselves (the problem of the previous chapter). Why, when we want an example of courage, or faith, or courageous faith, do we so quickly turn to the famous and the dead? What about the many examples of leadership, stewardship, and discipleship among the saints who have gathered that very day? What about the known and celebrated saints of years past who built and sustained this congregation through good times and tough ones? Should not their stories be remembered, retold, and celebrated? Of course they should.

Which brings to mind the caution issued in chapter 2 about the danger of the "holy" trinity: Martin Luther King Jr., Archbishop Desmond Tutu, and Mother Teresa. Once a year. Period. Yes, they are great, courageous, and heroic disciples of Jesus Christ. But if those are the examples you find yourself turning to more than annually, you need to both get out more and read more. One of the things you might want to read more of is the Bible.

When we use biblical examples in this biblically illiterate age, we have at least a twofold agenda, hoping to use the example to illumine, inform, and further our argument, while also teaching them a bit of Scripture. Gone are the days when we could make a reference to a biblical chapter or verse, even Psalm 23, and be confident everyone knows the meaning of the reference. I say "cloud of witnesses," and they say "Huh?" We have a responsibility in our preaching, over time, to reacquaint the congregation with their own biblical tradition. We need to do this persistently and patiently.

I also mentioned in chapter 2 that Fred Craddock is the master of this kind of teaching. He sets aside all temptation to say, "I shouldn't have to remind you of this, but I know you don't know the Bible, so here goes." Instead, he opens with something along the lines of "Now

you will recall . . . " Then he tells them what they need to know about
the biblical character or narrative in question, never belaboring it, and
at least in my hearing, always in the present tense. He recounts Abraham and Sarah laughing at God's promise (Gen. 17:17 and 18:12) as
if the oaks of Mamre were in the park across the street, and he had just
heard about the pregnancy at the grocery store. If we take care in telling
the biblical story, not rushing through it to get to *our* point, and if we
do not chide but seek to inform, then our twofold agenda may yield a
double blessing.

Story

You know where the sermon is going. You have exegeted well, come
to a prayerful conclusion about what the Holy Spirit wants the people
of God to hear from these texts on this occasion, and started mapping
your moves. A wonderful introduction has started to suggest itself to
you, and for a Thursday, things are looking good. By Friday it has
all really come together except for this huge gaping hole right where
the development of your penultimate theological claim should be. You
need a story. What would Jesus do? Jesus would make one up. Be a
good disciple and make one up yourself.

Why? There are more online sermon helps than we can ever possibly
use.[7] I have written my share of lectionary commentary, so I should
want you to buy my books. Surely my publishers do. Yes and no: yes,
because I think the biblical material at the heart of such books is useful;
no, because they are no substitute for you knowing where your sermon
is going and fabricating an appropriate story to help you and the audience get there. Your sermon may have a gaping hole, but that hole has
dimensions, and sewing someone else's unshrunk patch onto your sermon will only make the gap larger in the end. Here are three examples
from one sermon to start:

> The woman was lost in a country not her own, with scant skill in
> the language, and all she wanted to do was go to church. How hard
> could that be? Armed with a map she barely understood, an address,
> and the name of the pastor of the *Evangelische Freikirche*, she missed
> her bus stop, and things went downhill from there. Finally she found
> the right intersection, turned the corner, and as she walked up the
> steps to the church, she was met by a host of people walking out
> the doors. "Great," she thought, "I missed the service." Using what

little German she had, she pointed to the piece of paper with the pastor's name. "*Sommerferien*," she was told, on summer vacation. Crestfallen, she stuffed papers and map into her purse and began to retrace her steps when someone tapped her on the shoulder and said, "Hallo! Are you from America?" In English far superior to her German, the woman was invited to share her story, then invited home to share lunch with a large and friendly family, then a bicycle tour of the city, drinks and snacks in a café, and a late afternoon escort to the train station. What began so badly became one of the best days of her life, and a highlight of her trip.

On another corner in another part of the world a man in a wheelchair was not doing so well. Americans with Disabilities Act notwithstanding, there were no cuts in the curb and no ramp to the building. At least he could appreciate the bitter, perfect irony—he could not get across the street nor enter the building to see the lawyer handling his suit for workplace discrimination and accommodation.

School's started. It had been almost two weeks, and the shy new student remained overwhelmed by his situation. He roomed alone, sat by himself in the cafeteria, was afraid to speak in class, and the only conversation he recalled having in days was at the library to ask for a reserve book. He had been told this was such a friendly place, which was part of why he came to this school instead of one offering better financial aid, but so far the friendliness had passed him by. Whatever happened to Southern hospitality?

The first one happened in 1993, the last one came guiltily as I thought about moving our then teenage daughter to the third high school in nine months, and the second came out of nowhere. They were all fabricated. Not from whole cloth, and not only from my experience. And they came from thinking about the understanding of hospitality I wanted to develop in this sermon from Luke 14:1, 7–14/Jeremiah 2:4–13, contrasting God's hospitality with our reluctance to both accept it and practice it. I suppose I could have Googled "hospitality," but that yields 66 million hits.

Fabricators need to know what they are trying to make. That is the great advantage of homiletical fabrication: you know the thought, claim, or idea you are trying to develop, so presumably the issue of trying to fit someone else's illustrative square peg into your homiletical round hole will not be a problem. So you begin with, "The huge gaping hole in my sermon is about . . . " Hospitality? Forgiveness? Grace? The shape of a well-lived Christian life? Whatever that is, you work backward from there.

Suppose our sermon has been examining what it means to accept the surprise of grace. We want to be as concrete and specific in our concluding image as we were in describing the alienation, pain, and despair of a life cut off from God. Excellent idea, because we undermine our message by being more compelling in describing what we pray people will turn from than we are at describing what we invite them to turn to, a problem as old as Dante: *Purgatorio* is a lot more fun to read than *Paradiso*. How should we proceed? We could start by going through our mental Rolodex of people whose lives look like what we are talking about. Is there a saint in this congregation or community who fits the bill? Great, because not every story needs to be about the dead and famous. Can you name them by name, or should there be a little obfuscation in this fabrication?

What about this person do you want to highlight? Is she emblematic for faith in the face of loss, her commitment to social justice, or her sacrificial giving to things she cares deeply about? Does he have a way of making all feel welcome, or of quietly bearing his brothers' and sisters' burdens? The beauty of fabrication is that you get to tell the story in the way you want your listeners to remember. It serves to support the conclusion you were trying to make, to carry the sermon in the direction you intended.

Is the person you want to tell about a relative or a close personal friend? Then can you imagine changing enough of the details so that their identity need not be revealed, and the listeners do not have to hear about how important this person is/was to your life? Good, then they can devote their attention to imagining how the person models something for their own lives. As we saw in chapter 4, when you change the story so that you are not a part of it, you do not hide the truth of your experience, which is what you are really trying communicate.

Let me show you what I mean, from a sermon on Luke 15:1–10, the "Lost Sheep" and the "Lost Coin."

> Like Little Bo Peep we've lost our sheep. Or maybe we are the sheep, lost, like the old song, "We're poor little lambs / who have lost our way." And Bo Peep is particularly appropriate, come to think of it, because it is her philosophy that seems to be guiding us, now that we've lost it. But when you have lost it, and believe me, we have, then all you are left with is the Bo Peep School of Evangelism. "Leave them alone / and they'll come home." When you have lost

the ability, the desire, the passion, to look, to seek and save the lost, that is all you are left with. Wishful thinking.

In part it is because we have gotten this all turned around; being so conditioned by bad art and self-centered thinking, we can only imagine that *we* are the ones who need to be found. We've been finding ourselves, following our bliss, looking out for number one, and singing "I gotta be me" for so long that we think it is in *Hymnal 1982*. But the hymn that is in there says, "I once was lost, but now I'm found." To quote our Tuesday morning preacher's sister, "And then what happened?" Nothing. And why nothing? Because we have lost the ability to look, mistakenly thinking that the joy is in being found when the joy is in the finding.

A Hispanic colleague from my Baptist days told of a woman in his church who "came forward" at the altar call one Sunday. She was crying and waving her arms in the air and shouting, "Fill me up, Lord, fill me up." They prayed for her, laid hands on her, and led her back to her pew. Next week, same thing: "Fill me up, Lord, fill me up." And the Sunday after that, and the Sunday after that. Finally, as she rushed down the aisle one Sunday too many, crying, "Fill me up, Lord, fill me up," someone else called from the back of the church, "Don't fill her up, Lord. Plug the leak!"

Yes, Lord, plug the leak. Some of us are so low on air and energy and hope that we have all but given up. It is nice enough, don't you think? sitting with the other ninety-eight sheep. And frankly, I don't have the energy to light the lamp, sweep, and search for one lousy drachma. We'll just get by with what we've got. Maybe the show I have in mind is not *Lost* but *Survivor*. *Will the last Episcopalian to leave the church please turn out the lights?*

Here's the problem. We cannot get what we want without doing some things we think will make us uncomfortable. We *think* something will make us uncomfortable. We do not know that because we have not tried. The funny thing is that everyone I know who has tried brings back a report like Joshua: you will not believe what I saw. I saw children laughing, families bonding, the sick being cared for, the grieving loved. I saw people getting involved, making decisions, taking stands. I saw houses built, schools opened, hungry fed, prisoners visited. I saw Bibles studied, heard creeds affirmed, anthems sung, and carillon rung. I smelled it too, and tasted, oh, how I tasted. Taste and see; see what we are missing because we have lost the desire to look.

Amy practices what I preach. Her favorite hymn is "Amazing Grace," though she sings it without the "wretch." She looks, deeply, for people to help, and she prefers to do it without anyone knowing about it. She is the most joyous person you will ever hope to meet. Did I mention that she is confined to a wheelchair? You don't really notice it, the way she can get around. It is being visually impaired that you notice. Funny thing, that, with the "Amazing Grace" line "I once was blind / but now I see" you absolutely cannot use the word "blind" about Amy, because she sees the things the rest of us have long ago mastered the art of overlooking.

Amy was the first one to hear it. Initially, she told me, she did not hear a thing. Gradually she realized what she was hearing was silence, a heavenly silence. As time went on, the silence was replaced by a gentle weeping, occasionally racked with sighs too deep for words. Heaven, Amy told me, is weeping. She taught me how to listen, and I have heard it for myself. It is the saddest sound I have ever heard. When we lose our desire to look for the lost, it is not only our joy in finding that is lost. When the lost are not found, when the sinner does not repent, even heaven's joy is lost.

All of the above was made up, fabricated. In the case of the "plug the leak" story, it was a colleague's fabrication that I "borrowed," and the sound of heaven weeping from a song (Eric Clapton?) or poem (Emily Dickinson?) that I vaguely remembered but did not chase down because "heaven weeping" seemed to be in the public domain. "Amy" was complete fabrication, but I needed a closing story about the importance and power of seeking. The argument of this chapter has been that good preachers today, following the example of Jesus, the master preacher, need to learn how to make stuff up in order to bring interest, edge, and vibrance to their sermons. An example from a truly gifted practitioner may make this clearer.

A SERMON BY BARBARA BROWN TAYLOR

If there is a more beloved preacher than Barbara Taylor, I do not know who it is. Audiences in and out of church cannot hear or read her too often, making her books best sellers, her lectures packed, and her now-occasional sermons an event. She may have "left church" as parish priest, but when she comes back to speak, she draws a crowd. This sermon, preached at the chapel of Duke University, comes from Year A in the Revised Common Lectionary, Matthew's version of the "Supper/Banquet" parable, with the addendum, the "Guest without a Garment."

Exposed! The Imposter Syndrome

Matthew 22:1–14

If Matthew and Luke had churches in my town, I would definitely go to Luke's church. Every time I visit Matthew's church, I sit near the door. Things are so clear-cut for him. In his world, you are either a sheep or a goat, wheat or tare, a wise maiden or a foolish one. If you pretend to be one when you are in fact the other, then woe to you, you hypocrite—you wolf in sheep's clothing, you splinter picker with loggy eyes. Three guesses where you are headed when the kingdom comes!

In my part of the country, Matthew is what we call a fire-and-brimstone preacher. He gets really excited about hell, which he conceives as a burning trash dump where a lot of sorry hypocrites are going to grind their teeth for all eternity. Luke mentions the dump once, so maybe there is something to it, but Matthew cannot seem to get enough of it. Over and over, he puts hell in Jesus' mouth, filling the fiery furnace with sinners of every kind: evildoers, unfaithful stewards, wicked servants, and at least one poor guy who was so afraid of his master that he did not have the nerve to invest a single talent in the financial market. Imagine that!

"You wicked and lazy slave!" his master replied when he found out. "You knew, did you, that I reap where I did not sow, and gather where I did not scatter? Then you ought to have invested my money with the bankers, and on my return I would have received what was mine with interest" (25:26–27). I am pretty sure this guy worked for Lehman Brothers. Then he had his slave thrown into outer darkness as punishment for being afraid, but at least he did not cut him up first. In another story, another master cuts his wicked slave into pieces before sending him to the weeping and gnashing place (24:50–51).

I am not saying Jesus did not say these things. You will have to talk to your Bible teacher about that. I am just saying that Matthew sure seems to enjoy reporting them, the same way he seems to enjoy telling the parable of the wedding banquet.

The first part is bad enough. The king invites the A list to his son's wedding, but they do not show up. When he sends his slaves to fetch them, they not only make light of the invitation—they kill the messengers, which so enrages the king that he puts the roast ox and the fatted calves his chefs have prepared for them back in the oven while he rallies his troops to go and kill them all, burning their city to the ground.

Bad enough, right? But then he sends his slaves to bring in the B list, which also includes some people on the C, D, and F lists, most of whom were checking their e-mail, changing the oil in their pickup trucks, or just sleeping in the bushes until the shelter opened when they were summoned to the king's wedding banquet. Cool! I must have won the lottery! So they go. And you know what happens. The king notices one of them who is not dressed appropriately, acts as if that is some kind of big surprise, and—when the guy has nothing to say for himself—orders him bound hand and foot and thrown into the outer darkness, "where there will be weeping and gnashing of teeth."

Can we go to Luke's church, please?

No we can't. We are in Matthew's church this morning. It is his turn to give the sermon, and if you have a hard time sitting still, do not forget: it is his story, but it is not his Gospel. It is the Gospel according to Matthew, which every one of us and all of us together are allowed to engage according to the gospel that has given us life.

I have spent so much of my life changing bandages on people wounded by brutal religion that you have to keep an eye on me, to make sure I do not round off edges God means to keep sharp. My problem is that I really believe the gospel is good news—that even the hardest sayings, recorded by those with the angriest ears, have life in them somewhere, with truth I need to know.

In the case of this morning's parable, I am deeply relieved that someone knows about this awful dream I keep having. In one version of it, I am the guest preacher at some grand place like Duke Chapel, but I have forgotten my vestments, and there is nothing in the closet that fits me. My only choices are big baggy black things made for men twice my size or little angelic things made for choristers half my size. I keep trying them on and ripping them off again while the clock ticks the time away. The next thing I know, I am standing in church in something completely inadequate when it comes time for me to read the Gospel. I decide that posture is everything, holding my head high as I step into the pulpit to find that the Bible is written entirely in Swedish.

In another version, I have just learned that I am enrolled in a class I have not attended all semester—usually in advanced math or physics—but I also forgot to drop the class, which means that I have to take the final exam no matter what. I find the textbook. I cram and cram. I stay up all night, but I cannot do anything with the numbers. They keep swimming on the page like tadpoles. So I go to the exam next morning, knowing I will fail it, and when I walk through the door, the professor looks quizzically at me.

"And who are you?" he asks.

You know the dream I am talking about, right? At least I hope you do, or this is really embarrassing. People seem to have different versions of it, depending on their stations in life, but the dream always comes down to being somewhere you are not equipped to be—usually without any clothes on—waiting to be exposed for the imposter you are. As hard as you have worked to prevent it, it is finally going to happen. People are going to learn the truth about you: that you are stupid, that you have no business being here, that you do not know the language, do not know which fork to use, do not remember your host's name—that your body really is as bad as you thought it was, that people really are looking at you and there is nothing in reach—nothing at all—that you can use to cover yourself up.

Whatever else Matthew was up to in this parable, he got that part right. Everyone else at the banquet seems to have gotten a memo that the underdressed guest has not. When the magnificent king approaches him, with anger still radiating from his royal person over his first, disastrously received effort at being generous, the underdressed guest has no time to think, much less get the textbook.

"Friend," the king says to him (a lousy translation; "Buster" works much better).

"Buster," the king says to him, "how did you get in here without a wedding garment?"

Oh, God. It's one of those dreams.

Why do I think this story is a dream? Because real people do not turn down a king's dinner invitation, much less torture and kill the messengers who come to fetch them. Because once you have a whole ox and several fatted calves on serving platters, they will not keep while you wage war on a whole city, kill its inhabitants, and torch the place. Because who really expects someone nabbed in the middle of an oil change to have a clean wedding garment in the back of the truck?

Jesus called it a parable, which is almost the same thing as a dream. It is not a once-and-for-all story. It is a story you can walk around in, a story that wants a response from you—hopes for a response from you—one that changes as you change, so that it is different the tenth time you hear it than it was at the first.

Matthew was certainly looking for a response, but his reasons for recording the story do not exhaust our reasons for entering it. The king, the banquet, the dress code, the failure—the exposure of the failure, the judgment, the free fall into outer darkness—you know this story, don't you?

You even know why it is no good to be a hypocrite. It really is deadly, to keep two yous going—the public you and the private you, the you that you say you are and the you that you act like, the you that you dress like and the you that you really are. You say you are an environmentalist, but you gobble energy like a suburban mall. You say "Have a blessed day" to the lady at the bank and then pull into traffic like a demon straight from hell. You tell everyone who will listen how worried you are about the public schools, about the people who are losing their homes, about the election, but you do not do anything about these things. You say you will go to the vineyard, but you do not go.

Matthew seems to think that all this twoness is about gaining advantage over other people, but I think that is circumstantial. When Matthew wrote his Gospel, he was dealing with religious people who were living high on widows' mites, who were using their theological educations—their institutional privileges—to climb on top of other people. While that hypocrite's club still has plenty of members, Matthew stays so busy with them that he seems to lose sight of the people whose twoness has less to do with their inflated sense of their own worth than with their terrible fear that they are worth nothing at all.

It is just as deadly, this other hypocrisy. You look all pulled together, but you are really a wreck. You make a good salary, but you are on welfare in your heart. You can speak three languages. You have a college degree. You know which fork to use, and still you keep waiting for someone to come and arrest you—to ask you how you got in here—and when you cannot get a single word to pass your lips because you have been found out at last, you hold out your hands so the usher will have an easier time binding them. You are scared of the outer darkness, but it is no surprise, really. It is where you always feared you belonged.

Based on personal experience, I would have to say that the only thing worse than this kind of twoness is waiting for someone to find out about it. The only thing worse than showing up in your dream with the wrong clothes on—no clothes on?—is waiting for someone to notice. Then someone does, and while there can be real terror in that moment—especially if the noticer happens to be a really mad king—there can also be real relief in that moment—because someone finally noticed your twoness, and now you do not have to pretend anymore. Someone was not fooled by your pretense. Someone has reached past the two yous to tap the real you on the shoulder, and even if he calls you "Buster," the jig is up.

Here is the good news: because your twoness has been exposed, your wholeness is a real possibility, perhaps for the first time. Someone has paid attention to you long enough to notice what it was about you that did not fit—someone who has decided not to let you pass this time, who has the regal nerve to walk right up to you and say, "Which one's the lie? This isn't a Halloween party. Take off the mask."

Well. Now that the worst has happened, you have a chance to be made new. When this dream comes back, you are going to play it differently—because you can, now. When that king approaches you next time, you are going to let him know you got the point.

I am teaching a film class at Piedmont College this semester. Every other Tuesday night, nine students and I sit in a dark auditorium, watching deep and sometimes disturbing films such as *American Beauty*, *Pleasantville*, and *Magnolia*. On alternate Tuesdays we sit in the same place with the lights on, discussing the characters we watched come to life on the screen. Nine times out of ten, we know more about them than they know about themselves. The high-strung real estate agent cannot see how brittle her striving has made her, but we can. The man with testosterone poisoning cannot see how much he misses his dead mother, but we can.

Last Tuesday we were sitting there talking about why these characters are so dense when someone pointed out that they do not have the luxury of watching the movie as we do. They are in the movie, where they are so busy with their own dramas that they do not have much opening to think about their parts. They just keep playing their roles—acting like people we know they are not, saying things they do not really believe, and hurting the people they want to be near.

When their lives change—if their lives change—it is because someone gets close enough to tell them what they cannot see about themselves: that they are even worse than they feared, or that they are lovelier than they ever imagined, but in any case that their story does not have to turn out the same way every time unless they insist.

Since the characters are all different, so are the revelations that change their lives. There is no one-sized truth that fits all, except that the keys to their prisons are usually in other people's pockets—someone, anyone, who will stop, look, and refuse to be taken in by their carefully perfected acts. When that happens, the scrutiny pops their locks. It opens the door to their salvation—because someone got close enough to see past their twoness and call them to become whole.

I do not remember which student said this so well—probably the painfully shy girl who is brilliant on paper but almost never says a word out loud. Whoever it was, we got it: that we could not see ourselves any better than the people on the screen could see themselves. Who was watching our movies carefully enough to tell us what they saw? Who—in a whole room full of people who could see exactly how we were dressed—who would have the nerve to come up and say, "How did you get in here?" or "Didn't you see the garment with your name on it?" or "Would you like to dance?"

I guess you never know who that person will be—a mad king, a patient lover, a scary Matthew, a sweet Jesus. Since this is our gospel—our story, our hope of waking up to real life—then I guess that person could be you or me—dreaming God's dream as many times as it takes to put the fiery furnace out because everyone—I mean everyone—is inside the banquet hall, dancing the night away.

Analysis

Like most of Professor Taylor's sermons, this sermon is as filled with figurative language as any you will hear. It is why so many people adore her preaching, and her sermon collections from a dozen or more years ago are still popular. "How does she do it?" students want to know. Fred Craddock once said that she has her own rhythm: she writes a paragraph, then goes outside to feed the chickens, comes back and writes some more, then back outside to brush the horse, hang some laundry, go for a walk. Back and forth, sermon and life, life and sermon, letting the imagery emerge, not grinding away at the laptop.

And does the imagery ever emerge! Not just the focal metaphors, to which we will turn, but almost every phrase, made interesting by an artful turn of phrase or sharply drawn image. "You say you are an environmentalist, but you gobble energy like a suburban mall. You say, 'have a blessed day' to the lady at the bank and then pull into traffic like a demon straight from hell." Hypocrites indeed. This is craft, founded upon gift and experience to be sure, but still hard-won craft. Shaping sermons like this one takes time, time enough for the pattern and direction of the message to take form and the images to emerge, then more time to revise. Revise. When was the last time you took time, made time, found time, to *revise* a sermon. Not run SpellCheck, but revise?

Rather than looking at the sermon in terms of its "moves," it may be more helpful to consider the controlling, or focal, metaphors. My reading shows

1. Matthew's "church"—not his Gospel, or Christology, but his church. It is in this church, not Luke's, where we read the twin stories of banquet and garment.
2. The dream (nightmare?) of our "twoness"—the panic of being unprepared, underdressed, and unwelcome, which we have all felt.

3. The parables as dreams—Taylor applying her hermeneutical key, thinking of the parables as dreams, exploring the idea of "twoness" in her reading of Matthew, showing what it means, in the parables and in life, to be exposed.
4. Film class—The blessing of having someone help us see past our twoness and on to our wholeness.

The pivotal moment in the sermon is the suggestion that we think of the parables as dreams. Here again is how Professor Taylor puts it:

Oh, God. It's one of those dreams.

Why do I think this story is a dream? Because real people do not turn down a king's dinner invitation, much less torture and kill the messengers who came to fetch them. Because once you have a whole ox and several fatted calves on serving platters, they will not keep while you wage war on a whole city, kill its inhabitants, and torch the place. Because who really expects someone nabbed in the middle of an oil change to have a clean wedding garment in the back of the truck?

Dreams are not givens, with right and wrong interpretations. Dreams are impressions, possibilities, profound but elusive. Parables, like dreams, do not really happen, but are about things that happen, the *about* somehow more suggestive and insightful than the happening itself would be. If we actually found ourselves standing in the pulpit without sermon manuscript or notes, and without clothes, while the lessons were read in Swedish or Swahili, we would experience mortification, not insight into the human condition.

Not every metaphor, focal or peripheral, works as well as the preacher might like. Ideally we do not end with the least effective metaphor, but it happens, and in the case of this sermon, I think it did. The film class, the idea that like characters in a movie we do not see ourselves for who we are, but need someone, Jesus? to help us break through from twoness to wholeness, was not nearly as compelling. Perhaps because it strayed too far from the central biblical images focal to the rest of the sermon, calling for a fairly radical shift in perspective. What might have happened if we had stayed in Matthew's church, rather than gone to film class?

Students, however, have called my attention to another key to the sermon, the indirect, metaphorical moment of self-disclosure in the middle of the sermon. "I have spent so much of my life changing bandages on people wounded by brutal religion that you have to keep an eye on me, to make sure I do not round off edges God means to keep sharp." The preacher does not shout, "I know some find me inadequately orthodox, too open to the wisdom of other religious traditions, and say that in moving from parish to academy I have been said to have left the faith, and not just full-time parish ministry." She does say, "It is okay to keep an eye on me. In fact, I hope you will."

The sermon is certainly dialogical, dealing with questions of identity and the questions posed by thoughtful readers when hearing challenging Gospel texts. It is also proclamatory, though admittedly in a Taylor-esque way, the proclamation of less-well-trod way, to an understanding of God's kingdom where questions are honored and doubts not dismissed, but nevertheless a kingdom of profound hope. There is self-reference, and some self-disclosure, but appropriate to the occasion and to the expectations an audience has for a preacher back for a visit. Most of all, there is persistently figurative preaching, at every turn and almost every phrase, holding our interest from beginning to end, yet leaving no doubt about the sermon's focus.

Conclusion

When I shared an early draft of the first chapters of this book with Dr. Fred Craddock, he expressed some surprise that no one had written something like it before. There are at least two ways one can take such a comment, and knowing Dr. Craddock, that is exactly what he intended. Both "This is such a good idea I wonder why no one thought of it before?" and "If this is such a good idea, I wonder why no one thought of it before?" That no one has thought to publish the idea in book form is apparently true, perhaps a comment on the divide between biblical studies and homiletics my own work tries to bridge.

So here we are, having explored the preaching of Jesus, his and ours, in the hope that by better understanding *how* Jesus preached in Matthew, Mark, and Luke, we might more faithfully and effectively preach Jesus ourselves. If you have not been skipping past Brosend to get to Craddock, Curry, Long, and Taylor, you are well-indoctrinated in my characterization of Jesus' rhetoric as dialogical, proclamatory, occasionally self-referential, and persistently figurative. And you have been imagining how your preaching might take on more of those characteristics in sermons to come. The book began with a more audacious challenge, however, about not just pulpit effectiveness in general, but the public voice of the pulpit in particular. It is time to make that claim specific.

Somewhere between 1968 and 1998, we preachers lost something. Unkindly, one might say we lost our nerve, our confidence, and our sense of a higher calling. We were domesticated, perhaps lulled by a booming economy, the fall of the Berlin Wall, and the dismantling of the Soviet Union, with the resulting step back from the nuclear brink. We could pat ourselves on the back for being on the "right" side of the civil rights movement and the anti-Vietnam War protests, and women had sure come a long way. Some of us felt that we had run out of issues. Into that complacency, if that is what it was, came 9/11, the War in Iraq, and the collapse of the economy. Suddenly we had issues, but we had lost our voice. We were ashamed, if we were honest, but it seemed like the only choice was between strident opposition or patriotism, and we chose . . . Okay, we didn't really choose; we talked about the epistle or the psalm instead. And our nonchoice gave us and our listeners away.

If you have not discerned by now that I am a Yellow Dog Democrat who cast his first presidential vote (proudly) for George McGovern and his last presidential vote (joyfully) for Barack Obama, you have not been paying attention. But you know what? The economy collapsed for all of us. The body bags coming home from Iraq and Afghanistan hold Republicans and Democrats. Our denominations are as divided as ever over issues of human sexuality; we just draw the line at different points (Who is welcome at the Lord's Table? Who can be ordained? Who can be a bishop?). And issues of public education, accessibility of health care, immigration policy, and global climate changes know no partisan boundary: they impact us all. Yet most of us preach about none of them and congratulate ourselves for not "politicizing" the pulpit. Who are we kidding?

Jesus, and everybody he spoke to, knew nothing of our separation of "church" and "state." He was as political as could be: you do not use "kingdom" as your central metaphor without having something political in mind, after all. But he lived in a time when no one separated religion and politics, and also at a time when "politics" meant public, not partisan. *Polis*, after all, is just the Greek word for "city." Politicizing the pulpit simply means talking about things that effect the *polis*, the community. Heaven forbid preachers should start doing that!

You know where this is going. Preaching like Jesus—preaching that is dialogical, proclamatory, occasionally self-referential, and persistently figurative—will also turn out to be preaching that is profoundly political, because it will be preaching that responds to the questions and issues of the listeners, and because it will proclaim the kingdom that Jesus proclaimed. But—and this is a really, really, big but—because it will not be persistently self-referential and occasionally figurative, but the reverse, occasionally self-referential and persistently figurative, it will be fairly, if not always favorably, received. The sermon, dear preacher, will not be about you, and it will be presented in a way that engages even as it challenges the listener. This does not mean we turn worship into political rallies and sermons into stump speeches. It means that we follow the leader, Jesus, preaching sermons informed by his rhetoric and his topics, sermons that confront and resist empire, temple, and adversary, sermons that equip and encourage listeners for their own lives of faithful resistance.

Jesus came preaching. It was not the most obvious strategy of resistance, nor the simplest, safest career path. Jesus came preaching peace, yes, and he also came preaching love, forgiveness, and reconciliation. The topics, however, were not always blossoms and bouquets, even when he was considering the flowers of the field. He spoke of the flowers to remind us of our mortality and to challenge us to reorder our priorities in response. He talked of the preoccupation with money and possessions as if the residents of Capernaum were as addicted to shopping as the average American suburbanite. To a conquered and oppressed people, he preached a peace founded upon higher, deeper loyalties than loyalties to empire and temple. How can we in faith preach differently?

Remember also that as much as possible, we utilize the rhetoric of Jesus in its totality, not picking and choosing, deciding this week to be dialogical, next week persistently figurative, and once in a blue moon proclamatory. It worked so well for Jesus because he was almost always dialogical, proclamatory, occasionally self-referential, and persistently figurative. For our preaching to approach that level of effectiveness, we must do the same. With not a little fear and trembling, given the sermons that have earlier graced and blessed this study, I close with an example of my own, an effort to preach what I challenge us all to practice. The texts are overwhelming: the "sacrifice" of Isaac, Paul's glorious cry that "nothing will be able to separate us from the love of God in Christ Jesus our Lord," and the first "passion prediction," and Peter's passionate repudiation of it, in the Gospel of Mark.

What Were They Thinking?

Second Sunday of Lent (B): *Genesis 22:1–14; Romans 8:31–39; Mark 8:31–39*

Do you ever watch the start of a movie or television show and ask yourself, "What were they thinking?" Who said, "Let's cast Jennifer Lopez opposite Ben Affleck as mob enforcers who have to kill a special needs kid, and they fall in love, except she's gay, and . . . "? Maybe the same people who said, "Let's make a television show about a drug-addicted Episcopal priest whose father is a philandering bishop. We'll give him a nymphomaniac narc-dealing daughter, an alcoholic wife, and a gay son. Then we'll have Jesus drop in every now and then, looking like he came out of a five-year-old's pop-up Bible story book." You watch the deservedly forgettable movie *Gigli* or the blessedly short-lived television show *The Book of Daniel*, and you ask, "What were they thinking?" It's not just mass media, of course. Who can forget New Coke, the Edsel, or polyester suits? And it is not just funny, not by a long shot. Most of the time we hear what our politicians have in store for us—or in the case of the response to Hurricane Katrina in New Orleans, the War in Iraq, our health care system, and, well, don't get me started—what they don't have in store for us—and we wonder, "What are they thinking?" The same goes for suicide bombers, Muslims who riot and kill over Danish cartoons, sexually abusive priests, criminally negligent parents, and on and on. What were they thinking? It is also my first, second, and third reaction to the Scripture lessons for today. What were the authors of Genesis, Romans, and the Gospel of Mark thinking?

Many of us who read Romans wonder what Paul was thinking just about every other verse. The passage today, familiar from funerals and memorial services, is a glorious affirmation of God's unfailing presence and love and read out of context, we think that Paul knew exactly what he was thinking: he was thinking about how God's love affirms Paul's faith. Except the Letter to the Romans is much more of a struggle than these verses suggest, perhaps the mightiest theological struggle in Scripture. Paul is struggling with his faith, with what it means to be a Jew and a follower of Jesus, struggling with his own mortality, sinfulness, and spiritual inadequacy. The best-known verses in Romans preceding this affirmation are, "Wretched man that I am! Who will rescue me from this body of death?" (7:24) and "We do not know how to pray" (8:26). What kind of affirmation is that? Just how distant was Paul feeling from God that he was compelled to write, "I am convinced that . . .[nothing] will be able to separate us from the love of God in Christ Jesus our Lord"?

And then there is Peter, famously impetuous, notoriously loud-mouthed, historically unreliable Peter. The Peter who sparred frequently with Paul, and in today's Gospel, he spars with Jesus. Peter left everything to follow Jesus, but while he had hardly the slightest idea what he had signed on for, he knew for certain that he had not signed on for this, the first of what we often call the "passion predictions." What happens next is often misunderstood. The text reads, "And Peter took him aside and began to rebuke him" (Mark 8:32). This is the language the Gospels use for exorcism, as if Peter was trying to purge Jesus of an evil spirit. And it is language that explains what often seems to us like Jesus' overreaction: "Get behind me, Satan!" Peter, it seems, was not trying to change Jesus' mind, but change Jesus' spirit, and in what should be read as a kind of duel of exorcists, Jesus rebukes Peter right back.

But let's face it: as far as the lessons for this morning are concerned, Paul and Peter are decidedly minor characters. We want to know what in heaven Abraham was thinking! He has come such a long way, over such a long time, from Ur to Haran, Haran to Canaan, to Egypt and back; he went from childlessness to promise, a promise embodied in Isaac, the son of Sarah. But there was one more journey, to the land of Moriah, leaving Sarah behind and taking Isaac, the servants, a bundle of wood, and the fire.

What was Abraham thinking? How could he even consider it? Had he not learned enough about God to realize that if what he was being asked to do sounded too horrible to be true, it probably was? Forget about the evidence for the practice of child sacrifice in antiquity, both in and out of Scripture. Forget about Kierkegaard's powerful reflection on the "ontological suspension of the ethical" in Fear and Trembling. What was Abraham thinking?

As long as we are shamelessly speculating about the thought processes of biblical characters, why not ponder the musings of the ultimate character, God? What was God thinking when he sent Abraham to Mount Moriah, Mount Zion, Jerusalem? I know it is proleptic, but hadn't God read James 1:13, "God cannot be tempted by evil and he himself tempts no one"? If God wanted to teach Abraham about the wickedness of child sacrifice, did Isaac have to be scarred for life in the process? According to the rabbis, God knew all along Abraham would not have to go through with it, the meaning of the word "test" suggesting an artificial situation—or as Woody Allen put it in Without Feathers, "Abraham, do you believe every deep, resonant voice you hear?"[1] Christianity sees the binding of Isaac as a forerunner of the crucifixion, but that only works at a considerable level of abstraction 1,800 or so years before the fact, and still leaves us with the question: what was God thinking?

Which brings us to Jesus, who in the Gospels never mentions the binding of Isaac or suggests it influenced his self-understanding in the slightest. One of the wonderful things about the Gospel of Mark is the insight it gives us into what Jesus *was* thinking. When we read carefully, we are told not just what was said and done but why. If my reading of the conflict with Peter is correct, we are not dealing with an unimportant misunderstanding, yet again, by one of the Twelve, we are dealing with a fundamental challenge to Jesus' sense of himself, and by extension, of the meaning of discipleship, which makes Jesus' words distinctly important. "Get behind me, Satan" is not addressed to Peter, but to Satan, the adversary, who uses Peter to challenge Jesus, and the self-understanding Jesus has just shared with the Twelve. Satan is "in" Peter at this moment in the same way Satan was "in" Judas on the last night of Jesus' earthly life.

Paul, Peter, Abraham, God, and Jesus. Did I leave anyone out? Oh yes, you and me. What are you thinking? How are you making sense of this incredible mix of rich biblical material? Assuming we have learned the lesson of resisting child sacrifice and have, I pray, realized that this extends to child abuse and exploitation, what are we to make of Abraham, Paul, Peter, and Jesus? You will not be surprised when I say that I think the key is in the words of Jesus, but I have to tell you, I think I have for a very long time misunderstood what Jesus meant. Maybe you have too.

Jesus says, "Deny yourself." What was he thinking when he said that? What did he mean? I know where we usually go with this, but are we right? To deny myself is to sacrifice, like Abraham, and like Jesus. I have to give up something, give up some focal part of myself. Only then will I be worthy, be able, to follow. Does that sound familiar?

Who do you think you are kidding? If that is what it takes, what could you or I possibly do to render ourselves "worthy" to follow Jesus? And what have you ever known about Jesus that makes you think Jesus doesn't want all of you, doesn't love every smidgen of you? Every bit, even the bits you pretend are not there?

What "deny yourself" means, I am coming to believe, is to stop kidding ourselves about who we are. Drop the pretense, drop the privilege; drop all the hesitations, excuses, and justifications. Don't wait, don't try to smooth things out, stop fooling ourselves, and above all, stop trying to fool Jesus.

If we are wrong about self-denial, is it possible we also don't know what Jesus meant by "Take up your cross"? I think we are wrong, and in a quite similar way. Just as we think self-denial must mean some sort of self-abasement, so we think "Take up the cross" means looking around for something really terrible to lug around with us. We think we should imitate

Francis of Assisi and look for lepers to kiss. Or we think about all the people and things that annoy us, and if we don't call them the "thorn in our flesh" (cf. 2 Cor. 12:7), we say they are "our cross to bear."

Wrong again. Try this on for size: We are our cross. We are our cross. Denying ourselves is to quit the self-deception, and cross-bearing is bringing ourselves, our whole selves, along for the journey. We would rather maintain the illusions and only bring along that which is "worthy" of Jesus, and so we hope to leave behind our doubts, disappointments, and sins, especially our sins. Jesus says pick them up and bring them along.

These sins, these cross-worthy sins, are not just the vague generalities we intone each week, "what we have done and left undone," but specific thoughts and acts and attitudes. Some of them get between us and Jesus, some get between us and others, and some get between the church and its mission. One sin will serve as the "for example" because it is much on my mind, and how we deal with it is important to the ministry and mission of the church.

It was a movie that brought this home. Always being the last ones to see a good movie, Friday we went to see the Oscar-award-winner *Crash*. It was not what I expected, but it was what I needed, especially after spending Wednesday and Thursday in antiracism training periodically required of clergy by the church. After two days of patting myself on the back for what a swell, politically correct guy I am, it was frightening to realize how much I look like many of those in the movie, a mix of noble actions, blindly self-centered motives, and base behavior. Racist behavior.

Racism is everywhere, not just on the movie screen. Denying that we feel it, and not bringing it along with us as we follow Jesus—is not an option. If we pretend we are not capable of racially discriminatory thoughts and behavior, how in heaven is the Holy Spirit going to help us address it? If we act as if we do not hear and see when someone around us, maybe someone dear to us, acts or speaks in a prejudiced or discriminatory way, how are they going to grow and change? Jesus will have none of it. Jesus says, "Take it up. It is a part of you, and we both know it. The only way it is going to get better is if you follow me and we nail it to the cross along with everything else that belongs up there."

What was Paul thinking? He was thinking that God does not want anything, even our sinful selves, to separate us from the love that is ours in Christ Jesus. Not anything. Especially, come to think of it, our sinful selves.

Appendix

Analysis of Jesus' Sayings in the Synoptics

The columns below reflect an analysis of the sayings of Jesus in the Synoptic Gospels according to the characterization of the rhetoric of Jesus, as explained in the above chapters:

D   dialogical (see chap. 2)
P   proclamatory (see chap. 3)
SR   occasionally self-referential (see chap. 4)
F   persistently figurative (see chap. 5)

Mark	Matthew	Luke
	4:1–11 temptation D/P	4:1–13 temptation D/P
1:15 kingdom is near P	4:17 kingdom is near P	
		4:18–21 Scripture is fulfilled P/D/SR
		4:22–27 doctor, heal yourself D/P/F
1:17 follow me SR/P	4:19 follow me SR/P	5:10 you will catch people P
2:8–12 healing, forgiveness D/P/SR	9:2–8 healing, forgiveness D/P	5:20–25 healing, forgiveness D/P
2:15–17 strong/sick, call sinners D/ F	9:12–13 strong/sick; mercy/sacrifice D/F	5:31–32 strong/sick, call sinners D/F
2:19–20 sons of groom fast D/F	9:15 sons of groom fast D/F	5:34–35 sons of groom fast D/F

Mark	Matthew	Luke
2:21–22 patches & wineskins F	9:16–17 patches & wineskins F	5:36–38 patches & wineskins F 5:39 old wine is best F
2:23–28 grain on the Sabbath D	12:1–8 grain on Sabbath, mercy/sacrifice D	6:1–5 grain on Sabbath D
3:1–6 withered hand, do good on Sabbath D/P	12:9–14 withered hand, sheep in pit, do good on Sabbath; D/F	6:6–11 withered hand, do good on Sabbath D/P
3:20–30 Jesus and Beelzebul D/F/P	12:22–32 Jesus and Beelzebul D/F/P	11:14–22 Jesus and Beelzebul D/F/P
	12:38–42 Sign of Jonah D/F	11:29–32 sign of Jonah D/F
	12:43–45 return of evil spirit F	11:24–26 return of evil spirit F
3:31–35 mother and brothers D/F	12:46–50 mother and brothers D/F	8:19–21 mother and brothers D/F
4:1–9 allegory of seed and soils F/P	13:1–9 allegory of seed and soils F/P	8:4–8 allegory of seed and soils F/P
4:10–13 purpose of the parables D	13:10–17 purpose of the parables D	8:9–10 purpose of the parables D
4:14–20 allegory explained D	13:18–23 allegory explained D	8:11–15 allegory explained D
	13:24–30 weeds among the wheat F/P	
4:26–29 seed growing secretly F/P		
4:30–32 mustard seed F/P	13:31–32 mustard seed F/P	13:18–19 mustard seed F/P
	13:33 leaven F/P	13:20–21 leaven F/P

Mark	Matthew	Luke
	13:36–43 weeds/wheat explained D/F	
	13:44 treasure in a field F/P	
	13:45–46 pearl F/P	
	13:47–50 net F/P	
	13:52 treasures new and old F/P	
	5:3–12 beatitudes P	6:20b–23 blessings P
		6:24–26 woes P
9:49–50 salted with fire; saltiness lost F	5:13 salt of the earth F/P	14:34–35 saltiness lost F
4:21 lamp on lampstand F	5:14–16 light of the world, lampstand F/P	8:16 lamp on lampstand F
	5:17–20 fulfill law and prophets P	16:16–17 law won't pass away easily P/F
	5:21–26 antithesis on murder D/F	12:57–59 before the judge F
9:43–48 cut it off F	5:27–30 antithesis on adultery D/F	
	5:31–32 antithesis on divorce D/P	16:18 divorce and adultery P
	5:33–37 antithesis on oaths D/P	
	5:38–42 antithesis on retaliation D/P/F	6:29–30 turn the cheek F/P
	5:43–48 antithesis on love/hate D/P/F	6:27–28, 32–36 love your enemies P/F
	6:1–4 giving alms P/F	

Mark	Matthew	Luke
	6:5–6 on prayer P/F	
11:25 ask/receive forgiveness D/P	6:7–15 Lord's Prayer D/P	11:1–4 Lord's Prayer D/P
		11:5–8 friend at midnight F/P
	6:16–18 on fasting P/F	
	6:19–21 treasures P/F	12:33–34 treasures P/F
	6:22–23 the sound eye F	11:34–36 the sound eye F
	6:24 serving two masters F	16:13 serving two masters F
	6:25–34 be not anxious P/F	12:22–32 be not anxious P/F
4:24–25 measure given, received F	7:1–5 do not judge P/F	6:37–42 do not judge P/F
	7:6 pearls before swine F	
	7:7–11 ask, seek, knock P/F	11:9–13 ask, seek, knock P/F
	7:12 Golden Rule P	6:31 Golden Rule P
	7:13–14 narrow gate, hard way P/F	13:23–24 narrow door P/F
	7:15–20 known by fruits F	6:43–45 known by fruits F
	7:21–23 "Lord, Lord" P	6:46 "Lord, Lord" P
		13:25–30 "I do not know you" F

Mark	Matthew	Luke
	7:24–27 two foundations F	6:47–49 two foundations F
	8:11–12 Gentiles in kingdom P/F	13:28–30 Gentiles in kingdom P/F
	8:18–22 following, lay his head, burying the dead D/P/F	9:57–62 following, lay his head, burying the dead, hand to plow D/F
	9:37–38 harvest great, workers few F	10:2–12 harvest great, workers few F
6:1–6a in his hometown D/F	13:53–58 in his hometown D/F	4:16–30 in his hometown D/F
6:8–11 sending disciples P	10:5–16 sending disciples, sheep/wolves P/F	9:1–5 sending disciples, sheep/wolves P/F
	10:17–25 disciples' fate, persecution, disciple not above teacher P/F	6:40 disciple not above teacher P
	10:26–33 whom to fear P/F	12:2–9 whom to fear P/F
	10:34–36 not peace but sword, division P/F	12:51–53 not peace but sword, division P/F
	10:37–39 hating father & mother, take up cross, save/lose soul F/P	14:25–27 hating father & mother, take up cross, save/lose soul F/P
9:41 cup of water F	10:40–42 receives you/me, cup water F/P	10:16 hear/refuse you/me F/P

Mark	Matthew	Luke
	11:2–6 questions from John the Baptist D/P	7:18–23 questions from John the Baptist D/P
	11:7–19 Jesus on John the Baptist, children in marketplace P/F	7:24–35 Jesus on John the Baptist, children in marketplace P/F
	11:20–24 woes to unrepenting cities P/F	10:12–15 woes to unrepenting cities P/F
		10:17–20 return of 70, Satan falls F
	11:25–27 thanks to Father for wisdom revealed to children F	10:21–22 thanks to Father for wisdom revealed to children F
	13:16–17 blessed eyes and ears F	10:23–24 blessed for what you've seen F
		10:25–28 lawyer's question D
		10:29–37 Good Samaritan F/D
		10:38–42 Mary/Martha D
	11:28–30 come to me, you weary P/F	
7:1–23 traditions of elders, blind guides D/F/P	15:1–20 traditions of elders, blind guides D/F/P	11:37–54 against the Pharisees D/F
7:24–30 Syro-Phoenician woman D/F	15:21–28 Canaanite woman D/F	
8:11–12 Pharisees demand sign D/P	16:1–4 Pharisees & Sadducees demand sign D/F	

Mark	Matthew	Luke
8:15–21 leaven of Pharisees/Herod D/F	16:5–12 leaven of Pharisees & Sadducees D/F	
	16:18–19 you are Peter F	
8:31–33 first passion prediction; "Get behind me Satan" P/D	16:21–23 first passion prediction; "Get behind me Satan" P/D	9:22 first passion prediction P
8:34–9:1 take up your cross P/F	16:24–28 take up your cross P/F	9:23–27 take up your cross P/F
9:11–13 coming of Elijah D/P	17:10–13 coming of Elijah D/P	
9:31 second passion prediction P	17:22–23 second passion prediction P	9:44–45 second passion prediction P
	17:24–27 paying the temple tax D/F	
9:33–37 true greatness D/F	18:1–5 true greatness D/F	9:46–48 true greatness D/F
9:38–40 for/against us D/F		9:49–50 for/against us D
9:42–50 temptations, cut it off F/P	18:6–9 temptations, cut it off F/P	17:1–2 millstone around neck F/P
	18:10–14 lost sheep F/P	15:3–7 lost sheep D/F/P
	18:15–18 reproving a fellow member D/P	17:3 reproving a sinner D/P
	18:19–20 two/three together P	

Mark	Matthew	Luke
	18:21–22 seventy times seven F/P	17:4 seven times a day F/P
	18:23–35 the unforgiving servant F/P	
		12:13–15 life is not possessions P/D
		12:16–21 parable of rich fool F/P
		12:35–48 watchful slaves F/P
		12:49–53 divisions in household P
		12:54–56 signs of the times F/P
		13:1–9 parable of barren fig tree F/P
		13:32–35 warning to Herod D/P
	12:11–12 livestock in pit F	14:1–6 livestock in pit D/F/P
		14:7–14 places at table F
	22:1–14 wedding banquet, no robe F/P	14:15–24 great supper F/P
		14:25–33 cost of discipleship F/P
		[15:1–7 lost sheep F/P]
		15:8–10 lost coin F
		15:11–32 lost son F

Mark	Matthew	Luke
		16:1–9 unjust steward F
		16:10–15 faithful in little/much F/P
		16:14–15 reproving Pharisees D
		16:16–17 John the Baptist, kingdom, law P/D
		16:18 against divorce P
		16:19–31 rich man and Lazarus F
	17:20 mustard-seed faith D/F	17:5–6 mustard-seed faith D/F
		17:7–10 servant fixing supper F
		17:20–21 kingdom is among you P
		18:1–8 persistent widow F/P
		18:9–14 Pharisee and publican F/P
10:2–12 on divorce P/D	19:3–12 on divorce P/D	16:18 against divorce P
10:13–16 blessing the children D/P	19:13–15 blessing the children D/P	18:15–17 blessing the children D/P
10:17–22 rich man D	19:16–22 rich young man D	18:18–23 rich ruler D
10:23–31 riches and discipleship P/F	19:23–30 riches and discipleship P/F	18:24–30 riches and discipleship P/F

Mark	Matthew	Luke
	20:1–16 laborers in the vineyard F	
10:32–34 third passion prediction P	20:17–19 third passion prediction P	18:31–34 third passion prediction P
10:35–45 servant of all D/F/P	20:20–28 servant of all D/F/P	22:24–27 servant of all D/F/P
		19:1–10 Zacchaeus, save the lost D/P
		19:41–44 Jesus weeps over Jerusalem P/F
11:15–17 temple action, saying P	21:12–13 temple action, saying P	19:45–46 temple action, saying P
11:23–25 ask in prayer, receive (fig tree) P	21:20–22 ask and receive (fig tree) P	
11:27–33 by what authority? (John the Baptist) D	21:23–27 by what authority? (John the Baptist) D	20:1–8 by what authority? (John the Baptist) D
	21:28–32 parable of two sons D/F	
12:1–12 allegory of vineyard owner F	21:33–46 allegory of vineyard owner F	20:9–19 allegory of vineyard owner F
12:13–17 tribute to Caesar D	22:15–22 tribute to Caesar D	20:20–26 tribute to Caesar D
12:18–27 on the resurrection D/P	22:23–33 on the resurrection D/P	20:27–40 on the resurrection D/P
12:28–34 great commandment D/P	22:34–40 great commandment D/P	(10:25–28) the lawyer's question D
12:35–37a David's son? D	22:41–46 David's son? D	20:41–44 David's son? D

Mark	Matthew	Luke
12:37b–40 warning about scribes, Pharisees P/F	23:1–36 woe to scribes, Pharisees P/F	20:45–47 warning about scribes, Pharisees P/F
	23:37–39 lament over Jerusalem F	13:34–35 lament over Jerusalem F
12:41–44 widow's mite F/P/D		21:1–4 widow's mite F/P/D
13:1–2 not one stone D/P	24:1–2 not one stone D/P	21:5–6 not one stone D/P
13:3–8 signs before the end F/P	24:3–8 signs before the end F/P	21:7–11 signs before the end F/P
13:9–14 coming persecutions F/P	24:9–14 coming persecutions F/P	21:12–19 coming persecutions F/P
13:14–20 desolating sacrilege P	24:15–22 desolating sacrilege P	21:20–24 desolating sacrilege P
13:21–23 false christs P	24:23–28 false christs; stars fall P	(17:23–24) stars fall P/F
13:24–27 coming Son of Man P	24:29–31 coming Son of Man P	21:25–28 coming Son of Man P
13:28–32 fig tree's lesson P/F	24:32–36 fig tree's lesson P/F	21:29–33 fig tree's lesson P/F
13:33–37 Watch! F/P		21:34–36 Watch! P/F
	24:37–44 days of Noah F/P	(17:26–36) days of Noah P/F
	24:45–51 faithful, wicked servant F	(12:41–46) do not be anxious, P/F
	25:1–13 Ten Bridesmaids F	
	25:14–30 the Talents F	(19:11–27) the Pounds F

Mark	Matthew	Luke
	25:31–46 last judgment F	
14:6–9 in memory of her D	26:10–13 in memory of her D	7:36–50 forgive much, love much D/F
14:22–25 institution of the Eucharist P	26:26–29 institution of the Eucharist P	22:15–20 institution of the Eucharist P
14:61–62 are you the Christ? I am D/P	26:63–64 are you the Christ? I am D/P	22:67–70 you would not believe; seated at the right hand of power D/P

Notes

Introduction

1. Fred B. Craddock, *As One without Authority* (Enid, OK: Phillips University Press, 1971).

2. Timothy B. Tyson, *Blood Done Sign My Name* (New York: Three Rivers Press, 2005); Charles Marsh, *The Last Days: A Son's Story of Sin and Segregation at the Dawn of the New South* (New York: Basic Books, 2002).

3. Joachim Jeremias, *The Parables of Jesus*, trans. S. H. Hooke (London: SCM Press, 1972).

4. Amos N. Wilder, *The Language of the Gospel: Early Christian Rhetoric* (New York: Harper & Row, 1964).

5. James Dunn's emphasis on the interaction of saying, memory, and tradition in *Jesus Remembered* (Grand Rapids: Wm. B. Eerdmans Publishing Co., 2003) is helpful: "The Jesus tradition shows us *how* Jesus was remembered; its character strongly suggests again and again a tradition given its essential shape by regular use and reuse in oral mode. . . . This suggests in turn that that essential shape was given by the original and immediate impact made by Jesus as that was first put into words by and among those involved or eyewitnesses of what Jesus said and did. In that key sense, the Jesus tradition *is* Jesus remembered. And the Jesus thus remembered *is* Jesus, or as close as we will ever be able to reach back to him" (335, with original emphasis). While Dunn is stressing a historical claim, the rhetorical significance should not be lost: the tradition remembered Jesus' rhetoric in particular and consistent ways.

Chapter 1: Jesus the Preacher / Preaching Jesus

1. Charles L. Campbell, *The Word before the Powers: An Ethic of Preaching* (Louisville, KY: Westminster John Knox Press, 2002); John Howard Yoder, *He Came Preaching Peace* (Scottdale, PA: Herald Press, 1985).

2. Henri Nouwen, *In the Name of Jesus: Reflections on Christian Leadership* (New York: Crossroad Publishing Co., 1989).

3. See Fred B. Craddock, *Overhearing the Gospel* (Nashville: Abingdon Press, 1978 and other editions), 9–20. "It is not to be assumed that the gospel provides religious and moral constraints upon what we say but leaves how we say it to be governed solely by practical considerations of effectiveness. This simply is not

true" (19, with original emphasis). So also Wilder, *The Language of the Gospel:* "Form and content cannot long be held apart," 4.

4. Among their many published works on the historical Jesus, I have in mind especially: John Dominic Crossan, *The Historical Jesus* (New York: HarperSanFrancisco, 1991); N. T. Wright, *Jesus and the Victory of God* (Minneapolis: Fortress Press, 1996); Marcus J. Borg, *Meeting Jesus Again for the First Time* (New York: HarperSanFrancisco, 1994); John P. Meier, *A Marginal Jew: Rethinking the Historical Jesus,* 3 vols., Anchor Bible Reference Library (New York: Doubleday, 1991–2001); Luke Timothy Johnson, *The Real Jesus* (San Francisco: HarperSanFrancisco, 1996).

5. Borg, *Meeting Jesus Again,* 70.

6. E. P. Sanders, *Jesus and Judaism* (Philadelphia: Fortress Press, 1985), 11.

7. These four are not the only claims in my understanding of Jesus within history, but are the four of importance for consideration of Jesus as a preacher and teacher in first-century Palestine.

8. Borg, *Meeting Jesus Again,* 26–27.

9. Meier, *A Marginal Jew,* vol. 3, *Companions and Competitors,* 617.

10. Matt. 1:22; 2:5, 15, 17, 23; 4:4, 6–7, 10, 14; 8:17; 11:10; 12:17; 13:35; 21:13–14; 26:24, 31; 27:9.

11. Walter Wink, esp. the summary of The Powers trilogy, *The Powers That Be: A Theology for a New Millennium* (New York, Doubleday, 1998).

12. Sanders, *Jesus and Judaism,* 339.

13. John P. Meier, *A Marginal Jew,* 3:542; cf. 541: "Both Samaritanism and Judaism were latter-day forms of the ancient religion of Israel, a Palestinian religion that believed in and worshiped the God Yahweh as the unique God of Israel according to the prescriptions contained in the five books of Moses. Over the centuries, this religion had developed distinctive practices such as circumcision of infants, the prohibition of eating pork, the observance of every seventh day as a day of rest, an emphasis on the need to have one central sanctuary, and annual celebrations of special feasts of pilgrimage to this central sanctuary (e.g., Passover, Pentecost, Tabernacles). This core religion of Israel experienced various traumas, transformations, and developments under the assaults and influences of the Assyrian, Babylonian, Persian, and Hellenistic empires. During the last centuries before the turn of the era—though at different times and in different ways—Samaritanism and Judaism emerged from the crucible of all this historical turmoil as two major expressions of the ancient religion of Israel, the ancient worship of Yahweh."

14. Richard A. Horsley, *Galilee: History, Politics, People* (Valley Forge, PA: Trinity Press International, 1995); Sean Freyne, *Galilee and Gospel,* Wissenshaftliche Untersuchungen zum Neuen Testament 125 (Tübingen: Mohr Siebeck, 2000).

15. James D. G. Dunn, *Jesus Remembered, Christianity in the Making* (Grand Rapids: Wm. B. Eerdmans Publishing Co., 2003), 295.

16. N. T. Wright, *The New Testament and the People of God* (Minneapolis: Fortress Press, 1992), 168: "The Torah assumed new importance in border territory. As we shall see, it acquired some of the functions and features of the Temple itself."

17. Dunn, *Jesus Remembered*, 300.

18. Crossan, *The Historical Jesus*, 18–19; J. Andrew Overman, "Who Were the First Urban Christians? Urbanization in Galilee in the First Century," in Society of Biblical Literature 1988 Seminar Papers, ed. David Lull (Atlanta: Scholars Press, 1988), 160–68.

19. Author's notes from an unpublished speech delivered to the American Baptist Peace Conference, Calvary Baptist Church, Washington, DC, November 1982.

20. "The Pay at the Top," *New York Times*, April 28, 2009.

21. Richard A. Horsley, *Jesus and Empire* (Minneapolis: Fortress Press, 2003), 60.

22. Ibid., 35.

23. Meier, *A Marginal Jew*, 3:619–20.

24. Wright, *Jesus and the Victory of God*, 159.

25. Dunn, *Jesus Remembered*, 310.

26. Ibid., 315–17. On 317, Dunn notes the likelihood of a pious upbringing, education in Torah, familiarity with Scripture and temple, Sabbath observance, synagogue attendance, and concludes: "[Jesus] himself was a pious Jew who took his religious obligations seriously."

27. Meier, *A Marginal Jew*, vol. 2, *Mentor, Message, and Miracles* (1994), 450.

28. K. L. Schmidt, "Basileia . . . ," in *Theological Dictionary of the New Testament* [TDNT], ed. Gerhard Kittel, trans. Geoffrey W. Bromiley, 10 vols. (Grand Rapids: Wm. B. Eerdmans Publishing Co., 1964–76), 1:576–93.

29. See Pss. 10:16; 24:8, 10; 29:10; 47:2; 84:3; 93:1; 95:3; 96:10; 97:1; 98:6; 99:1; Isa. 6:1, 5; 33:22; 43:15; 44:6; Jer. 10:10; Ezek. 20:33; Zeph. 3:15; Zech. 14:9; Mal. 1:14.

30. Sanders, *Jesus and Judaism*, 127, with original emphasis.

31. Ibid., 126.

32. Wright, *Jesus and the Victory of God*, 199.

33. See J. Behm and E. Würthwein, "Metanoeō, metanoia," in TDNT 4:975–1008; R. Bultmann and A. Weiser, "Pisteuō . . . ," in TDNT 6:174–228.

34. Dunn, *Jesus Remembered*, 761–62.

35. Ben Witherington III, *Jesus the Sage* (Minneapolis: Augsburg Fortress, 1994).

36. Vernon K. Robbins, *Jesus the Teacher* (Philadelphia: Fortress Press, 1984).

37. Leander E. Keck, *Who Is Jesus?* (Columbia: University of South Carolina Press, 2000), 65.

38. Dunn, *Jesus Remembered*, 697. In addition to 5 instances in the triple tradition (Matt. 19:16/Mark 10:17/Luke 18:18; Matt. 22:16/Mark 12:14/Luke

20:21; Matt. 22:24/Mark 12:19/Luke 20:28; Matt. 22:36/Mark 12:32/Luke 10:25; Matt. 26:18/Mark 14:14/Luke 22:11) and 2 Mark/Luke parallels (Mark 5:35/Luke 8:49; Mark 9:17/Luke 9:38), there are 14 single uses of "teacher" (*didaskolos*) in reference to Jesus (Matt. 8:19; 9:11; 12:38; 17:24; Mark 4:38; 9:38; 10:20, 35; 13:1; Luke 7:40; 11:45; 12:13; 19:39; 20:39; 21:7), for a total of 22.

39. Borg, *Meeting Jesus Again*, 80; cf. Ben Witherington III, *Jesus the Sage* (Minneapolis: Fortress Press, 1994), 201: "Jesus taught a Wisdom that entailed a counterorder, and often it was a Wisdom from below, not one that propped up the status quo or supported the values of the wealthy few."

40. Hans Dieter Betz, *The Sermon on the Mount, Hermeneia* (Minneapolis: Augsburg Fortress, 1995), 198–328.

41. Sanders, *Jesus and Judaism*, 256: "It is a general principle that greater stringency than the law requires is not illegal."

42. Wright, *Jesus and the Victory of God*, 290.

43. Uriel Rappaport, "How Anti-Roman Was the Galilee?" in *The Galilee in Late Antiquity*, ed. Lee I. Levine (New York: Jewish Theological Seminary of America, 1992), 95–102.

44. Dunn, *Jesus Remembered*, 805–18.

45. See Gregory Dix, *The Shape of the Liturgy* (London: Continuum, 1945), esp. 110–25; and chap. 9, "The Meaning of the Eucharist," 238–67.

46. Wright, *Jesus and the Victory of God*, 479–81.

47. See William Brosend, *Conversations with Scripture: The Parables* (Harrisburg, PA: Morehouse Publishing, 2006), 63–65.

48. K. C. Hanson and Douglas E. Oakman, *Palestine in the Time of Jesus: Social Structures and Social Conflicts* (Minneapolis: Fortress Press, 1998), 113–16.

49. Keck, *Who Is Jesus?* 121.

50. Robbins speaks of the five textures of biblical texts: inner- (how the author uses language to create meaning), inter- (various citations, allusions, references, and parallels to other biblical texts), sociocultural (historical, social, economic, and other backgrounds critical to understanding the world of the text), ideological (discernible perspectives and biases in the text, and social and confessional biases held by the interpreter), and sacred (views of the sacred explored and proclaimed in the text). I cannot commend his work too highly. His insights are appreciated equally by students from high school age on, from church basement to seminary classroom. It is fairly pointed out that his "taxonomy" is not really new, but the clarity it brings to the discussion of biblical texts is important and refreshing. See Vernon K. Robbins, *Exploring the Texture of Texts* (Harrisburg, PA: Trinity Press International, 1996); and idem, *The Tapestry of Early Christian Discourse* (London: Routledge, 1996).

51. The "first/last" saying, while perhaps connecting the entire unit to the pericope on blessing the children, which precedes Mark 10:17–30, obviously has no clear connection to the material in the pericope itself.

52. Robbins, *Jesus the Teacher*, 101–8.

53. The words and actions of Jesus and the people of Nazareth never seem to connect, so that when Jesus "passed through the midst of them" in 4:30, he enacts the already obvious verbal disconnect.

54. See my *Conversations with Scripture*, 28–34.

55. Wilder, *Language of the Gospel*, 78, 84.

56. Thomas B. Long, "No News Is Bad News," in *What's the Matter with Preaching Today?* ed. Mike Graves (Louisville, KY: Westminster John Knox Press, 2004), 145.

57. *Harper's Magazine*, July 1928, 133–41.

58. David G. Buttrick, "Preaching Today: The Loss of a Public Voice," in *The Folly of Preaching*, ed. Michael P. Knowles (Grand Rapids: Wm. B. Eerdmans Publishing Co., 2007), 3, 4–5, emphasis.

59. Barbara Brown Taylor, "The Weekly Wrestling Match," in Graves, *What's the Matter with Preaching Today?* 172.

60. The literature is as voluminous as it is contentious. See Bob Woodward's trilogy on the Bush administration's plans for and conduct of the War in Iraq, especially *State of Denial* (New York: Simon & Schuster, 2007); and Thomas E. Ricks, *Fiasco* (New York: Penquin, 2007).

61. Aristotle, *The Art of Rhetoric*, trans J. H. Freese, Loeb Classical Library (Cambridge: Oxford University Press, 1926), 1.1.11–1.2.9 (8–21).

62. C. H. Dodd, *The Parables of the Kingdom* (New York: Charles Scribener's Sons, 1961), 5.

Chapter 2: Dialogical Preaching

1. Among others, see Fred B. Craddock, *Preaching* (Nashville: Abingdon Press, 1985), chap. 5, "The Listeners"; and Roger E. Van Harn, *Pew Rights: For People Who Listen to Sermons* (Grand Rapids: Wm. B. Eerdmans Publishing Co., 1992).

2. Adela Y. Collins, *Mark: A Commentary* (Minneapolis: Fortress Press, 2007), 202 n. 128.

3. E. P. Sanders, *Jesus and Judaism* (Philadelphia: Fortress Press, 1985), 267.

4. Vernon Robbins, *Exploring the Texture of Texts* (Harrisburg, PA: Trinity Press International, 1996), 40–47.

5. See Collins, *Mark*, 352: "This vow is a clever way in which a son can prevent his parents from using any of his property. . . . In other words, the son is making cynical use of the biblical vow, a cultic form, in order to evade his obligations related to the commandment to honor one's father and mother."

6. "He said to him, 'Teacher, I have kept all these since my youth.' Jesus, looking at him, loved him" (Mark 10:20–21a). "When Jesus saw that he answered wisely, he said to him, 'You are not far from the kingdom of God'" (Mark 12:34).

7. Halvor Moxnes, *Putting Jesus in His Place* (Louisville, KY: Westminster John Knox Press, 2003), 52.

8. John Dominic Crossan, *The Historical Jesus: The Life of a Mediterranean Jewish Peasant* (New York: HarperSanFrancisco, 1991), 421.

9. Marcus J. Borg, *Meeting Jesus Again for the First Time* (New York: HarperSanFrancisco, 1994), 81.

10. http://libweb.ptsem.edu/collections/barth/faq/quotes.aspx?menu=296&subText=468.

11. William Rainey Harper, "Bible Study and the Religious Life," republished in *Religion and the Higher Life: Talks to Students* (Chicago: University of Chicago Press, 1904).

12. John S. McClure, *The Roundtable Pulpit* (Nashville: Abingdon Press, 1995).

13. Timothy B. Tyson, *Blood Done Sign My Name* (New York: Three Rivers Press, 2005); Charles Marsh, *God's Long Summer: Stories of Faith and Civil Rights* (Princeton, NJ: Princeton University Press, 2008); Marsh's memoir, *The Last Days: A Son's Story of Sin and Segregation at the Dawn of the New South* (New York: Basic Books, 2002), is also excellent.

14. Mark Chaves, *Congregations in America* (Cambridge, MA: Harvard University Press, 2004).

15. Loren B. Mead, *The Once and Future Church: Reinventing the Congregation for a New Mission Frontier* (Washington, DC: Alban Institute, 1991).

16. David J. Lose, *Confessing Jesus Christ: Preaching in a Postmodern World* (Grand Rapids: Wm. B. Eerdmans Publishing Co., 2003).

17. Thomas G. Long, "Taking the Listeners Seriously in Biblical Interpretation," in *The Folly of Preaching*, ed. Michael P. Knowles (Grand Rapids: Wm. B. Eerdmans Publishing Co., 2007), 73.

18. Thomas H. Troeger and H. Edward Everding Jr., *So That All Might Know: Preaching That Engages the Whole Congregation* (Nashville: Abingdon Press, 2008), 7, 5.

19. Long, "Taking the Listeners Seriously," 73–74.

20. John S. McClure, *The Roundtable Pulpit* (Nashville: Abingdon Press, 1995).

21. Fred B. Craddock, *Overhearing the Gospel* (Nashville: Abingdon Press, 1978), 121, with original emphasis.

Chapter 3: Proclamatory Preaching

1. "When a righteous man fled from his brother's wrath, she guided him on straight paths; she showed him the kingdom of God [basileian theou], and gave him knowledge of holy things; she prospered him in his labors, and increased the fruit of his toil" (Wis. 10:10).

2. Walter Wink, *Engaging the Powers: Discernment and Resistance in a World of Domination*, vol. 3 of *The Powers* (Minneapolis: Fortress Press, 1992), esp. chap. 6, "God's Domination-Free Order: Jesus and God's Reign," 109–37.

3. Khaled Hosseini, *The Kite Runner* (New York: Riverhead Trade, 2004), 319.

4. Charles L. Campbell, *The Word before the Powers* (Louisville, KY: Westminster John Knox Press, 2002), 74.

5. John Tierney, "The Advantage of Closing a Few Doors," *New York Times*, February 26, 2008, S1: "They wasted so many clicks rushing back to reopen doors that their earnings dropped 15 percent. Even when the penalties for switching grew stiffer—besides losing a click, the players had to pay a cash fee—the students kept losing money by frantically keeping all their doors open. Why were they so attached to those doors? The players . . . would probably say they were just trying to keep future options open. But that's not the real reason. . . . Even if a door vanished from the screen, players could make it reappear whenever they wanted. But even when they knew it would not cost anything to make the door reappear, they still kept frantically trying to prevent doors from vanishing.

"Apparently they did not care so much about maintaining flexibility in the future. What really motivated them was the desire to avoid the immediate pain of watching a door close. 'Closing a door on an option is experienced as a loss, and people are willing to pay a price to avoid the emotion of loss,' Dr. [Dan] Ariely says."

6. John Dominic Crossan and Jonathan L. Reed, *Excavating Jesus: Beneath the Stones, behind the Texts* (New York: HarperSanFrancisco, 2001), 136.

7. Arthur Paul Boers, *Never Call Them Jerks: Healthy Responses to Difficult Behavior* (Washington, DC: Alban Institute, 1999).

8. Walter Wink, *Naming the Powers: The Language of Power in the New Testament*, vol. 1 of *The Powers* (Philadelphia: Fortress Press, 1984).

9. Barbara Brown Taylor, *Speaking of Sin: The Lost Language of Salvation* (Cambridge, MA: Cowley Publications, 2001); Martin L. Smith, *Reconciliation: Preparing for Confession in the Episcopal Church* (Cambridge, MA: Cowley Publications, 1985).

10. The miter is the head garment worn by a bishop and is symbolically shaped to suggest the tongues of fire that rested on the heads of the apostles on the day of Pentecost.

11. David Buttrick, *Homiletic: Moves and Structures* (Philadelphia: Fortress Press, 1987), esp. 23–53.

Chapter 4: Self-Reference in Preaching

1. Walter Wink, *The Human Being* (Minneapolis: Augsburg Fortress, 2002), 23.

2. Phillips Brooks, *Lectures on Preaching* (New York: E. P. Dutton, 1877).

3. Aristotle, *The Art of Rhetoric*, trans. J. H. Freese, Loeb Classical Library (Cambridge, MA: Harvard University Press, 1926), 1.2.3 (p. 17).

4. Ibid., 1.2.4–5 (p. 17).

5. Frederick Buechner, *Telling the Truth: The Gospel as Tragedy, Comedy, and Fairy Tale* (New York: Harper Collins, 1977), 22–23.

6. Karl Barth, *The Word of God and the Word of Man* (New York: Harper, 1957), 107.

7. Terry Waite on the BBC program *Listener's Tales*, http://www.bbc.co.uk/worldservice/specials/1339_listener/page12.shtml.

8. Paul Tillich, *The Shaking of the Foundations* (New York: C. Scribner's Sons, 1948), 10.

Chapter 5: Persistently Figurative Preaching

1. William Brosend, *Conversations with Scripture: The Parables* (Harrisburg, PA: Morehouse Publishing, 2006).

2. J. D. Crossan, ed., "Paul Ricoeur on Biblical Interpretation," *Semeia: An Experimental Journal for Biblical Criticism* 4 (1975): esp. 75–106.

3. William Brosend, "The Letter of Jude: A Rhetoric of Excess or an Excess of Rhetoric?" *Interpretation: A Journal of Bible and Theology* 60, no. 3 (July 2006): 292–305.

4. Richard Lischer, A Maundy Thursday sermon preached at the Chapel of Duke University, March 24, 2005, http://www.chapel.duke.edu/sermons/2005.html.

5. Thomas Troeger and H. Edward Everding Jr., *So That All Might Know: Preaching That Engages the Whole Congregation* (Nashville: Abingdon Press, 2008).

6. Aristotle, *The Art of Rhetoric*, trans. J. H. Freese. Loeb Classical Library (Cambridge, MA: Harvard University Press, 1926), 2.20.2–3 (272–73).

7. A Google search for "sermon helps" yields 480,000 "hits."

Conclusion

1. Woody Allen, *Without Feathers* (New York: Ballantine Books, 1986).